6/07

To the Fitchburg Public Library, Best Wishes Rip Pallotta

ONE DAY IN MUDVILLE

A look at some of the most unique baseball games of all time

RIP PALLOTTA

Bloomington, IN   authorHOUSE®   Milton Keynes, UK

In memory of

Kenneth Mansfield

from

Sara Mansfield Munson

AuthorHouse™
1663 Liberty Drive, Suite 200
Bloomington, IN 47403
www.authorhouse.com
Phone: 1-800-839-8640

AuthorHouse™ UK Ltd.
500 Avebury Boulevard
Central Milton Keynes, MK9 2BE
www.authorhouse.co.uk
Phone: 08001974150

This book is a work of non-fiction. Unless otherwise noted, the author and the publisher make no explicit guarantees as to the accuracy of the information contained in this book.

First published by AuthorHouse 3/1/2007

ISBN: 978-1-4259-7899-0 (sc)

Printed in the United States of America
Bloomington, Indiana

This book is printed on acid-free paper.

ACKNOWLEDGMENTS

THERE ARE SEVERAL PEOPLE WHO deserve my thanks for the help and encouragement that they gave me as I wrote this book.

First of all, I want to thank Joanne Connors-Wade. Joanne is an excellent author in her own right; she's authored two books, *A Thread of Evidence* and *No Tomorrows*. Joanne proofread this entire book for me and for that; I owe her a great deal.

I want to thank my good friend Bob Morgan. Bob is a former sports journalist in Central Massachusetts. Bob has a very keen memory of baseball in the forties and fifties. His insightful comments are very much appreciated. Bob read every chapter as I wrote them and added stories that were simply fascinating.

I want to thank my good friend Art Johnson. Art was a major league pitcher in the forties with the Boston Braves. His willingness to fill me in on his memories and also his friendship will always be remembered by me.

I can't say enough good things about the website Retrosheet.org. This is by far the best baseball website there is and it was put together by volunteers led by Dave Smith. I thank them for their help.

Thanks also go to Rich Letarte, author of *That One Glorious Season*. Rich has a great baseball mind.

In addition, I want to thank Don Culp and Mark Miller. Don was once a baseball player in Ohio and was coached by the great Ty Cobb. Mark is an Ohio resident and an expert on the life and career of Harvey Haddix.

My best wishes go to Paul Bergman, a terrific baseball fan from Pittsburgh, Pa.

I thank former major league umpire Art Frantz.

I'd like to thank Paul Keating, former owner of the Albany Yankees.

Finally, I want to thank the following former major league baseball players for their willingness to spend time with me recalling their experiences in the games that I covered in this book. Billy Bryan, Rico Petrocelli, Bill Monboquette, Paul La Palme, Ken Wood, Ted Lepcio, Carl Willey, Bob Hendley, Chris Krug, Jim King, Milt Pappas, Joe Hicks, Billy Rohr, Russ Gibson, John Paciorek, Jack Hamilton, John Herrnstein, Frank Bolling, Jake Gibbs, Jim Bouton, Vern Benson, and Dick Kryhofski. The lineup that I just named is my Hall of Fame, believe me.

DEDICATION

I WOULD LIKE TO DEDICATE this book to my lovely wife, Melanie, and my three fabulous children, Alison, Randy, and Christopher.

Melanie is not a baseball fan, but has accompanied me to many a game all over the country, and her presence has made it that much more fun for me.

I'll never forget Alison running around Holman Stadium in Nashua, New Hampshire with her *Nashua Pirates* hat. I'd love to turn back the clock and take her to those games again. As I write this (2006), Alison is expecting a baby. Another baseball fan?

When the Red Sox won the World Series in 2004, it was my son Randy who made it extra special. When the Sox beat the Cardinals in four straight games, Randy, who was watching with his friends, called me up in the first inning of the clinching game to make sure I was awake. He called me again in the sixth to make sure again that I hadn't fallen asleep. He wanted to make sure that I saw the Sox win their first World Championship in 86 years. He told me that he would call me again in the ninth. He didn't. As the ninth inning began, I heard footsteps in the house. Randy had come home. He told me that he didn't want to be with anyone else when the Red Sox became World Champs.

Christopher and I have made several trips to games, but three stand out. Once we drove all the way to Detroit, once to Montreal, and once to Baltimore. All from our home in Massachusetts. I can't wait for the next one.

FORWARD

BASEBALL IS A WONDERFUL GAME. Ever since I was of single digit age, I've been drawn to baseball. It really is a very big part of my life. I've seen so many changes through the years. However, the classic time for me would have to be the 60's. When the 60's began, I was five years old. When they ended, I was sixteen. My formative years - and the baseball players of that era were like a second family to me. I just loved it. I collected all the cards, read all of the stats. My sister Janis used to say that that's why I could read so well so young, because of the baseball cards.

Baseball was very different then. Everything was about the game, not what happened around the game. The sports pages were about box scores and statistics. They were about commentary on the game, what happened on the field. Today, we read about union squabbles, strikes (work stoppages, not a well-pitched ball), steroids, contract negotiations and the like. Dick Radatz, the great Red Sox relief pitcher from the sixties once said, "In my day we used to pass a copy of *The Sporting News* around the locker room. Nowadays they pass around copies of the *Wall Street Journal*."

We used to have a lot of fun with trades. Talent for talent. Trades were big news. Even a trade from a team that wasn't your favorite team was something to talk about with other fans. Today, trades have to do with salary and years remaining on ones contract. Talent is the least important part of the recipe.

Baseball in the sixties was fun. That's what this book is about. It's about unique things that happened on the baseball field. Most of the games, not all, occurred during the sixties. Some funny, some bizarre, some shocking, some tragic, some impressive, but all of them interesting.

I've identified several games that were unique. These aren't the great games of the era, but each of them has a unique twist. In most cases, before the game began, no one could have possibly predicted that what was about to happen would happen. These games were not expected to be historic, but in some way, they were. You'll read about a home run champion who came off the bench to pitch and win the game! You'll read about a 59-year-old major league player. A 33-inning game. A guy who ran around the bases backwards!

You'll also read about a man who broke a very important racial barrier in the game. In addition, a twenty-two-year-old slugger who lost so much in one game.

Writing this book was an absolute joy. I've been such a devoted fan for so many years - writing a book about baseball was something that I always wanted to do. For the longest time, though, I didn't know what I could write that wasn't written already. There are lots of baseball books about players and many baseball books about teams. However, there aren't many books that have been written about individual games. That's what this book is all about. *One Day in Mudville* is a book that I hope will be fun and interesting to read. I hope you enjoy reading it as much as I enjoyed writing it.

CONTENTS

CHAPTER ONE

Saturday September 25, 1965
Boston Red Sox at Kansas City Athletics

Satchel Paige, 59 - The Oldest Major Leaguer

ON FRIDAY, SEPTEMBER 25, 1965, the baseball season was nearing its end for the '65 season. With a week to go, we all looked toward the post season. In those days, there were no playoffs. The American League and the National League each had ten teams, no divisions, making post season simple. The first place teams played a best of seven World Series.

The Minnesota Twins had a seven and one half game lead over the Baltimore Orioles with eight games to go and a magic number of two. Any combination of Twin wins and Oriole losses totaling two, would clinch the championship for the Twins. In the National League, a real pennant race was going on. The San Francisco Giants, Los Angeles Dodgers and Cincinnati Reds were neck and neck for first place. The week would prove interesting for the senior circuit. In the end, the Dodgers would prevail and go on to win the World Series, four games to three.

In Kansas City, Missouri, the game scheduled for that evening between the Boston Red Sox and the Kansas City Athletics was a far cry from a pennant race. With a week to go in the season, the

Red Sox were in ninth place out of ten teams and the Athletics were dead last. The Red Sox were thirty-seven games out of first place, a game and a half ahead of the Athletics, so here we were, with a late season game between the two worst teams in the American League. The attendance was less than ten thousand fans.

Some unique events came down that night. Hard to believe, but there were six men in uniform who were present or future Hall of Famers. Two Athletics coaches were immortals - Luke Appling and Gabby Hartnett. The Athletics also had a rookie pitcher Jim 'Catfish' Hunter. The 'Cat' was ending his rookie season with the Athletics, a season that saw him get eight wins with eight losses. Not bad for a last place team. 'Catfish' Hunter would become a perennial champion with both the Oakland Athletics and the New York Yankees and be enshrined in 1987.

The Red Sox had a twenty-six-year-old outfielder who led the league in batting in 1963, Carl Yastrzemski. 'Yaz' would go on to win the Triple Crown in two years and launch himself into a seventeen-year run that would get him in the Hall of Fame in his first year of eligibility, 1989. The Red Sox manager, a former National League second baseman, was Billy Herman. Herman would be enshrined in 1975.

No one could possibly have predicted one of the managers that night would ultimately own the other team. Haywood Sullivan was the manager of Kansas City for the last part of 1965. In just a few weeks, he would leave this organization owned by Charlie Finley, the maverick owner of the Kansas City team, and join the Red Sox front office. He climbed the corporate ladder with Buddy Leroux, a guy who would soon become the Red Sox trainer, of all things, and eventually own the Red Sox in the late 70's.

All of the above being so, the real treat of the night was, those fewer than ten thousand fans would see the man who was arguably the greatest pitcher of all time, future Hall of Famer, Leroy 'Satchel' Paige.

If not the greatest of all time, he was definitely among them. A comparison of statistics between Paige and the others might leave the casual fan wondering. Cy Young, after all, won 511 major league games lifetime. Walter Johnson won 416; Christy Mathewson won 373 and Warren Spahn, 363. Satchel Paige won a total of twenty-eight games. He lost thirty-one. How, then, could he be considered among the greats?

The answer? Plain and simple. Satchel Paige, an African American was a legend for many years in the Negro Leagues. In the pre-Jackie Robinson era, the years African American players were not welcome in the majors, Satchel Paige was lighting up baseball stadiums all over the place. He was a member of the Kansas City Monarchs, the Chattanooga Black Lookouts, the Memphis Red Sox and many more. He was nothing short of awesome.

His career began almost forty years prior to this September night. As far as we can tell, his first year in pro ball was 1926 with the Chattanooga Black Lookouts. He was twenty years old that year, or so we think. There has long been some question about Satchel's age - no one is certain. The date of birth historians most regard as his proper date of birth is July 7, 1906. He was born in Mobile, Alabama. His mother was asked years later to clarify Satchel's date of birth. She was either unable or unwilling to clarify.

She once told a sportswriter, "I can't rightly recall whether Leroy was my first born or my fifteenth."

As a young boy, Leroy acquired his nickname because he made a few bucks carrying luggage or 'satchels' at a railroad station.

In 1926, Satchel brought an incredible arm to the game, bringing great notice to the Negro Leagues. He was, to the Negro Leagues, what Babe Ruth was to the Majors, raising the level every time he performed.

Paige was a power pitcher with great speed, in addition to his famous 'hesitation pitch'. This was a unique change up and it's never been duplicated.

For the next two decades, Satchel dazzled fans and opponents alike as he pitched in every corner of the United States. Even though the Negro League teams played only each other in official games, the teams played major league teams often in exhibition games. He faced the Yankees in spring training, and Joe DiMaggio referred to him as "the best and fastest pitcher I ever faced."

Satchel pitched year round. When the Negro League season ended, he played winter ball in the Caribbean.

Paige had some quirky work habits. He didn't work out. He said he got stronger the more he pitched and didn't like to warm up. He believed he was wasting pitches that could be used in the game. He often claimed he started twenty-nine games in one month pitching in Bismarck, North Dakota. He also claimed he went 104-1 in 1934.

Satchel Paige was well paid. In the forties, he made $40,000 per year, making him the highest paid pro baseball player **in all of baseball.**

During World War II, Satchel led a team that barnstormed throughout the country and played against many major league teams. This was at the time the idea of someone breaking the color barrier was getting steam.

Satchel wanted to be the guy to do it and made no secret of it. As we know, Jackie Robinson was the guy who broke the color barrier. In my opinion, it was for the best that it came down that way for a couple of reasons. For one thing, Satchel Paige was a lot older than Jackie. When Robinson was signed, he started out in the minors in Montreal. It would have been an insult to Paige to start out in the minors. Paige was a pitcher and this is somewhat of a retaliatory position to begin with. What I mean is, when a batter hangs over the plate, a good pitcher will throw a 'brush back' or 'chin music' to get back some of the plate. Occasionally batters are hit by a pitch in these situations. A 'brush back' is good strategy; however, if Satchel Paige were the first black player, a 'brush back' would have been construed as aggression, not strategy.

In Satchel's autobiography, he states, "Signing Jackie like they did still hurts me deep down. I'd been the guy who'd started all that big talk about letting us in the big time. I'd been the one who'd opened the major league parks to colored teams. I'd been the one who the white boys wanted to go barnstorming against."

He also called Robinson "the greatest colored player I've ever seen." Jackie Robinson was the right guy for the job. For the next decade, Jackie was forced to steer a boat through incredibly rocky seas. Make no mistake about it; the boat Jackie Robinson steered was built by Satchel Paige.

Satchel finally got his chance to play in the major leagues. In 1948, he was signed by the Cleveland Indians. At age forty-two, he was the oldest rookie in major league history. He played for the Indians that year, winning six and losing one with a 2.48 earned run average helping the Indians win the world championship.

For two years, he pitched for the Indians, and then was released.

In 1950, he was back in the Negro League, but in 1951, he returned to the majors with the St. Louis Browns. The Browns were owned by Bill Veeck, the same guy who owned the Cleveland Indians when Paige pitched for them. He played three years for the Browns, through 1953. In 1952, he made the All Star team winning twelve and losing ten for the Browns, a team that went 64-90. In 1953, he pitched in fifty-seven games, won three, lost nine for the last place Browns. Once again, he was released.

Bob Morgan, a friend of mine, was a long-time sportscaster in New England. He has great recall of Satchel Paige. He saw Satchel pitch in a game on August 24, 1953; Browns against the Red Sox in Boston.

The game went into extra innings and with the score tied, the Red Sox loaded the bases with no outs in the bottom of the tenth. Satchel was summoned from the bullpen to keep the game going. With none out, 'Satch' struck out George Kell for the first out. Next batter up was player-manager Lou Boudreau. 'Satch' anticipated exactly what Boudreau was going to do. Boudreau was Satchel's manager when they were with Cleveland in the late forties. The only trouble was, Satchel couldn't convince anyone that he knew what was about to happen.

According to Bob, "Satchel, on the mound, called time and trying to be subtle, gestured to the third baseman, Jim Dyck, to come in for the bunt. Dyck didn't move, so Satchel just shrugged and threw a strike. The ball went back to him and again he gestured to the third baseman to move in for the bunt. Again, Dyck didn't move, so 'Satch' threw it way outside because obviously he knew what Boudreau was thinking. Everybody can see him, he's trying to wave Dyck in as if to say, 'go in, I know what he's going to do'...but Dyck never moved. Satch just shrugged his shoulders, got on the mound and threw a fastball right down the middle. What do you think Boudreau did? He pulled a suicide squeeze, driving in the winning run. Instead of throwing Boudreau out at first, Satchel Paige took the ball, flipped it up in the air and threw his glove at the third baseman and walked into the dugout."

Satch was up for a challenge. If Boudreau was going to beat him, he wanted it to be with a hit, not a bunt.

After the 1953 season, it was back to the Negro Leagues and barnstorming again. In 1955, he tacked on with the Miami Marlins of the International League. He pitched with them through 1957. By now, Satchel was fifty-one years old. This wasn't all, in 1961, at the age of fifty-five; he resurfaced with the Portland Beavers of the Pacific Coast League.

For the next few years, Satchel barnstormed again, making money at the one thing he knew - baseball. It seemed his career was finally over. In his mid fifties, after a lifetime of dedication to baseball, Satchel had very little money and no pension. This was a sad situation for Satchel. As for the baseball establishment, it was a shameful situation. Then came 1965.

While he barnstormed around the nation, the Kansas City Athletics were playing the worst baseball in the American League. They were owned by a maverick, Charles Finley, the master of promotion. Finley, a self-made man, had a soft spot in his heart for Satchel Paige. He came up with a way to help him. By putting Paige on the roster, Satchel would get some valued major league time and put him over the required time to qualify for a major league pension. Thus, he was signed. Charlie did this to not only help himself and promote his team; he also helped a man who deserved so much more than he ever got from baseball.

I had the opportunity to talk to Billy Bryan, catcher for the Kansas City Athletics that year. He caught old Satch's pitches that night. Bill is a real gentleman and had only good things to say about Satchel Paige. He remembered a time before Paige joined the team when "we (the Athletics) were going someplace and going through the airport, Satch was sitting there on a bench.

"Haywood Sullivan said, 'Hey, there's old Satch'. We went over and talked to him for a little while and Sully asked him, 'Satch, how many years you been pitching?' Old Satch looked up and said, 'forty some odd years'...Satch never called anybody by name. It was 'hey kid, hey pitch.'"

"I spent a lot of time in the bullpen too when Finley brought him in and he got him a rocking chair. He sat in the bullpen in a rocking chair...He didn't throw hard at that age and I don't think Satch even knew how old he was. He had his famous *Hesitation Pitch*...it was a changeup actually, with a lot of motion to it. Satch was tall and thin, with long arms and all. He'd follow through with his left foot and then his arm would come through after his whole body had completed its motion." Bryan told me he never saw this pitch by anyone else.

Paul La Palme was a pitcher for the Pittsburgh Pirates in the early 50's. His team faced Satchel's St. Louis Browns teams in spring training and he remembers Satchel and the *Hesitation Pitch* very well.

"I saw him pitch a couple of times. I was with the Pirates and we took spring training in California. On our way back, we were playing the St. Louis Browns quite a bit back in those days. Oh God! He pitched a couple of times and he was an elderly gentleman then, but what a great guy. Sometimes we'd be sitting around the hotel and he'd be in the lobby...I wish I had a tape recorder. He told some stories!"

"You had to see him pitch. You had to see him. He was phenomenal. I remember one play in particular. I think we were playing in Alpine, Texas and Satchel was pitching that day. Somebody hit the ball down the baseline and he lumbered like, he was so lanky and smooth, he lumbered over, picked up the ball and then took a couple of steps and he threw it underhand He just flipped it, like BOOM! And he just got the hitter by a half-step".

I asked Paul how he remembered the *Hesitation Pitch*.

"His arms and legs and everything moved, but the ball wasn't coming out of his hand! He had coordination up his bazoo!"

Rico Petrocelli, a member of the Red Sox Hall of Fame, was a rookie shortstop in 1965. He didn't play in this game, but remembers it well.

"He gave up one hit, a double to Yaz. He had a great sinker and it's all he threw. He was a great pitcher."

The winning pitcher that day was Red Sox pitcher Bill Monboquette. It turns out; this was the last game and last win for Monboquette as a member of the Red Sox. He's now a member of the Red Sox Hall of Fame. After the season ended, he was traded to the Detroit Tigers. He batted against Paige and struck out. While Monboquette was on the mound, he struck out Paige.

'Monbo' told me, "He had better swings off me than I had off him."

Here we were, late September 1965. A baseball game between the 'cellar dwellers' of the American League.

The starting lineups were announced and the Kansas City Athletics came out from the dugout and took their positions on the field. It was game time.

Walking toward the mound was a legend of baseball. A fifty-nine-year-old pitcher was about to face major league players in their twenties.

The Star Spangled Banner played, and the game began. Here is what happened.

Boston Red Sox 5, Kansas City Athletics 2

Game Played on Saturday, September 25, 1965 (N) at Municipal Stadium

```
BOS A    0  0  0    0  0  0    2  3  0  -  5  7  0
KC  A    1  0  0    0  0  1    0  0  0  -  2  7  1
```

BATTING

Boston Red Sox	AB	R	H	RBI	BB	SO	PO	A
Gosger cf	4	1	1	0	0	0	0	0
Jones 3b	3	0	0	0	0	1	0	0
Malzone ph,3b	1	0	0	0	0	1	1	0
Yastrzemski lf	4	1	2	0	0	1	6	0
Conigliaro rf	3	2	2	2	1	0	2	0
Thomas 1b	3	1	1	2	1	0	9	0
Mantilla 2b	4	0	1	0	0	1	0	4
Bressoud ss	4	0	0	0	0	1	2	1
Ryan c	4	0	0	0	0	0	7	1
Monbouquette p	4	0	0	0	0	3	0	2
Totals	34	5	7	4	2	8	27	8

FIELDING -
DP: 1. Mantilla-Bressoud-Thomas.

BATTING -
2B: Yastrzemski (44,off Paige).
HR: Thomas (21,7th inning off Segui 1 on 0 out); Conigliaro (31,8th inning off Wyatt 1 on 2 out).
Team LOB: 4.

Kansas City Athletics	AB	R	H	RBI	BB	SO	PO	A
Campaneris ss	4	0	0	0	0	0	1	3
Tartabull cf	4	1	2	0	0	1	2	0
Causey 3b	3	0	0	0	1	0	2	0
Bryan c	4	1	2	1	0	1	8	1
Green 2b	4	0	2	1	0	0	2	1
Rosario 1b	4	0	1	0	0	0	6	1
Hershberger rf	3	0	0	0	0	0	2	0
Reynolds lf	3	0	0	0	0	1	3	0
Paige p	1	0	0	0	0	1	0	0
Segui p	1	0	0	0	0	1	1	0
Stahl ph	1	0	0	0	0	1	0	0
Mossi p	0	0	0	0	0	0	0	0
Wyatt p	0	0	0	0	0	0	0	0
Aker p	0	0	0	0	0	0	0	0
Totals	32	2	7	2	1	6	27	6

FIELDING -
E: Rosario (1).

PB: Bryan 2 (16).

BATTING -
2B: Bryan (10,off Monbouquette).
Team LOB: 4.

BASERUNNING -
CS: Tartabull (5,2nd base by Monbouquette/Ryan).

PITCHING

Boston Red Sox	IP	H	R	ER	BB	SO	HR
Monbouquette W(10-18)	9	7	2	2	1	6	0

Kansas City Athletics	IP	H	R	ER	BB	SO	HR
Paige	3	1	0	0	0	1	0
Segui	4	3	2	2	1	4	1
Mossi L(5-7)	0.1	1	1	1	0	1	0
Wyatt	0.1	2	2	2	1	1	1
Aker	1.1	0	0	0	0	1	0
Totals	9	7	5	5	2	8	2

WP: Segui (8), Wyatt (12).

Umpires: Bill Valentine, Bill McKinley, Hank Soar

Time of Game: 2:14   Attendance: 9289

Starting Lineups:

Boston Red Sox		Kansas City Athletics	
1. Gosger	cf	Campaneris	ss
2. Jones	3b	Tartabull	cf
3. Yastrzemski	lf	Causey	3b
4. Conigliaro	rf	Bryan	c
5. Thomas	1b	Green	2b
6. Mantilla	2b	Rosario	1b
7. Bressoud	ss	Hershberger	rf
8. Ryan	c	Reynolds	lf
9. Monbouquette	p	Paige	p

RED SOX 1ST: Gosger popped to first; Jones reached on an error by Rosario [Jones to second]; Jones was out trying to advance to third; Yastrzemski doubled; Conigliaro made an out to left; 0 R, 1 H, 1 E, 1 LOB. Red Sox 0, Athletics 0.

ATHLETICS 1ST: Campaneris popped to catcher in foul territory; Tartabull singled; Causey grounded out (first unassisted) [Tartabull to second]; Bryan singled [Tartabull scored]; Green lined to left; 1 R, 2 H, 0 E, 1 LOB. Red Sox 0, Athletics 1.

RED SOX 2ND: Thomas popped to third; Mantilla grounded out (shortstop to first); Bressoud made an out to right; 0 R, 0 H, 0 E, 0 LOB. Red Sox 0, Athletics 1.

ATHLETICS 2ND: Rosario singled; Hershberger made an out to left; Reynolds struck out; Paige struck out; 0 R, 1 H, 0 E, 1 LOB. Red Sox 0, Athletics 1.

RED SOX 3RD: Ryan popped to shortstop; Monbouquette struck out; Gosger grounded out (shortstop to first); 0 R, 0 H, 0 E, 0 LOB. Red Sox 0, Athletics 1.

ATHLETICS 3RD: Campaneris grounded out (pitcher to first); Tartabull singled; Tartabull was caught stealing second (catcher to shortstop); Causey walked; Bryan struck out; 0 R, 1 H, 0 E, 1 LOB. Red Sox 0, Athletics 1.

RED SOX 4TH: SEGUI REPLACED PAIGE (PITCHING); Jones grounded out (first to pitcher); Yastrzemski struck out; Conigliaro singled; Bryan allowed a passed ball [Conigliaro to second]; Thomas popped to first; 0 R, 1 H, 0 E, 1 LOB. Red Sox 0, Athletics 1.

ATHLETICS 4TH: Green singled; Rosario grounded into a double play (second to shortstop to first) [Green out at second]; Hershberger made an out to right; 0 R, 1 H, 0 E, 0 LOB. Red Sox 0, Athletics 1.

RED SOX 5TH: Mantilla singled; Segui threw a wild pitch [Mantilla to second]; Bressoud grounded out (second to first) [Mantilla to third]; Ryan grounded out (shortstop to first); Monbouquette was called out on strikes; 0 R, 1 H, 0 E, 1 LOB. Red Sox 0, Athletics 1.

ATHLETICS 5TH: Reynolds grounded out (pitcher to first); Segui struck out; Campaneris made an out to left; 0 R, 0 H, 0 E, 0 LOB. Red Sox 0, Athletics 1.

RED SOX 6TH: Gosger made an out to right; Jones was called out on strikes; Yastrzemski popped to second; 0 R, 0 H, 0 E, 0 LOB. Red Sox 0, Athletics 1.

ATHLETICS 6TH: Tartabull was called out on strikes; Causey grounded out (second to first); Bryan doubled; Green singled [Bryan scored]; Rosario grounded out (second to first); 1 R, 2 H, 0 E, 1 LOB. Red Sox 0, Athletics 2.

RED SOX 7TH: Conigliaro walked; Thomas homered [Conigliaro scored]; Mantilla made an out to left; Bressoud struck out; Ryan made an out to center; 2 R, 1 H, 0 E, 0 LOB. Red Sox 2, Athletics 2.

ATHLETICS 7TH: Hershberger made an out to left; Reynolds lined to left; STAHL BATTED FOR SEGUI; Stahl struck out; 0 R, 0 H, 0 E, 0 LOB. Red Sox 2, Athletics 2.

RED SOX 8TH: MOSSI REPLACED STAHL (PITCHING); Monbouquette struck out; Gosger singled; MALZONE BATTED FOR JONES; WYATT REPLACED MOSSI (PITCHING); Bryan allowed a passed ball [Gosger to second]; Malzone struck out; Yastrzemski singled [Gosger to third]; Wyatt threw a wild pitch [Gosger scored, Yastrzemski to second]; Conigliaro hit an inside the park homer to center [Yastrzemski scored]; Thomas walked; AKER REPLACED WYATT (PITCHING); Mantilla struck out; 3 R, 3 H, 0 E, 1 LOB. Red Sox 5, Athletics 2.

ATHLETICS 8TH: MALZONE STAYED IN GAME (PLAYING 3B); Campaneris lined to right; Tartabull grounded out (first unassisted);

Causey popped to third; 0 R, 0 H, 0 E, 0 LOB.   Red Sox 5,
Athletics 2.

RED SOX 9TH: Bressoud made an out to left; Ryan popped to
second; Monbouquette made an out to center; 0 R, 0 H, 0 E, 0
LOB.   Red Sox 5, Athletics 2.

ATHLETICS 9TH: Bryan grounded out (second to first); Green made
an out to left; Rosario grounded out (first unassisted); 0 R, 0
H, 0 E, 0 LOB.   Red Sox 5, Athletics 2.

Final Totals	R	H	E	LOB
Red Sox	5	7	0	4
Athletics	2	7	1	4

CHAPTER TWO

Sunday June 23, 1963
Philadelphia Phillies at New York Mets

Jimmy Piersall homers and runs the bases backwards.

JIMMY PIERSALL WAS ONE OF the most unforgettable players that ever played the game. He was a classic. Never one like him before, nor since.

Jimmy Piersall was what they used to call a 'flake'. He was colorful and unpredictable. People bought a ticket just to see Jimmy Piersall.

He is the guy who introduced me to baseball - starting my journey as a die-hard fan. I was about five-years-old, or so, I'm not exactly sure. I can't recall if he was a member of the Boston Red Sox or the Cleveland Indians - he was traded from Boston to Cleveland around that time.

What I do recall is my mother taking me to the local A & P grocery store because Jimmy Piersall was going to be there signing autographs and meeting people, so off we went. I remember being in awe of the rugged major leaguer. I also remember him being very nice to me and very friendly to my mother. He said I had great teeth.

He said to my mom, "I wish my kids had teeth like that." He autographed a picture for me; I took it home and never forgot that meeting with him.

I got to be a huge fan of his. I became aware of his story, how he dealt with mental illness early in his career with the Red Sox. I got his book from the library, *Fear Strikes Out*. I watched the movie of the same name.

When I first started watching baseball with some serious intensity, he was a member of the Washington Senators. I lived (and still do) in central Massachusetts, so I could only see him on television when the Senators played the Red Sox. Later on, when he was with the Angels, I would ask my father to take me to Fenway Park only when the Angels were the visiting team so that I could see Piersall.

Once we went to New York City and I saw Jimmy play for the Angels against the New York Yankees at Yankee Stadium.

One game I'll never forget. September 13, 1964 (I still have the score sheet).The Angels played the Red Sox at Fenway Park and Jimmy Piersall hit a home run into the screen above the green monster. I can still see it, a line drive that continued to rise when it went over the wall. I was sitting behind third base and I recall seeing a big smile on Jimmy's face as he rounded the bases. Jimmy Piersall loved playing baseball. He was a guy who played hard and had fun doing so.

In 1952, early in his career, he dealt with mental illness and the game wasn't much fun. He accounts for it all in his book *Fear Strikes Out*. This book is considered one of the greatest sports biographies of all time. His description of his feelings when he was sick really puts the reader in his place. He was under extreme pressure; at least he felt extreme pressure.

He said that he always had a headache, every minute of every day. Sometimes it was more subtle than other times, but every minute of every day, he had a headache. Then he describes the treatment that he underwent at Westborough State Hospital in Massachusetts. A book I recommend.

I had the great opportunity to talk to Ken Wood about Jim Piersall. Ken was a teammate of Jim's with the Red Sox in 1952. He remembers the entire goings on when Jimmy was a rookie.

"I knew Jimmy before that and in my personal opinion, he got a lot of publicity with the writers, they would write something about

Jimmy and he would just go wild. He would do something else to get publicity and I think that's what happened to him really. He was a good boy, a good kid."

That year the Red Sox tried something that didn't work out too well with Piersall. Though he was a trained outfielder and a very good fielder, the Red Sox wanted to make Jimmy their shortstop, even though he never played that position. Ken Wood remembered that well.

"I could never figure out, I don't want to say too much because I was just a scrubeenie on the club, but they had four or five kids that they brought up from the minor leagues that were in the opening day lineup. You had (Billy) Goodman sitting on the bench, Gene Stephens, I think, was on the bench on opening day and maybe Walt Dropo, I'm not sure. They had Ted Lepcio at second base and Piersall opened the season at shortstop. He played there about a month and then they moved him to the outfield."

His roommate with the Red Sox was infielder Ted Lepcio. Ted is a terrific guy who spoke with me at length about his former roommate.

"He was my roommate for seven years. We didn't know anything about it (mental illness), but at times, that type of performance aggravated everybody because he was wound a little tight and did a few unusual things. It's well documented that he had to go to the hospital in Westborough for a little while, obviously he was troubled with something, but then he came out, we roomed together again."

"They asked me 'What do you think'? I said he's the same kid I knew (before mental illness), whether he went up there (Westborough) or not."

He spoke about Piersall's fielding ability and simply stated, "None better."

Bob Morgan, my sportscaster friend remembers Jimmy as a hustler.

"Every time he played, he hustled. He had a great arm. Defensively he was as good as Dwight Evans was. He was as good as anybody was. If he hit a ground ball back to the pitcher, he would run to first. That was Jimmy Piersall."

With his mental illness behind him, Jimmy returned to baseball and had a very good career. His final stats, 104 home runs, a .274 lifetime batting average in 17 major league seasons were stats any one would be proud of. His lifetime outfielders fielding average of .990 make him one of the greatest fielding outfielders of all time. He had a great arm, though he injured it in an unfortunate way.

On May 10, 1953, Piersall robbed Mickey Mantle of a home run with a fabulous catch reaching into the Red Sox bullpen in right-center field at Fenway. One month later, on June 10, 1953, he went six for six in a game between the Red Sox and the St. Louis Browns.

Jimmy Piersall was best known for doing 'nutty' things. He never backed down from a fight. He had some famous fights with Billy Martin. On May 24, 1952, he and Martin got into a real donnybrook in Boston. Teammates broke up the fight, and Piersall had to go to the clubhouse to change his bloody shirt. Later that day, he and Mickey McDermott, a Red Sox teammate, got into a fight, no one seems to remember why.

On May 10, 1953, something weird happened. Teammate Billy Goodman got into a heated argument with American League umpire Jim Duffy. Piersall broke up the argument and physically tried to pull Goodman into the dugout. He had Goodman in a bear hug and in trying to drag him into the dugout, he injured Goodman's ribs, and Goodman was out of the lineup for three weeks.

On August 16, 1954, there was an exhibition game between the Red Sox and the National League New York Giants. As part of the festivities, there was a throwing contest between Jimmy Piersall and Willie Mays. In this contest, Jimmy hurt his arm. He played only part of the game. His arm was never the same after that.

In 1961, he was one of the best batters in the game, batting .322 as a member of the Cleveland Indians. Three years later, while playing for the Los Angeles Angels, he batted .314 and was named the American League's Comeback Player of the Year.

On July 23, 1960, he was playing for the Indians against the Red Sox, and his old friend and teammate Ted Williams was at bat and

Piersall was in center field. To distract Williams, Piersall started doing jumping jacks and a war dance in center field. He got thrown out of the game for doing so. It was the sixth time that season that he was thrown out of a game.

On September 13, 1962, while he was a Washington Senator, he was in Baltimore and was heckled by an obnoxious fan. He went into the stands and attacked the fan. He was arrested and charged with disorderly conduct. The next day, after his hearing, he left the court building and was knocked unconscious by a revolving door.

Late in his career, Piersall was a bench player with the Angels. He came out to warm up the pitcher as the catcher put on his gear. While he was behind home plate, Jimmy noticed the home plate umpire, Emmet Ashford looking out toward the outfield. Piersall completely buried home plate with dirt. When Ashford went back to call balls and strikes, there was no visible home plate.

All of that being said, the crowing glory of Jimmy Piersall's nuttiness occurred on June 23, 1963. On this beautiful Sunday afternoon, the Philadelphia Phillies were at the Polo Grounds in Flushing, New York to play the New York Mets. Piersall was a member of the Mets. It was not a good year for either team. The Phillies were in eighth place out of ten teams, ten games behind the league leading St. Louis Cardinals. The Mets were in their second season of existence. In 1962, they were the worst team in the league, forty wins, and one hundred twenty losses. They were not much better in 1963. On this day, they were 26-44, in last place and fifteen and one half games behind the first place Cardinals.

However, the Mets were lovable. Their manager was Casey Stengel, one of the greatest and most colorful managers of all time. He was seventy-two years old at the time, and used to fall asleep in the dugout. You'd think that Piersall would be the ideal player for Stengel, two showmen, but they didn't get along all that well.

The Commissioner of Baseball was Ford Frick. The major league offices were in New York City and Frick often attended Yankee or Met games. He happened to be in the stands this day. He wasn't crazy about what happened.

In a game that was otherwise just another game, Jimmy Piersall hit his one hundredth home run of his career. An achievement to be proud of for sure, but a whole lot of guys have hit one hundred home runs. It's not exactly front-page news. This time it was.

To insure he got all the attention for this event, Jimmy Piersall ran around the bases backward. That's right, backward.

He made front-page news in the sports pages. The next day, if you look at the lead story in the New York Times sports section, the headline included "ymmiJ llasreiP of the Mets (who else?) Makes Backward Run After Hitting One Hundredth Homer."

Bob Morgan remembers this game very well.

"What a lot of people don't know, Casey Stengel who was managing the Mets at that time was really mad, he was really ripping. He told the press that he told Piersall 'I don't have to worry about this again because you'll never get to two hundred (home runs). Don't you ever do that again. You want to know why, sir?' Piersall asked 'Why?' Because I'm the vaudevillian, I'm the funny man, not you'".

What inspired Piersall for this act was the great Duke Snider. Duke played for the Mets that year as well and the future Hall of Famer hit his 400th lifetime home run. Piersall was excited when that happened and the next day purchased all the newspapers. There was only a small reference to Snider's 400th home run. In his book, *The Truth Hurts*, Piersall explains that he decided then that should he hit his 100th, it was going to be big.

He told Duke Snider," Hey, I got 99 homers, Duke, and when I get my 100th, I'm going coast to coast. See you later."

On June 23, they were playing the Phillies. It was a very nice Sunday afternoon. He had no home runs on the season, and Dallas Green was pitching for the Phils. The game was at the Polo Grounds, with its 247 feet foul lines. He was trying for the home run at first, but then the count went to three and two. In his book, Jimmy explained what happened next.

"The count went to three and two, and then I just wanted to hit the ball. Green let the next pitch go, and I got jammed and hit it straight down the right field line. It stayed fair, 248 feet, and dropped into the seats. So, I ran around the bases backward."

"And I ran fast backward because I'd practiced for this, back-pedaling. Anyway, running backward, I rounded first, second, and when I got to third I shook hands with Cookie Lavagetto, our third base coach, and then continued on to home plate. The place was going wild. But when I passed Stengel in the dugout, he didn't even smile."

"The next morning, I felt I was really going to get some ink on this. Well, there were about eight newspapers in New York then, and it was big in all of them. In one newspaper, there was a whole sequence of pictures of me running around the bases backward-not on a sports page, but on the front page of the paper. I bought copies of all of them and brought them out to the stadium later that day. I gave them all to Snider."

The Mets pitcher that day was Carl Willey. Carl pitched for the Milwaukee Braves and the New York Mets in his career and actually pitched the best game of his career, a two hit shutout.

The memory of Jimmy Piersall made him chuckle with affection for his old teammate. Funny thing was when I asked him about the game, he didn't remember his own performance, but did remember the backwards run by Piersall.

According to the former pitcher, "He kept saying he was going to do that, nobody believed him. He finally did it! He was a dandy! I saw Piersall climb the light tower in Birmingham, Alabama one day in the Southern Association."

At that time, they were on different teams, in different dugouts. The players on the visiting team became aware that something unusual was happening on high.

"Finally we looked up; there was Piersall, way up the light tower." I asked him if anyone knew why he climbed the light tower.

He said, "No, I don't think he does, either."

He remembered the Father and Sons game they had that year (1963) in New York.

"We had a father-son game in New York one time and my son hit the ball and just stood there. Piersall was umpiring and took him under his arm and ran to first base with him."

(He didn't mention whether or not he carried his son around the bases forward or backward.)

After his playing days, Jimmy did many things, starting in Public Relations for the California Angels, then bounced around a bit. He went on to work for the Oakland Athletics and Charles Finley. He called that experience a "fiasco" and called Finley "an awful person."

Later, Billy Martin, the guy he went many rounds with when they were playing got him a job with the Texas Rangers when Martin was managing the team. Piersall never mellowed, spoke his mind on all of these jobs, which is probably why there were so many of them. His last stop before retirement was as a broadcaster in Chicago. He did color for White Sox games. I don't need to point out that he was very outspoken and very controversial. Richie Phillips, the attorney and head of the umpires union actually wrote him a letter complaining about the way he went after umpires on his broadcasts.

Many broadcasters have found themselves in hot water because the players they covered didn't like them. Jim Piersall is the only guy that got into hot water because the players' wives didn't like him. The last straw was when he referred to them as "just horny broads that wanted to get married, and they wanted a little money, a little security, and they wanted a big, strong ball player."

His last broadcasting gig was as a sports shock jock talk show host on a radio station in Chicago. As I write this (2006), Jimmy is 77 years old, and enjoying his retirement at his home in Wheaton, Illinois.

Back in 1963, he did what no one else ever did, before or after. He circumnavigated the base paths backwards, and shook the third base coach's hand with his left hand, not his right.

Jimmy, I'd give anything to have another one like you.

Here we are at the Polo Grounds on Sunday June 23, 1963.

New York Mets 5, Philadelphia Phillies 0 (1)

Game Played on Sunday, June 23, 1963 (D) at Polo Grounds V

```
PHI N    0  0  0    0  0  0    0  0  0  -   0   2  2
NY  N    0  0  1    0  1  0    3  0  x  -   5  10  0
```

BATTING

Philadelphia Phillies	AB	R	H	RBI	BB	SO	PO	A
Taylor 2b	4	0	1	0	0	2	1	2
Callison rf	4	0	1	0	0	0	1	0
Gonzalez cf	4	0	0	0	0	0	1	0
Sievers 1b	3	0	0	0	0	0	4	2
Demeter lf	3	0	0	0	0	1	0	0
Dalrymple c	2	0	0	0	0	0	7	3
Baldschun p	0	0	0	0	0	0	0	0
Wine ss	3	0	0	0	0	0	3	2
Amaro 3b	3	0	0	0	0	0	1	1
Green p	1	0	0	0	0	1	2	2
Torre ph	1	0	0	0	0	1	0	0
Short p	0	0	0	0	0	0	0	0
Boozer p	0	0	0	0	0	0	0	0
Bennett p	0	0	0	0	0	0	0	0
Oldis c	1	0	0	0	0	1	4	0
Totals	29	0	2	0	0	6	24	12

FIELDING -
DP: 2. Dalrymple-Wine-Dalrymple, Taylor-Wine-Sievers.
E: Wine (10), Amaro (5).

BATTING -
3B: Callison (3,off Willey); Taylor (5,off Willey).
HBP: Dalrymple (3,by Willey).
Team LOB: 3.

New York Mets	AB	R	H	RBI	BB	SO	PO	A
Piersall cf	5	1	3	1	0	1	1	0
Harkness 1b	3	2	0	0	2	2	8	0
Hunt 2b	4	0	1	0	1	1	0	0
Snider lf	3	0	2	1	1	1	4	0
Kanehl pr,lf	0	1	0	0	0	0	0	0
Kranepool rf	3	0	0	0	0	1	1	0
Hickman ph,rf	1	1	0	0	0	0	0	0
Coleman c	3	0	2	0	0	0	6	0
Thomas ph	1	0	1	1	0	0	0	0
Jackson pr	0	0	0	0	0	0	0	0
Sherry c	0	0	0	0	0	0	3	0
Neal 3b	4	0	1	0	0	1	3	0
Moran ss	2	0	0	0	2	1	1	4

Willey p	4	0	0	0	0	2	0	2
Totals	33	5	10	3	6	10	27	6

BATTING -
2B: Piersall (3,off Baldschun).
HR: Piersall (1,5th inning off Green 0 on 0 out).
IBB: Snider (7,by Boozer).
Team LOB: 10.

BASERUNNING -
SB: Harkness (1,2nd base off Boozer/Dalrymple).
CS: Piersall (1,2nd base by Green/Dalrymple); Hunt (3,Home by Green/Dalrymple)

PITCHING

Philadelphia Phillies	IP	H	R	ER	BB	SO	HR
Green L(1-2)	5	7	2	2	3	4	1
Short	0.2	1	0	0	1	0	0
Boozer	1	0	2	0	2	2	0
Bennett	0	0	1	0	0	0	0
Baldschun	1.1	2	0	0	0	4	0
Totals	8	10	5	2	6	10	1

New York Mets	IP	H	R	ER	BB	SO	HR
Willey W(6-6)	9	2	0	0	0	6	0

WP: Short (3), Bennett (1), Baldschun (2).
HBP: Willey (3,Dalrymple).
IBB: Boozer (3,Snider).

Umpires: Frank Secory, Bill Jackowski, Paul Pryor, Vinnie Smith

Time of Game: 2:34

Starting Lineups:

	Philadelphia Phillies		New York Mets	
1.	Taylor	2b	Piersall	cf
2.	Callison	rf	Harkness	1b
3.	Gonzalez	cf	Hunt	2b
4.	Sievers	1b	Snider	lf
5.	Demeter	lf	Kranepool	rf
6.	Dalrymple	c	Coleman	c
7.	Wine	ss	Neal	3b
8.	Amaro	3b	Moran	ss
9.	Green	p	Willey	p

PHILLIES 1ST: Taylor popped to first in foul territory; Callison lined to left; Gonzalez lined to left; 0 R, 0 H, 0 E, 0 LOB. Phillies 0, Mets 0.

METS 1ST: Piersall singled to right; Harkness struck out; Piersall was caught stealing second (catcher to shortstop); Hunt singled to center; Snider singled to center [Hunt to third]; Kranepool grounded out (first to second to pitcher); 0 R, 3 H, 0 E, 2 LOB. Phillies 0, Mets 0.

PHILLIES 2ND: Sievers lined to third; Demeter struck out;

Dalrymple made an out to center; 0 R, 0 H, 0 E, 0 LOB. Phillies
0, Mets 0.

METS 2ND: Coleman singled to center; Neal forced Coleman
(pitcher to shortstop); Moran forced Neal (third to second);
Willey struck out; 0 R, 1 H, 0 E, 1 LOB. Phillies 0, Mets 0.

PHILLIES 3RD: Wine popped to catcher in foul territory; Amaro
made an out to left; Green struck out; 0 R, 0 H, 0 E, 0 LOB.
Phillies 0, Mets 0.

METS 3RD: Piersall made an out to center; Harkness walked; Hunt
walked [Harkness to second]; Snider singled to right [Harkness
scored, Hunt to third]; Kranepool struck out while Hunt was
caught stealing home (catcher to shortstop to catcher); 1 R, 1
H, 0 E, 1 LOB. Phillies 0, Mets 1.

PHILLIES 4TH: Taylor struck out; Callison tripled to center;
Gonzalez reached on a fielder's choice [Callison out at home
(shortstop to catcher)]; Sievers made an out to left; 0 R, 1 H,
0 E, 1 LOB. Phillies 0, Mets 1.

METS 4TH: Coleman singled to center; Neal made an out to right;
Moran walked [Coleman to second]; Willey grounded into a double
play (second to shortstop to first) [Moran out at second]; 0 R,
1 H, 0 E, 1 LOB. Phillies 0, Mets 1.

PHILLIES 5TH: Demeter grounded out (first unassisted); Dalrymple
was hit by a pitch; Wine made an out to right; Amaro popped to
third in foul territory; 0 R, 0 H, 0 E, 1 LOB. Phillies 0, Mets
1.

METS 5TH: Piersall homered; Harkness grounded out (first to
pitcher); Hunt grounded out (pitcher to first); Snider was
called out on strikes; 1 R, 1 H, 0 E, 0 LOB. Phillies 0, Mets 2.

PHILLIES 6TH: TORRE BATTED FOR GREEN; Torre struck out; Taylor
tripled to right; Callison grounded out (pitcher to first);
Gonzalez grounded out (shortstop to first); 0 R, 1 H, 0 E, 1
LOB. Phillies 0, Mets 2.

METS 6TH: SHORT REPLACED TORRE (PITCHING); Kranepool popped to
third in foul territory; Coleman grounded out (first
unassisted); Neal singled to right; Moran walked [Neal to
second]; Short threw a wild pitch [Neal to third, Moran to
second]; BOOZER REPLACED SHORT (PITCHING); Willey struck out; 0
R, 1 H, 0 E, 2 LOB. Phillies 0, Mets 2.

PHILLIES 7TH: Sievers popped to first in foul territory; Demeter
popped to third; Dalrymple popped to shortstop; 0 R, 0 H, 0 E, 0
LOB. Phillies 0, Mets 2.

METS 7TH: Piersall was called out on strikes; Harkness walked;
Harkness stole second; Hunt grounded out (catcher to first);
Snider was walked intentionally; KANEHL RAN FOR SNIDER; BENNETT
REPLACED BOOZER (PITCHING); HICKMAN BATTED FOR KRANEPOOL;
Bennett threw a wild pitch [Harkness to third, Kanehl to
second]; Hickman reached on an error by Amaro [Harkness scored
(unearned), Kanehl to third, Hickman to first]; THOMAS BATTED
FOR COLEMAN; BALDSCHUN REPLACED DALRYMPLE (PITCHING); OLDIS

REPLACED BENNETT (PLAYING C); Thomas singled to center [Kanehl scored (unearned), Hickman to third]; JACKSON RAN FOR THOMAS; Baldschun threw a wild pitch [Hickman scored (unearned), Jackson to second]; Neal was called out on strikes; 3 R, 1 H, 1 E, 1 LOB. Phillies 0, Mets 5.

PHILLIES 8TH: HICKMAN STAYED IN GAME (PLAYING RF); KANEHL STAYED IN GAME (PLAYING LF); SHERRY REPLACED JACKSON (PLAYING C); Wine grounded out (shortstop to first); Amaro popped to catcher in foul territory; Oldis was called out on strikes; 0 R, 0 H, 0 E, 0 LOB. Phillies 0, Mets 5.

METS 8TH: Moran was called out on strikes; Willey reached on an error by Wine [Willey to first]; Piersall doubled to right [Willey to third]; Harkness struck out; Hunt struck out; 0 R, 1 H, 1 E, 2 LOB. Phillies 0, Mets 5.

PHILLIES 9TH: Taylor struck out; Callison grounded out (shortstop to first); Gonzalez grounded out (pitcher to first); 0 R, 0 H, 0 E, 0 LOB. Phillies 0, Mets 5.

Final Totals	R	H	E	LOB
Phillies	0	2	2	3
Mets	5	10	0	10

CHAPTER THREE

September 9, 1965
Chicago Cubs at Los Angeles Dodgers

The Greatest Pitched Game in History: Unforgettable Game

WHEN I MADE UP MY list of games for this book, my goal was to come up with games in my memory that were unusual. The first two games I covered were one-of-a-kind. One game featured a fifty-nine-year-old major leaguer and one game featured a batter who rounded the bases backwards after hitting a home run. Unusual, for sure, but you wouldn't call them GREAT games.

Well, the game I'm covering now was certainly unusual and it was indeed GREAT. One of the greatest games of all time.

It happened on September 9, 1965. The Chicago Cubs took on the Los Angeles Dodgers in Los Angeles. It was a mid-week late season game with no real importance in the standings for the Cubs. The fans were there to see the Dodgers who had a chance to be in the post season.

At game time, the Dodgers were 79-61, tied with the Cincinnati Reds, both teams one-half game behind the San Francisco Giants. A heated pennant race was going on, so a win today would be important for the Dodgers, for sure.

The Cubs were in eighth place. Sixty-five wins, seventy-six losses, fifteen games behind. Cub fans had nothing to anticipate for the post season.

Pitching for the Dodgers that day was Sandy Koufax, one of the greatest pitchers of all time. Going into the game, the twenty-nine-year-old left-handed Koufax had twenty-one wins against seven losses on the season. He was headed to a Cy Young award as well as the World Series.

The Dodgers eventually won the National League pennant and the World Championship as they beat the American League champion Minnesota Twins in seven games of the World Series.

Pitching that day for the Cubs was a twenty-six-year-old lefty named Bob Hendley. His record as the day began was two wins, two losses on the season. He was pitching for the third team in his career, and second of the season. He pitched for the Milwaukee Braves from 1961 to 1963 going on to pitch for the San Francisco Giants in 1964. He started the 1965 season with the Giants, but after getting into eight games, was traded to the Cubs. His lifetime record on September 9, 1965 was thirty-seven wins, forty-two losses.

So here we were, Dodger Stadium in Los Angeles, a night game in September, Koufax vs. Hendley, and the Dodgers vs. the Cubs. There were 29000 fans in attendance. I guarantee you not one player, umpire, batboy, concession worker, or anyone else could have predicted they were about to witness the **greatest pitched game in the history of baseball.**

Indeed, it was exactly that. When it was over, both pitchers combined for seventeen innings pitched, one hit allowed, one base on balls, seventeen strikeouts, and only one unearned run. The final score, Dodgers 1, Cubs 0. The only hit of the game was by the Dodgers and it had absolutely nothing to do with the game's only run. In addition to that, it was the major league's eighth perfect game.

Twenty-seven Cubs came up and went down. Not one reached first base. This was the greatest game ever pitched by Koufax, and he had many great ones. This was also the greatest game pitched by Bob Hendley in his career, even though it was a loss.

Major league batters went one for fifty-one that day, for a batting average of .020. It was simply an awesome, unforgettable game, and one that could never have been predicted. This is the kind of game that makes baseball great.

Sandy Koufax's career was an interesting one. He played with the Dodgers only, both in Brooklyn and Los Angeles. He was indeed a native of Brooklyn. He never played a day in the minor leagues and his career lasted twelve seasons.

A comparison of his first six years and his second six years is startling. After his sixth year, Koufax had a lifetime record of thirty-six wins, forty losses, with an earned run average of 4.10. That was the record he took to spring training in 1961. How about if I told you, at that time, this guy was going to be a first time inductee into the Hall of Fame in only eleven years. You'd think I was crazy. What he did from then on was unbelievable.

For his second six years in the majors, he won 129 games, lost 47, and had an earned run average of 2.19. Most notably, the last four of those six years he won ninety-seven, lost twenty-seven, with an earned run average of 1.86.

During those four years, I was eight to twelve years old. It was my great honor to see many of the games he pitched. Back then, we had the NBC game of the week every Saturday. The Dodgers were on probably more than any other team, at least that's what my memory says.

Koufax became a color commentator on those games after his career ended at the end of the 1966 season. His career was cut short by severe elbow troubles. No one has ever had a four year run like that. He was only thirty when he pitched his last game in the majors, and is to date (2006) the youngest Hall of Fame inductee at the age of thirty-six.

I'd like to report that I spoke to Koufax about this game and his career, but I cannot. Sandy Koufax is simply not available for comment. Since leaving television, he has guarded his privacy very closely. He's never interviewed. How many times do you see ex-players interviewed on ESPN? You never see Koufax.

He simply doesn't want to be part of the hoopla and hype of it all. He's not a hermit; he does get around, he just doesn't get near a microphone or TV camera.

In 1999, the All-Star game was played at Fenway Park, Boston. Before the game, the all-century team was introduced. Ted Williams was there and no one will forget the scene when he was brought onto the field in a golf cart and given a tremendous ovation from his Boston fans.

Pete Rose was given an exemption to his lifetime ban from baseball for gambling and allowed to appear. He too received a big ovation from the fans. Roger Clemens was there. The former Red Sox great was now a Yankee, and was not on the American League All-Star team that year, but he came back to Boston to be introduced to his Boston fans as one of the all time greats.

Many other greats were there, and, Sandy Koufax was there. He came out, took a bow, got a great ovation and took his place beside the greats of the game. He looked good, but after that was over, he was gone. Somehow, he escaped the cameras and the microphones and 'got out of Dodge'.

Sandy Koufax makes appearances for BAT, the Baseball Alumni Team. BAT is a group of ex-players that care for the other ex-players who are under duress in life, be it financial, health, or otherwise. Those who meet him say he is a very nice man - very polite to those he meets. Occasionally he turns up at the Dodgers spring training to work with the younger pitchers. When he does, he avoids the media.

Bob Hendley also ended his career at a young age due to elbow troubles. He pitched for the Cubs into the 1967 season going on to New York and finished the season and his career with the New York Mets. He was twenty-eight when he pitched his last game in the majors. His overall record in the majors was forty-eight wins, fifty-two losses.

After his career as a player, he became a teacher and baseball coach at a high school in Georgia. I had the opportunity to speak to him about the game. I found him to be very gracious in his comments to me.

"I was a professional and you take the wins, you take the losses. Obviously it was a historical game, but at the same time it was in one sense (just) another game."

He went on to say, he considers it his greatest game and has great respect for Sandy Koufax.

As great as this game was, the story doesn't end with the last out. Five days after this game was played, the Cubs and Dodgers met again, this time in Chicago. Again, it was Koufax vs. Hendley, and this time, Hendley would prevail.

Koufax left the game after six innings, but Hendley went all the way for the Cubs, a nine inning complete game win. The score was 2-1.

Looking at the stats for both pitchers for both games, you see that, on balance Hendley kept right up with Koufax. After the two games, both pitchers had one win and one loss. Hendley pitched seventeen innings, Koufax fifteen. Each pitcher gave up five hits, two runs, one unearned. Koufax showed his brilliance by walking none and striking out seventeen. Bob Hendley walked only four and struck out ten.

For the two games, Koufax ERA was 0.60. Hendley's was 0.53. All in all, a great week for Bob Hendley.

In the book *Aaron to Zipfel*, Hendley said, "In the game Koufax pitched a no-hitter, his fastball was rising and his curveball was coming off a tabletop."

"We knew he would be tough to hit that night. That game certainly motivated me a little more when I pitched against him a few days later."

Another oddity; the one run that scored was on no official at-bats. What happened was, Lou Johnson walked and was sacrificed to second. He stole third and catcher Chris Krug tried to get him at third. The throw went past third baseman Ron Santo and Johnson scored. One run, no at-bats.

One guy who really loves the memory of this game is Bob Hendley's catcher, Chris Krug. Krug's given name is Everett but was nicknamed Chris because he was born on Christmas Day. His uniform number was 25.

It was Krug's error that caused the unearned run, the only run of the game. He reminded me of that fact and chuckled as he did so. I asked him how good Hendley's stuff was that day.

"Oh, it was excellent! Keep in mind; anytime you face big league players and the Dodgers didn't have the greatest hitting reputation in the big leagues at that time, they were stealing runs, which served a purpose for winning the World Series."

"You still have to get big leaguers out and Bob had excellent stuff. I caught him the next week in Chicago against Koufax and we beat him. You just go on to the next game."

He went on to say he had no regrets about the way things turned out.

About his error, "It brought me more notoriety than anything good I've done and that's okay! I mean, I'd rather be remembered, period!"

"As I've told Sandy...everybody has fifteen minutes of fame, you extended my fifteen minutes to the rest of my life."

Although, he didn't feel that way the day after.

"I had a problem the next day...the next day we flew to San Francisco and we were getting ready to play there. The sportswriters came by and really assaulted me verbally for throwing the ball away because that was a close race at that time. I ignored it, which was the best thing to do."

"I had talked to Bob that next day during BP at Candlestick and apologized to him. He said 'Hey, if I had held him on, you wouldn't have had to throw it'...and quite frankly, there's a little controversy on how bad the throw was. Johnson had the base stolen. I should never have thrown it but you react...that's what you do, you react and throw. I have a photo of Lou sliding into third and I see Ronnie (Santo) just getting there. He's knocking Ronnie over and it's showing the ball - it was a high throw, but if Ronnie doesn't get knocked over, catches it and we still might be playing."

"You know, I was the first hitter in the ninth. The first two times up I flied out to Davis in center and grounded to Wills. Wills threw the ball in the dirt to Wes Parker (first base) and Wes dug it out.

If I had been anything but a catcher, I'd have beat it out, but as it turned out it wasn't an error and Wes bailed them out on that one, but I struck out on that last time at bat. When I swung on that last pitch, I don't know how I missed it. I have no clue because I thought I was right on it."

"After that game I sat in the dugout with most of my teammates just in awe of the whole situation...it was just electrifying...we knew we were in something big, but it got a life of its own and it has just kept going."

The only hit of the game came in the seventh inning. It did not create a run.

Krug says, "It was a little flair over Ernie's (Banks) head at first base. It barely reached the outfield."

Chris Krug played with the Cubs and later the San Diego Padres. After baseball, he became a contractor and specialized in building baseball fields. He was, in fact, the guy who built the 'If you build it, they will come' field for the movie *Field of Dreams*. He also owns a horse farm in California.

Bob Hendley said it was just one game, but there has not been another like it. Here's how it all came down.

Los Angeles Dodgers 1, Chicago Cubs 0

Game Played on Thursday, September 9, 1965 (N) at Dodger Stadium

```
CHI N    0  0  0    0  0  0    0  0  0  -   0  0  1
LA  N    0  0  0    0  1  0    0  0  x  -   1  1  0
```

BATTING

Chicago Cubs	AB	R	H	RBI	BB	SO	PO	A
Young cf	3	0	0	0	0	1	5	0
Beckert 2b	3	0	0	0	0	1	2	1
Williams rf	3	0	0	0	0	2	0	0
Santo 3b	3	0	0	0	0	1	1	2
Banks 1b	3	0	0	0	0	3	12	0
Browne lf	3	0	0	0	0	1	1	0
Krug c	3	0	0	0	0	1	3	0
Kessinger ss	2	0	0	0	0	0	0	2
Amalfitano ph	1	0	0	0	0	1	0	0
Hendley p	2	0	0	0	0	2	0	5
Kuenn ph	1	0	0	0	0	1	0	0
Totals	27	0	0	0	0	14	24	10

FIELDING -
E: Krug (5).

Los Angeles Dodgers	AB	R	H	RBI	BB	SO	PO	A
Wills ss	3	0	0	0	0	0	0	2
Gilliam 3b	3	0	0	0	0	0	0	1
Kennedy 3b	0	0	0	0	0	0	0	0
W. Davis cf	3	0	0	0	0	0	2	0
Johnson lf	2	1	1	0	1	0	2	0
Fairly rf	2	0	0	0	0	0	3	0
Lefebvre 2b	3	0	0	0	0	2	1	0
Tracewski 2b	0	0	0	0	0	0	0	0
Parker 1b	3	0	0	0	0	0	4	0
Torborg c	3	0	0	0	0	0	15	0
Koufax p	2	0	0	0	0	1	0	0
Totals	24	1	1	0	1	3	27	3

BATTING -
2B: Johnson (19,off Hendley).
SH: Fairly (13,off Hendley).
Team LOB: 1.

BASERUNNING -
SB: Johnson (11,3rd base off Hendley/Krug).

PITCHING

Chicago Cubs	IP	H	R	ER	BB	SO	HR
Hendley L(2-3)	8	1	1	0	1	3	0

Los Angeles Dodgers	IP	H	R	ER	BB	SO	HR
Koufax W(22-7)	9	0	0	0	0	14	0

Umpires: Ed Vargo, Chris Pelekoudas, Bill Jackowski, Paul Pryor

Time of Game: 1:43   **Attendance:** 29139

Starting Lineups:

Chicago Cubs		Los Angeles Dodgers	
1. Young	cf	Wills	ss
2. Beckert	2b	Gilliam	3b
3. Williams	rf	W. Davis	cf
4. Santo	3b	Johnson	lf
5. Banks	1b	Fairly	rf
6. Browne	lf	Lefebvre	2b
7. Krug	c	Parker	1b
8. Kessinger	ss	Torborg	c
9. Hendley	p	Koufax	p

CUBS 1ST: Young popped to second; **Debut game for Don Young;** Beckert was called out on strikes; Williams was called out on strikes; 0 R, 0 H, 0 E, 0 LOB. Cubs 0, Dodgers 0.

DODGERS 1ST: Wills grounded out (pitcher to first); Gilliam made an out to center; W. Davis popped to third; 0 R, 0 H, 0 E, 0 LOB. Cubs 0, Dodgers 0.

CUBS 2ND: Santo popped to catcher in foul territory; Banks struck out; **according to Scully, strikeout was on a forkball;** Browne lined to center; **Debut game for Byron Browne;** 0 R, 0 H, 0 E, 0 LOB. Cubs 0, Dodgers 0.

DODGERS 2ND: Johnson popped to first in foul territory; Fairly made an out to center; Lefebvre flied to center; 0 R, 0 H, 0 E, 0 LOB. Cubs 0, Dodgers 0.

CUBS 3RD: Krug flied to center; Kessinger flied to right; Hendley was called out on strikes; 0 R, 0 H, 0 E, 0 LOB. Cubs 0, Dodgers 0.

DODGERS 3RD: Parker grounded out (shortstop to first); Torborg grounded out (third to first); Koufax grounded out (pitcher to first); 0 R, 0 H, 0 E, 0 LOB. Cubs 0, Dodgers 0.

CUBS 4TH: Young popped to first in foul territory; Beckert flied to right; Williams was called out on strikes; 0 R, 0 H, 0 E, 0 LOB. Cubs 0, Dodgers 0.

DODGERS 4TH: Wills grounded out (first unassisted); Gilliam flied to center; W. Davis popped to second in foul territory; **Excellent one-handed running catch by Beckert;** 0 R, 0 H, 0 E, 0 LOB. Cubs 0, Dodgers 0.

CUBS 5TH: Santo flied to left; Banks struck out; Browne grounded out (shortstop to first); 0 R, 0 H, 0 E, 0 LOB. Cubs 0, Dodgers

0.

DODGERS 5TH: Johnson walked; Fairly out on a sacrifice bunt (pitcher to second) [Johnson to second]; Hendley may have had a play at 2nd. **Scully says he dropped ball and then had to go to 1st;** Johnson stole third [Johnson scored (unearned) (error by Krug)]; Lefebvre struck out; Parker grounded out (pitcher to first); 1 R, 0 H, 1 E, 0 LOB. Cubs 0, Dodgers 1.

CUBS 6TH: Krug grounded out (shortstop to first); **throw in the dirt dug out by Parker;** Kessinger grounded out (third to first); close play, Gilliam playing close for bunt; Hendley struck out; 0 R, 0 H, 0 E, 0 LOB. Cubs 0, Dodgers 1.

DODGERS 6TH: Torborg flied to center; Koufax was called out on strikes; Wills grounded out (second to first); 0 R, 0 H, 0 E, 0 LOB. Cubs 0, Dodgers 1.

CUBS 7TH: Young struck out; **ball 2 very high & wide - to the backstop;** Beckert flied to right; Williams flied to left; 0 R, 0 H, 0 E, 0 LOB. Cubs 0, Dodgers 1.

DODGERS 7TH: Gilliam grounded out (third to first); W. Davis grounded out (first unassisted); Johnson doubled to first; Fairly grounded out (shortstop to first); 0 R, 1 H, 0 E, 1 LOB. Cubs 0, Dodgers 1.

CUBS 8TH: KENNEDY REPLACED GILLIAM (PLAYING 3B); Santo was called out on strikes; Banks struck out; Browne struck out; 0 R, 0 H, 0 E, 0 LOB. Cubs 0, Dodgers 1.

DODGERS 8TH: Lefebvre struck out; Parker grounded out (pitcher to first); **nice play by Banks to save throwing error on high throw;** Torborg flied to left; **at bullpen gate;** 0 R, 0 H, 0 E, 0 LOB. Cubs 0, Dodgers 1.

CUBS 9TH: TRACEWSKI REPLACED LEFEBVRE (PLAYING 2B); Krug struck out; AMALFITANO BATTED FOR KESSINGER; Amalfitano struck out; KUENN BATTED FOR HENDLEY; Kuenn struck out; 0 R, 0 H, 0 E, 0 LOB. Cubs 0, Dodgers 1.

Final Totals	R	H	E	LOB
Cubs	0	0	1	0
Dodgers	1	1	0	1

CHAPTER FOUR

Wednesday, September 12, 1962
Washington Senators at Baltimore Orioles

Most Strikeouts by a Pitcher in a Major League Game

IN APRIL OF 1986, ROGER Clemens of the Boston Red Sox pitched a complete game win against the Seattle Mariners and struck out twenty batters.

The next day it was the top story in all the sports pages because it was the first time a pitcher ever did that in a nine-inning game. For years, the record was nineteen and although it was tied many times, it had never been broken. In April, 1986, Clemens broke the record. Ten years later, Roger Clemens struck out twenty Detroit Tigers in a nine-inning game. He's the only guy to do it twice.

In 1998, Kerry Wood of the Chicago Cubs struck out twenty and in 2001, Randy Johnson of the Arizona Diamondbacks struck out twenty in the first nine innings of an extra inning game.

Four great accomplishments by three great pitchers. I take nothing away from them...but something has been taken away from another pitcher. Never talked about is a pitcher who struck out TWENTY-ONE batters in a major league game.

Tom Cheney, pitching for the Washington Senators in 1962 struck out twenty-one batters. The game went sixteen innings and Cheney pitched every one of them...all sixteen innings! You see where I'm going? The Clemens and Wood record was for strikeouts in a <u>nine-inning</u> game, not just a major league game.

The record for a game, regardless of innings, is twenty-one strikeouts. Tom Cheney is the only one who's ever hit the magic number **21.**

Who could have imagined this? When the game began, it was a late season, cold night in Baltimore between two teams that were way out of the pennant race. When the day began, Baltimore had a record of 72-74 and was in sixth place out of ten teams and fourteen games behind the league-leading New York Yankees.

The Washington Senators had a 56-92 record, in last place; thirty-one games behind the Yankees. There were only a few weeks to go until the season would mercifully be over for both teams.

Both teams were only an hour or so apart from each other, possibly the only thing to draw people to the ballpark. Fans of both teams could easily drive to the game. However, that didn't happen. Only 4,098 fans attended the game.

Tom Cheney entered the game with a record of five wins and eight losses on the season. His lifetime record going into this one was eight wins against fifteen losses. Even the greatest clairvoyant could not predict that this game would turn out to be a piece of baseball history. Something was about to happen that had never happened before or since and I'll bet never will again.

In baseball of today, managers religiously follow pitch counts and bullpens by committee. When a pitcher reaches one hundred pitches in a game, unless he's pitching a no-hitter the pitcher is not likely to go much further.

On this night, Cheney pitched a total of 238 pitches. He walked only four in sixteen innings. Randy Johnson actually had a chance to beat the record on his twenty-strikeout night. The game was tied after nine innings and Johnson was taken out of the game at that point. Had he stayed in, he could have tied or surpassed Cheney's record.

I had the opportunity to speak to Joe Hicks about this game. Joe was an outfielder on the Senators that year and played the whole game in center field.

He recalls, "He (Cheney) couldn't raise his hand the next day. He threw a lot of pitches. It was a cold night." Joe went on to say that although pitching this many innings in a game was unusual and would never happen today, it did happen occasionally back then.

"The first year I came up, I was with the White Sox, and we went into Baltimore for a twi-night doubleheader. The first game went sixteen innings and both pitchers went the distance. The second game went twelve innings and both pitchers went the distance. That would never happen today. The starters go six innings and then the bullpen takes over...the game has changed a lot."

I asked Joe if he was tired after playing sixteen innings in a game.

"Not really, no, I didn't get a chance to play every day. In the minor leagues I played all the time, but in the major leagues they 'platooned' me and it was hard on me because I wasn't used to that. Being in and out of the lineup, I had a hard time getting my time in."

Another player that I spoke to about this game was Jim King. He was an outfielder who had an eleven-year career in the major leagues with the St. Louis Cardinals, San Francisco Giants, and the Washington Senators. Jim is now retired and living in Elkins, Arkansas recovering from open-heart surgery. He has many memories of this game.

"He had good stuff that night...That was one of those nights when with anything he threw, he could find the plate with it."

I asked him if while it was happening he thought it was odd that a pitcher stayed in the game for so long.

"Well, no, not back then, hello, they didn't have closers, they had relief pitchers, but there weren't too many closers like there are now. The game has changed a lot. It's just run different now. Nowadays they just don't do it...He was getting ahead good, I can remember that. I mean he wasn't throwing behind, he was throwing a lot of pitches."

He went on to say that, what Cheney did was like pitching maybe four games now.

The starting pitcher that night opposing Cheney was Milt Pappas. Milt was a pitcher for many years in the major leagues. We'll be discussing Milt Pappas in another chapter in this book. On that night, Milt was a 23-year-old pitcher making a name for himself with the Baltimore Orioles. He is a very friendly guy and I had the opportunity to speak with him about this game. He laughed when I asked him if a pitcher would ever pitch sixteen innings in today's game.

"God, No! They're lucky if they go six innings."

When I asked him if he had any thoughts about what he was seeing while it was going on, he said "No, not really, I don't think anyone was really totally aware of the situation...you'll never see that again."

Let me tell you about Tom Cheney. He was a Georgia boy who began his pro career in 1953. He worked his way through the minor leagues and made it to the majors in 1957 with the St. Louis Cardinals.

He began the season in the major leagues, got into four games, started three, lost his only decision and finished the season in the minors. Two years later, he appeared in the majors, again with the Cardinals. In 1960, he was in eleven games with the Pittsburgh Pirates. In 1961, after pitching one game with Pittsburgh, he went on to Washington where he got into ten games.

In 1962, he spent the whole year with the Washington Senators, pitching as a starter and reliever. He started twenty-three games and got into fourteen as a relief pitcher. He ended the 1962 season with a record of seven wins, nine losses.

He would pitch three more years in the major leagues, all with the Senators; nine wins, thirteen losses and end his major league career after the 1966 season.

Tom Cheney retired with a lifetime record of nineteen wins, twenty-nine losses. He was a flamethrower. When he was on, he could strike you out. He started seventy-one games in his career and struck out ten or more eight times, a pretty good ratio. In the other seven times, two of them were in less than nine innings. When he was hot, he was hot, with decent control.

When Roger Clemens struck out twenty Seattle Mariners on April 29, 1986, the manager of the Mariners was Chuck Cottier.

Cottier was Cheney's second baseman in 1962. A few weeks after the Clemens game in 1986, Chuck Cottier was fired as manager of the Mariners and replaced by Dick Williams. Williams was a Baltimore Oriole when Cheney struck out twenty-one, in fact, Williams was the twenty-first strikeout. It was the final out of the game. He struck out looking. What a coincidence.

Tom Cheney's career ended quietly after the 1966 season. He was thirty-one when he hurled his final pitch in the major leagues. He returned to Georgia and according to Rich Marazzi and Len Fiorito in their book, *Aaron to Zipfel*, Tom Cheney became a truck driver for Green's Propane in Leesburg, Georgia.

He passed away on November 1, 2001 in Rome, Georgia. He is buried in the town he was born, Morgan, Georgia. He was sixty-seven years old.

Cheney, was a journeyman pitcher with a mediocre, at best, life-time record...but, on one September night, he accomplished something no other pitcher has ever done. He'll never be in the Hall of Fame, but he'll always stand alone in the record book.

Thanks Tom, may you rest in peace.

Washington Senators 2, Baltimore Orioles 1

Game Played on Wednesday, September 12, 1962 (N) at Memorial Stadium

WAS A	1	0	0	0	0	0	0	0	0	0	0	0	0	0	0	1	-	2 10
BAL A	0	0	0	0	0	0	1	0	0	0	0	0	0	0	0	0	-	1 10

BATTING

Washington Senators	AB	R	H	RBI	BB	SO	PO	A
Kennedy ss	6	0	1	0	1	2	0	2
Stillwell 2b	3	1	1	0	1	0	0	1
King ph	1	0	1	0	0	0	0	0
Cottier 2b	2	0	0	0	0	0	2	1
Hinton rf	7	0	1	0	0	0	1	0
Zipfel 1b	7	1	3	2	0	2	11	0
Retzer c	7	0	0	0	0	0	22	1
Osteen pr	0	0	0	0	0	0	0	0
Schmidt c	0	0	0	0	0	0	1	0
Hicks cf	5	0	1	0	1	1	4	0
Schaive ph	1	0	0	0	0	0	0	0
Piersall cf	0	0	0	0	0	0	1	0
Lock lf	7	0	1	0	0	2	4	0
Brinkman 3b	5	0	1	0	2	0	3	4
Cheney p	6	0	0	0	0	1	0	2
Totals	57	2	10	2	5	8	48	11

BATTING -
2B: Hinton (22,off Pappas); Hicks (4,off Pappas).
HR: Zipfel (6,16th inning off Hall 0 on 1 out).
SH: Cheney (6,off Pappas).
Team LOB: 13.

BASERUNNING -
CS: Kennedy (1,2nd base by Hall/Landrith).

Baltimore Orioles	AB	R	H	RBI	BB	SO	PO	A
Adair ss	6	0	2	0	1	1	4	5
Snyder rf	7	0	2	0	0	3	4	0
B. Robinson 3b	5	0	1	0	2	1	1	4
Gentile 1b	7	0	1	0	0	3	13	1
Powell lf	6	0	1	0	1	0	4	0
Nicholson cf	7	0	1	0	0	3	4	0
Landrith c	6	0	0	0	0	1	12	1
Brandt ph	1	0	0	0	0	0	0	0
Breeding 2b	6	1	1	0	0	3	5	3
Williams ph	1	0	0	0	0	1	0	0
Pappas p	2	0	0	0	0	2	1	1
Lau ph	1	0	1	1	0	0	0	0
Hall p	3	0	0	0	0	3	0	1

Hoeft p	0	0	0	0	0	0	0	0
Stock p	0	0	0	0	0	0	0	0
Totals	58	1	10	1	4	21	48	16

FIELDING -
E: Adair (16), Breeding (7).

BATTING -
2B: Snyder (18,off Cheney); Adair (24,off Cheney); Gentile (20,off Cheney);
Breeding (10,off Cheney).
Team LOB: 13.

BASERUNNING -
SB: Adair (6,2nd base off Cheney/Retzer).

PITCHING

Washington Senators	IP	H	R	ER	BB	SO	HR
Cheney W(6-8)	16	10	1	1	4	21	0

Baltimore Orioles	IP	H	R	ER	BB	SO	HR
Pappas	7	4	1	1	3	4	0
Hall L(6-6)	8.1	5	1	1	1	4	1
Hoeft	0.1	1	0	0	0	0	0
Stock	0.1	0	0	0	1	0	0
Totals	16	10	2	2	5	8	1

WP: Cheney (6).
BK: Pappas (1).

Umpires: Bill McKinley, Nestor Chylak, Frank Umont, Bob Stewart

Time of Game: 3:59   **Attendance:** 4098

Starting Lineups:

Washington Senators		Baltimore Orioles	
1. Kennedy	ss	Adair	ss
2. Stillwell	2b	Snyder	rf
3. Hinton	rf	B. Robinson	3b
4. Zipfel	1b	Gentile	1b
5. Retzer	c	Powell	lf
6. Hicks	cf	Nicholson	cf
7. Lock	lf	Landrith	c
8. Brinkman	3b	Breeding	2b
9. Cheney	p	Pappas	p

SENATORS 1ST: Kennedy grounded out (third to first); Stillwell
singled to shortstop; Hinton doubled to right [Stillwell to
third]; Zipfel grounded out (first unassisted) [Stillwell
scored, Hinton to third]; Retzer made an out to center; 1 R, 2
H, 0 E, 1 LOB. Senators 1, Orioles 0.

ORIOLES 1ST: Adair singled to left; Snyder made an out to left;
B. Robinson singled to center [Adair to third]; Gentile popped
to third in foul territory [B. Robinson to second]; Powell
grounded out (second to first); 0 R, 2 H, 0 E, 2 LOB. Senators

1, Orioles 0.

SENATORS 2ND: Hicks walked; Lock made an out to center; Brinkman singled to right [Hicks to second]; Cheney struck out; Kennedy forced Brinkman (shortstop to second); 0 R, 1 H, 0 E, 2 LOB. Senators 1, Orioles 0.

ORIOLES 2ND: Nicholson struck out; Landrith popped to catcher in foul territory; Breeding made an out to center; 0 R, 0 H, 0 E, 0 LOB. Senators 1, Orioles 0.

SENATORS 3RD: Stillwell grounded out (third to first); Hinton grounded out (shortstop to first); Zipfel grounded out (second to first); 0 R, 0 H, 0 E, 0 LOB. Senators 1, Orioles 0.

ORIOLES 3RD: Pappas was called out on strikes; Adair struck out; Snyder doubled; B. Robinson walked; Gentile struck out; 0 R, 1 H, 0 E, 2 LOB. Senators 1, Orioles 0.

SENATORS 4TH: Retzer made an out to shortstop; Hicks lined to pitcher; Lock lined to third; 0 R, 0 H, 0 E, 0 LOB. Senators 1, Orioles 0.

ORIOLES 4TH: Powell made an out to left; Nicholson struck out; Landrith grounded out (pitcher to first); 0 R, 0 H, 0 E, 0 LOB. Senators 1, Orioles 0.

SENATORS 5TH: Brinkman made an out to right; Cheney grounded out (shortstop to first); Kennedy grounded out (third to first); 0 R, 0 H, 0 E, 0 LOB. Senators 1, Orioles 0.

ORIOLES 5TH: Breeding struck out; Pappas struck out; Adair doubled to center; Snyder was called out on strikes; 0 R, 1 H, 0 E, 1 LOB. Senators 1, Orioles 0.

SENATORS 6TH: Stillwell walked; Pappas balked [Stillwell to second]; Hinton made an out to right; Zipfel struck out; Retzer grounded out (second to first); 0 R, 0 H, 0 E, 1 LOB. Senators 1, Orioles 0.

ORIOLES 6TH: B. Robinson popped to catcher in foul territory; Gentile doubled to right; Powell made an out to center; Nicholson was called out on strikes; 0 R, 1 H, 0 E, 1 LOB. Senators 1, Orioles 0.

SENATORS 7TH: Hicks doubled to left; Lock struck out; Brinkman walked; Cheney out on a sacrifice bunt (pitcher to second) [Hicks to third, Brinkman to second]; Kennedy struck out; 0 R, 1 H, 0 E, 2 LOB. Senators 1, Orioles 0.

ORIOLES 7TH: Landrith made an out to center; Breeding doubled; LAU BATTED FOR PAPPAS; Lau singled to right [Breeding scored]; Adair made an out to third; Snyder singled to third [Lau to third]; B. Robinson popped to first in foul territory; 1 R, 3 H, 0 E, 2 LOB. Senators 1, Orioles 1.

SENATORS 8TH: HALL REPLACED LAU (PITCHING); Stillwell grounded out (pitcher to first); Hinton made an out to left; Zipfel struck out; 0 R, 0 H, 0 E, 0 LOB. Senators 1, Orioles 1.

ORIOLES 8TH: Gentile was called out on strikes; Powell singled to center; Nicholson made an out to left; Landrith was called out on strikes; 0 R, 1 H, 0 E, 1 LOB. Senators 1, Orioles 1.

SENATORS 9TH: Retzer lined to second; Hicks struck out; Lock popped to catcher in foul territory; 0 R, 0 H, 0 E, 0 LOB. Senators 1, Orioles 1.

ORIOLES 9TH: Breeding grounded out (third to first); Hall struck out; Adair walked; Adair stole second; Snyder struck out (catcher to first); 0 R, 0 H, 0 E, 1 LOB. Senators 1, Orioles 1.

SENATORS 10TH: Brinkman made an out to catcher; Cheney made an out to right; Kennedy walked; KING BATTED FOR STILLWELL; King singled to center [Kennedy to third]; Hinton made an out to center; 0 R, 1 H, 0 E, 2 LOB. Senators 1, Orioles 1.

ORIOLES 10TH: COTTIER REPLACED KING (PLAYING 2B); B. Robinson was called out on strikes; Gentile struck out; Powell walked; Nicholson forced Powell (third to second); 0 R, 0 H, 0 E, 1 LOB. Senators 1, Orioles 1.

SENATORS 11TH: Zipfel singled to left; Retzer made an out to center; Hicks forced Zipfel (first to shortstop) [Hicks to second (error by Adair)]; Lock made an out to left; 0 R, 1 H, 1 E, 1 LOB. Senators 1, Orioles 1.

ORIOLES 11TH: Landrith made an out to second; Breeding struck out; Hall struck out; 0 R, 0 H, 0 E, 0 LOB. Senators 1, Orioles 1.

SENATORS 12TH: Brinkman grounded out (shortstop to first); Cheney popped to catcher in foul territory; Kennedy struck out; 0 R, 0 H, 0 E, 0 LOB. Senators 1, Orioles 1.

ORIOLES 12TH: Adair grounded out (shortstop to first); Snyder grounded out (second to first); B. Robinson grounded out (third to first); 0 R, 0 H, 0 E, 0 LOB. Senators 1, Orioles 1.

SENATORS 13TH: Cottier made an out to left; Hinton grounded out (second to first); Zipfel singled to left; Retzer made an out to shortstop; 0 R, 1 H, 0 E, 1 LOB. Senators 1, Orioles 1.

ORIOLES 13TH: Gentile popped to third in foul territory; Powell grounded out (shortstop to first); Nicholson made an out to center; 0 R, 0 H, 0 E, 0 LOB. Senators 1, Orioles 1.

SENATORS 14TH: Hicks made an out to right; Lock struck out; Brinkman grounded out (shortstop to first); 0 R, 0 H, 0 E, 0 LOB. Senators 1, Orioles 1.

ORIOLES 14TH: Landrith made an out to right; Breeding struck out; Hall struck out; 0 R, 0 H, 0 E, 0 LOB. Senators 1, Orioles 1.

SENATORS 15TH: Cheney made an out to left; Kennedy singled to left; Kennedy was caught stealing second (catcher to shortstop); Cottier made an out to second; 0 R, 1 H, 0 E, 0 LOB. Senators 1, Orioles 1.

ORIOLES 15TH: Adair grounded out (third to first); Snyder struck out; B. Robinson walked; Cheney threw a wild pitch [B. Robinson to second]; Gentile made an out to left; 0 R, 0 H, 0 E, 1 LOB. Senators 1, Orioles 1.

SENATORS 16TH: Hinton popped to first in foul territory; Zipfel homered; Retzer reached on an error by Breeding; OSTEEN RAN FOR RETZER; SCHAIVE BATTED FOR HICKS; HOEFT REPLACED HALL (PITCHING); Schaive popped to catcher in foul territory; Lock singled to left [Osteen to second]; STOCK REPLACED HOEFT (PITCHING); Brinkman walked [Osteen to third, Lock to second]; Cheney forced Brinkman (third to second); 1 R, 2 H, 1 E, 3 LOB. Senators 2, Orioles 1.

ORIOLES 16TH: SCHMIDT REPLACED OSTEEN (PLAYING C); PIERSALL REPLACED SCHAIVE (PLAYING CF); Powell grounded out (pitcher to first); Nicholson singled to right; BRANDT BATTED FOR LANDRITH; Brandt made an out to center; WILLIAMS BATTED FOR BREEDING; Williams was called out on strikes; 0 R, 1 H, 0 E, 1 LOB. Senators 2, Orioles 1.

Final Totals	R	H	E	LOB
Senators	2	10	0	13
Orioles	1	10	2	13

CHAPTER FIVE

Friday April 14, 1967
Boston Red Sox at New York Yankees

First Major League Game for Billy Rohr and Russ Gibson

I WAS 12 YEARS OLD, and will never forget this game. Anyone who heard it on the radio will remember it forever.

I routinely came home from school and turned on the radio. The Red Sox and Yankees met at Yankee Stadium. It was the third game of the early season and both teams had one win and one loss so far on the year.

Thirty-seven-year-old Dick Williams, the youngest manager in the major leagues, led the Red Sox. This game was only the third of his major league managing career. He had managed the prior two years in Toronto with the Red Sox triple A team in the International League. Williams would go on to a long and successful managerial career.

We all sensed something different about this team. The Red Sox had a winning record in spring training and Dick Williams had made a prediction to all the fans. "I honestly think we'll win more games than we lose...we'll have a hustling ball club, and they won't quit."

"They didn't quit on me in Toronto, I don't expect to have anybody quit on me here." No one did.

Only six months prior, the Red Sox ended the 1966 season in ninth place out of ten teams. They finished one-half game ahead of the 'cellar dwellers' New York Yankees. The Red Sox went on to win the American League championship and went to the seventh game of the World Series against the St. Louis Cardinals.

Dick Williams had taken several players with him from Toronto. Among them were Mike Andrews and Reggie Smith. Andrews was a second baseman and Smith, a center fielder batted .320 at Toronto in 1966. The Red Sox had great expectations of these two rookies and as it turned out, both delivered.

In addition to Smith and Andrews, Williams brought up two other members of the 1966 Toronto Maple Leafs, Billy Rohr and Russ Gibson. Neither had as much ink as Smith and Andrews. Rohr was a twenty-one-year-old pitcher with a record of fourteen wins and ten losses in 1966 with the AAA team.

Gibson was a twenty-seven-year-old catcher beginning his eleventh year of professional baseball. He was a local guy from Fall River, Massachusetts so many fans were routing for their local hero from Durfee High School. Ten years in the minor leagues is a long time and toward the end of that tenure, Gibson was actually a player/coach. In 1966, to everyone's surprise he had a .292 batting average.

I've had the opportunity to meet many former major league players. Every one of them remembers their debut game. Each of them can tell you about the first pitcher they faced or in the case of the pitchers, the first batter they faced. They'll tell you what it felt like kneeling in the on-deck circle for their first major league at-bat.

On April 14, 1967, Billy Rohr and Russ Gibson made their major league debuts. Back then, we called the pitcher and catcher the 'battery', a term seldom used today but commonly used then. With the 'battery' making their major league debut, what could one expect? What we got was a great deal of folklore that lasts to this day.

Billy Rohr pitched and Russ Gibson caught a one-hit shutout for the Red Sox that day. The one hit came with two outs and two strikes on the batter in the ninth inning. The Red Sox were one strike away from a no-hitter when Elston Howard singled to right, ending the no-hit bid. Charlie Smith followed Howard and flied out to right field to end the game and put the lid on what could have been the greatest debut for a pitcher and catcher in the history of the game. Moreover, wouldn't you know; the guy who broke up the no-hit bid would soon join the Red Sox!

Pitching for the Yankees that day was future Hall of Famer Whitey Ford. Whitey was close to the end of his career that started in 1950 and would end thirty-seven days after this game. He pitched well, giving up only three runs on seven hits in eight innings pitched. However, he got the loss.

Two other Hall of Famers were in the game. For the Yankees, Mickey Mantle came up as a pinch hitter and Carl Yastrzemski played left field for the Red Sox. Late in the game, Yastrzemski made an outstanding catch to keep the no-hit bid alive.

The Red Sox started well. Reggie Smith led off with a home run to give the Red Sox an instant lead, which they never gave up. Rohr came in to pitch the bottom of the first and got three quick outs. Inning after inning, he kept mowing them down.

The shortstop for the Red Sox was the great Rico Petrocelli. He has very fond memories of this game.

"Billy Rohr's game was great. His control was just unbelievable. He hit the corners all day and then the one hit...Elston Howard hit it off the handle of the bat and it plunked into right field, and that was it. But it was a great game by Rohr."

I had the opportunity to talk to both Russ Gibson and Billy Rohr about this game. They were both terrific to talk with. Remember, Russ Gibson was a New England kid. Two dreams came true for him that day.

"The two best things were to end up playing for the Red Sox, which I really wanted to do and playing in Yankee Stadium, which I really loved. That place is absolutely beautiful."

I asked him about Rohr's stuff that day.

"He had a sinker and his curve ball was crazy. Plus, being a rookie, these guys (the Yankees) had never seen him before."

When I asked him if he thought he got the chance to catch that day because of his familiarity with Rohr the year before, he said,

"We had three catchers at the time and Dick had told me that I'd be catching in New York, but I don't know if it just happened that Rohr was going to have his first start or what, he didn't say."

Then I asked, what he was thinking during the game with a no-hitter going on in his debut.

"You know, I was just thrilled to be in Yankee Stadium, that's the greatest feeling in the world to be there. I had two hits off Whitey Ford so I was on top of the world. No-hitters, you don't really even think about them until about the seventh inning."

"Everybody has caught a thousand six-inning no-hitters. When it started getting up near the end, that's when I thought, 'this kid could do it', and in the ninth inning, I'll tell you what, Tresh hit one, he was the opening batter, and I said 'there goes the no-hitter' and Yaz made the greatest catch I've ever seen. It was over the shoulder, he was flat out. He had his hand over his head, when it went into his glove. I said 'this is definitely going to be a no-hitter'. Then we got the second guy out and Ellie Howard came up and we worked Ellie to two and two and he (Rohr) threw a fastball right down the middle. He (Howard) took it and I jumped up and said, 'That's it!' and he (home plate umpire Cal Drummond) called it a ball. I said 'You got to be kidding!' but the guy called such a great game, what the heck could I say? We tried to throw a curve ball, three and two and he (Rohr) didn't break it and it got up high. He (Howard) just lofted it into right field. The next guy popped up and it was all over."

Russ and I reflected on his career and his ten years in the minor leagues. When I asked if it was discouraging along the way and if he ever considered giving up, he said,

"Oh yes, definitely. In fact, I had met Williams two years earlier because I had a great year in Seattle, which was triple A on the west coast, and I went to spring training with the Sox and had a great spring too. I was leading the club in hitting and everything else. Even the trainer said, 'Gibby you got it.' Then they had one cut left and two guys to go and I can't believe he (then Sox manager Johnny Pesky) cut me."

He said Pesky told him he would be up soon, and they would make a trade to make room for him. That trade never happened.

"So I drove all the way to Florida, and on my way down, I said, 'screw this.' If I couldn't do it that year...simply because the other catcher hit about .200 the year before and I know I was a better catcher than he was. So, when I got there, I told Dick "I think I'm going to give it up, if I can't make it this year, I'll never make it' so he said, 'look, hang around, go play golf for a couple of days, and then I want you to come with me and be a player-coach for me.' He said, 'I'm going to take over the Red Sox. I'll put in a couple of years here and I'll take over.'" Dick Williams kept his word.

Russ spoke at length about his former manager. "He didn't have any friends. He's the best manager I ever played for, but he didn't make any friends, that's for sure."

Russ played for the Red Sox in the World Series that year and became involved in a controversial call. In the first inning of the first game, Lou Brock, one of the greatest base stealers in history was on first for the Cardinals. He broke for second and Russ tried to throw him out. It looked like he got him. Russ agrees and is still upset about it.

"That kills me. I'll tell you what, I threw him out, they called him safe...they gave him the benefit of the doubt."

Russ stayed with the Red Sox through 1969, a total of three years. He went on to the San Francisco Giants and played for another three years. He loved San Francisco and played with several future Hall of Famers such as Willie Mays, Gaylord Perry, Willie McCovey and Juan Marichal. He spoke well of Willie Mays.

"He was really a good friend. I played golf with him quite a bit. He really helped me out, out there,...I thought I was going to be in the World Series twice my first year out there. We had a great club... we won the western division in the National League and then we played Pittsburgh who won the east. We had beaten Pittsburgh nine out of ten times during the year and they ended up beating us three games to two in the playoffs."

After the 1972 season, Russ Gibson's career was over and for the next ten years, he lived in San Francisco, worked for Bank of America, then came home to Massachusetts and worked with the Massachusetts Lottery for twenty-five years.

He retired a few years ago and says, "I love it." Presently he lives in Swansea, Massachusetts.

Billy Rohr was very friendly and affable. He enjoyed talking about the game and has fond memories of both the game and his catcher. I began by asking about the ball that Tom Tresh hit in the ninth inning that resulted in the fantastic catch by Carl Yastrzemski. Did he think then, this was the near hit of the game and he would now get his no-hitter?

"In retrospect, I did, but I can't remember having that thought at the time. Actually, there was a ball hit earlier in the game by Bill Robinson that ricocheted off my shin. Either Joy Foy or Rico threw him out at first. That would have been a ground ball hit back up the middle as sure as shooting, but it hit me. But yeah, I thought if that thing doesn't go for a hit, then maybe this is going to happen."

With two men out, Elston Howard came to bat for the Yankees and with a two and two count he took ball three. Rohr believes that not only he, but also Gibson and even Howard thought it was strike three.

"Absolutely. Russ has told me that Ellie started to cross home plate as if to go back to the Yankee dugout...Gibby started to stand up... I mean it looked like it was all over...the rest, as they say, is history."

This game has a great deal of folklore for baseball fans in New England. I've often wondered if it would be remembered as much if it had been a no-hitter. I think not. I think the way this game ended made it a one-of-a-kind game that will probably never be matched. It is far more unique than a routine no-hitter. I asked Rohr what he thought about my theory.

"If you stop and think about it, two outs in the ninth and a full count, that's about as far as you can take it. So, in some respects, I suppose that's true, it has some sense of uniqueness that perhaps a no-hitter doesn't have."

A few months following this game, Elston Howard was sold from the Yankees to the Red Sox. He had spent his whole career with the Yankees and now was on his way to Boston. He would be Gibson and Rohr's teammate.

Bill Rohr said, "I got to pitch to him and... what a nice man; an absolute gentleman." When I asked him if he and Ellie Howard joked about the hit, he said, "Oh absolutely, he gave me grief consistently about it...I remember Ellie saying that was the only time he ever got booed in Yankee Stadium for getting a hit."

A few days after the one hitter, Rohr faced the Yankees again, this time at Fenway Park in Boston.

"Friday night and colder than a mother-in-laws kiss" is the way he described it. Bill Rohr won the game. Here he was at a young age and a quick record of two wins and no losses as a major league pitcher. It would have been hard to believe that he would win only one more game as a major league pitcher and retire with a record of three wins and three losses. He pitched for the Cleveland Indians in 1968 and became injured.

"I hurt my arm in Cleveland in 1968...it was a slight rotator cuff tear. I was trying to pitch different kinds of ways so that it wouldn't hurt and what have you, but it wasn't going to happen."

What did happen; Bill Rohr became a trial attorney. He jokingly said,

"I couldn't get an honest job when I got out of prison, so I became a lawyer."

He lives in Palm Springs and continues to practice law in Southern California.

Elston Howard passed away in 1980.

Every ball player has clear memories of their debut game. This is certainly true for these two guys. What makes this game so unique is, it has some strong and never-ending memories for lots of folks... and those memories will stay strong for a very long time.

Boston Red Sox 3, New York Yankees 0

Game Played on Friday, April 14, 1967 (D) at Yankee Stadium

```
BOS A    1  0  0    0  0  0    0  2  0  -   3  8  1
NY  A    0  0  0    0  0  0    0  0  0  -   0  1  0
```

BATTING

Boston Red Sox	AB	R	H	RBI	BB	SO	PO	A
Smith 2b	5	1	1	1	0	1	3	2
Foy 3b	3	1	1	2	1	0	0	2
Yastrzemski lf	4	0	2	0	0	1	2	0
Conigliaro rf	4	0	1	0	0	1	4	0
Scott 1b	4	0	0	0	0	2	11	1
Thomas cf	4	0	0	0	0	1	3	0
Petrocelli ss	3	0	1	0	1	0	1	6
Gibson c	4	1	2	0	0	0	2	0
Rohr p	2	0	0	0	1	0	1	1
Totals	33	3	8	3	3	6	27	12

FIELDING -
DP: 1. Petrocelli-Smith-Scott.
E: Rohr (1).

BATTING -
HR: Smith (1,1st inning off Ford 0 on 0 out); Foy (1,8th inning off Ford 1 on 2 out).
SH: Rohr (1,off Ford).
Team LOB: 7.

New York Yankees	AB	R	H	RBI	BB	SO	PO	A
Clarke 2b	3	0	0	0	1	0	4	1
Robinson rf	3	0	0	0	1	0	1	0
Tresh lf	3	0	0	0	1	1	0	0
Pepitone cf	3	0	0	0	1	0	0	0
Howard c	4	0	1	0	0	0	8	0
Smith 3b	4	0	0	0	0	0	1	3
Barker 1b	2	0	0	0	1	1	10	1
Kennedy ss	2	0	0	0	0	0	1	2
Mantle ph	1	0	0	0	0	0	0	0
Amaro ss	0	0	0	0	0	0	1	0
Ford p	2	0	0	0	0	0	1	6
Clinton ph	1	0	0	0	0	0	0	0
Tillotson p	0	0	0	0	0	0	0	0
Totals	28	0	1	0	5	2	27	13

FIELDING -
DP: 1. Smith-Clarke-Barker.

PITCHING

Boston Red Sox	IP	H	R	ER	BB	SO	HR
Rohr W(1-0)	9	1	0	0	5	2	0

New York Yankees	IP	H	R	ER	BB	SO	HR
Ford L(0-1)	8	7	3	3	1	5	2
Tillotson	1	1	0	0	2	1	0
Totals	9	8	3	3	3	6	2

Umpires: Cal Drummond, Bill Haller, Jim Honochick, Nestor Chylak

Time of Game: 2:11   **Attendance:** 14375

Starting Lineups:

Boston Red Sox		New York Yankees	
1. Smith	2b	Clarke	2b
2. Foy	3b	Robinson	rf
3. Yastrzemski	lf	Tresh	lf
4. Conigliaro	rf	Pepitone	cf
5. Scott	1b	Howard	c
6. Thomas	cf	Smith	3b
7. Petrocelli	ss	Barker	1b
8. Gibson	c	Kennedy	ss
9. Rohr	p	Ford	p

RED SOX 1ST: Smith homered; **Debut game for Billy Rohr;**
Foy walked; Yastrzemski singled to right [Foy to third];
Conigliaro reached on a fielder's choice [Foy out at home (third
to catcher), Yastrzemski to second]; Scott grounded out (pitcher
to first) [Yastrzemski to third, Conigliaro to second]; Thomas
struck out; 1 R, 2 H, 0 E, 2 LOB. Red Sox 1, Yankees 0.

YANKEES 1ST: Clarke grounded out (third to first); Robinson made
an out to center; Tresh grounded out (shortstop to first); 0 R,
0 H, 0 E, 0 LOB. Red Sox 1, Yankees 0.

RED SOX 2ND: Petrocelli singled to left; Gibson grounded into a
double play (third to second to first) [Petrocelli out at
second]; **Debut game for Russ Gibson;** Rohr grounded out
(pitcher to first); 0 R, 1 H, 0 E, 0 LOB. Red Sox 1, Yankees 0.

YANKEES 2ND: Pepitone made an out to center; Howard grounded out
(shortstop to first); Smith grounded out (shortstop to first); 0
R, 0 H, 0 E, 0 LOB. Red Sox 1, Yankees 0.

RED SOX 3RD: Smith grounded out (shortstop to first); Foy made
an out to third; Yastrzemski grounded out (first to pitcher); 0
R, 0 H, 0 E, 0 LOB. Red Sox 1, Yankees 0.

YANKEES 3RD: Barker grounded out (first unassisted); Kennedy
made an out to second; Ford grounded out (shortstop to first); 0
R, 0 H, 0 E, 0 LOB. Red Sox 1, Yankees 0.

RED SOX 4TH: On a bunt Conigliaro singled to third; Scott struck
out; Thomas made an out to right; Petrocelli popped to first in
foul territory; 0 R, 1 H, 0 E, 1 LOB. Red Sox 1, Yankees 0.

YANKEES 4TH: Clarke made an out to right; Robinson walked; Tresh struck out; Pepitone walked [Robinson to second]; Howard made an out to center; 0 R, 0 H, 0 E, 2 LOB. Red Sox 1, Yankees 0.

RED SOX 5TH: Gibson grounded out (pitcher to first); Rohr made an out to second; Smith popped to catcher in foul territory; 0 R, 0 H, 0 E, 0 LOB. Red Sox 1, Yankees 0.

YANKEES 5TH: Smith grounded out (shortstop to first); Barker walked; Kennedy made an out to second; Ford grounded out (first to pitcher); 0 R, 0 H, 0 E, 1 LOB. Red Sox 1, Yankees 0.

RED SOX 6TH: Foy grounded out (pitcher to first); Yastrzemski struck out; Conigliaro struck out; 0 R, 0 H, 0 E, 0 LOB. Red Sox 1, Yankees 0.

YANKEES 6TH: Clarke made an out to left; Robinson grounded out (pitcher to third to first); Tresh walked; Pepitone forced Tresh (second to shortstop); 0 R, 0 H, 0 E, 1 LOB. Red Sox 1, Yankees 0.

RED SOX 7TH: Scott struck out; Thomas made an out to shortstop; Petrocelli grounded out (pitcher to first); 0 R, 0 H, 0 E, 0 LOB. Red Sox 1, Yankees 0.

YANKEES 7TH: Howard popped to first in foul territory; Smith made an out to first; Barker struck out; 0 R, 0 H, 0 E, 0 LOB. Red Sox 1, Yankees 0.

RED SOX 8TH: Gibson singled to center; Rohr out on a sacrifice bunt (pitcher to second) [Gibson to second]; Smith grounded out (shortstop to first); Foy homered [Gibson scored]; Yastrzemski singled to second; Conigliaro forced Yastrzemski (third to second); 2 R, 3 H, 0 E, 1 LOB. Red Sox 3, Yankees 0.

YANKEES 8TH: MANTLE BATTED FOR KENNEDY; Mantle made an out to right; CLINTON BATTED FOR FORD; Clinton reached on an error by Rohr; Clarke walked [Clinton to second]; Robinson grounded into a double play (shortstop to second to first) [Clarke out at second]; 0 R, 0 H, 1 E, 1 LOB. Red Sox 3, Yankees 0.

RED SOX 9TH: AMARO REPLACED MANTLE (PLAYING SS); TILLOTSON REPLACED CLINTON (PITCHING); Scott popped to first in foul territory; **Debut game for Thad Tillotson;** Thomas made an out to shortstop; Petrocelli walked; Gibson singled to center [Petrocelli to second]; Rohr walked [Petrocelli to third, Gibson to second]; Smith struck out; 0 R, 1 H, 0 E, 3 LOB. Red Sox 3, Yankees 0.

YANKEES 9TH: Tresh made an out to left; Pepitone made an out to right; Howard singled to right; Smith made an out to right; 0 R, 1 H, 0 E, 1 LOB. Red Sox 3, Yankees 0.

Final Totals	R	H	E	LOB
Red Sox	3	8	1	7
Yankees	0	1	0	6

CHAPTER SIX

Sunday September 29, 1963
New York Mets at Houston Colt 45's

Mr. Perfect

IN 1961 AND 1962, BASEBALL expanded from sixteen to twenty teams. The American League expanded in 1961 by two teams, the Los Angeles Angels and the Washington Senators. The National League followed suit one year later. The two added by the National League were the Houston Colt 45's and the New York Mets. Both teams were lovable losers. In 1963, the second year of existence for both teams, the Houston team finished ninth out of ten teams. The reason they didn't finish last was; that honor was reserved for the New York Mets.

In late 1963, a young man named John Paciorek came up to the major leagues for his shot at making it in the show. It was a chance any eighteen-year-old would kill for. John Paciorek signed with the Houston Colt 45's at the age of seventeen and played his first professional season in 1963 with Modesto of the California League.

The California League was a Class A league, slightly above entry level, three steps below the major leagues. After the minor league season, John Paciorek got his chance. He would play one game, the last game of the season in right field for the Houston Colt 45s.

John Paciorek came from a baseball family. He and three brothers played pro ball. Along with him, two of his ball-playing brothers made it to the major leagues. Tom Paciorek had a distinguished eighteen-year career in the major leagues for several teams. Another brother, Jim Paciorek had a short run with the Milwaukee Brewers and then played good ball in Japan. A third brother, Mike, was a first baseman in the minors for a time.

On the last day of the season in 1963, these two teams played the final game of the season for both teams. The game was played in Colt Stadium in Houston. There were about 3,900 in attendance that Sunday.

On September 29, 1963, it was John Paciorek's shot at the major leagues and he did everything right. You see, John came up to the plate five times in this game and reached base all five times. Two were by bases on balls, and the other three were singles. He scored four runs and drove in three, a fantastic debut for this young guy.

What makes this game so unique is, this wasn't only John Paciorek's debut, it was also his finale. John Paciorek started and ended his major league career on this day; and he was perfect. Although he played pro ball for several more years, he would never again get the chance to play in the major leagues. He ended up with a batting average of 1.000, an on-base percentage of 1.000 and a fielding average of 1.000.

I was able to reach John Paciorek at his home in California. I found him to be a real gentleman, and he seemed to enjoy talking about his game.

"When I signed out of high school, I was seventeen years old and considered if not their biggest prospect, one of them and they were looking for me to be up in the big leagues quickly. I went to winter baseball in the fall, right after I signed, then I went to spring training at Apache Junction with the big club. I had a good spring training and they had to figure out what they wanted to do because I did so well. They were thinking about keeping me up there, but they decided I probably wouldn't get that much chance to play if I stayed in the big leagues, so they sent me to the minor leagues. From there,

I went to Modesto, California. During the course of the season, I developed a little bit of a back problem."

It was that back problem that ultimately prevented John from playing more baseball in the major leagues.

"I went home afterward and they were all expecting me to make it in the big leagues the next year. Everything was going well, but my back was bothering me so badly. I didn't know what I was going to do. I did a lot of exercises over the break and I thought I was going to come back, but when I was at spring training, they gave me every opportunity to make the club. I was hurting badly, but I didn't tell anybody. I was doing just horribly. I couldn't bend down. Every time I would bend down, I had a knife shot through my back. They ended up sending me again to the minor league spring training and from there I eventually ended up telling everybody how bad my back was hurting. They brought me up and I had the operation."

I wondered if the injury was caused by a specific play in a game.

Paciorek replied, "I really don't know. I developed torn muscles in my upper back. I used to play hard, diving for balls and throwing hard."

"When I first hurt it, I was playing for Dave Philley, the manager, and he was known as a real blood and guts kind of guy when he played ball. He would say that he would be taped up from foot to head and still play, so I kept playing. Eventually, I couldn't even lift my arm anymore. I was sitting on the bench waiting to recuperate when I noticed my lower back was bothering me. It got worse and worse. I was out for two years."

John had his operation and came back to play pro ball through the 1969 season, but the back was never the same.

"I was always hurt. I never hurt before, maybe a pulled muscle or something, but after the operation, I was always hurt."

He played in the Houston system through 1967.

"I was finally released by Houston, they hated to release me. I was just so erratic and hurt most of the time, they said 'He's never going to do anything' then I went home."

"Houston released me when I couldn't even lift up my arm. I couldn't even play first base, I couldn't throw or anything. Over the off-season, my arm got better. I was watching my brother (Tom) play at the University of Houston, and there was a scout there who remembered me. He asked how I was feeling and I told him I was feeling really good. He was from Cleveland (Indians). He made some calls and they gave me the chance to come to spring training and I did really well."

The Indians signed him. He spent the 1968 season with Rock Hill of the Western Carolinas League and Reno of the California League.

He ended up having the best year of his career, hitting 20 home runs in only 95 games.

"With a relatively limited amount of at-bats, they were impressed with that. The next season, I was even more hurt. I would have to come out hours before and everybody else and stretch out. After that, I was in Waterbury and they finally released me."

Mr. Paciorek said he was actually glad it was over. At the time, he said to himself,

"I'm just so happy not to have to do that anymore."

With his baseball career behind him, John Paciorek entered the world of education.

"I'm a physical education teacher and coach. I graduated from the University of Houston. Now I'm working at a small private school in San Gabriel, California."

He continues to keep in touch with his brothers. He told me his brother Tom just became the color man for the Washington Nationals broadcasting team. He worked for the White Sox for a while with Hawk Harrelson. 'Jimbo' (he calls his brother Jim) is living in Seattle, Washington and now retired. John's brother Mike, is married, lives in California and works with another brother who didn't play ball.

The brothers were all born and raised in Detroit, Michigan, but got into baseball and left that area.

John realizes he is the answer to a very interesting trivia question. The question; who is the only player in history to reach base in his only five plate appearances in his major league career? You got it, John Paciorek.

John Paciorek knows what it feels like to hit in the big leagues, drive in runs in the big leagues, round third and score in the big leagues.

He also knows what it feels like to play perfect defense in the big leagues. He experienced it all on one glorious September day.

Houston Colt .45s 13, New York Mets 4

Game Played on Sunday, September 29, 1963 (D) at Colt Stadium

```
NY  N    0  0  1    3  0  0    0  0  0  -   4   9  2
HOU N    0  2  0    5  4  1    1  0  x  -  13  13  2
```

BATTING

New York Mets	AB	R	H	RBI	BB	SO	PO	A
Kranepool rf	5	0	1	1	0	0	2	0
Carmel cf	3	0	0	0	1	2	0	0
Hunt 2b	3	0	2	0	0	0	3	2
Harkness 1b	3	1	1	0	1	1	8	0
Hickman 3b	4	1	1	0	0	1	1	1
Schreiber 3b	0	0	0	0	0	0	1	0
Hicks lf	4	0	0	0	0	0	0	0
Coleman c	2	1	1	1	0	0	6	0
Cannizzaro c	2	0	0	0	0	0	2	0
Moran ss	2	0	0	0	0	1	0	0
Fernandez ph,ss	2	0	0	0	0	0	1	2
Bearnarth p	2	1	2	2	0	0	0	0
Bauta p	0	0	0	0	0	0	0	1
Stallard p	0	0	0	0	0	0	0	0
Thomas ph	1	0	0	0	0	0	0	0
Powell p	0	0	0	0	0	0	0	2
Smith ph	1	0	1	0	0	0	0	0
Totals	34	4	9	4	2	5	24	8

FIELDING -
DP: 2. Harkness, Powell-Hunt-Harkness.
E: Carmel (6), Hicks (3).

BATTING -
2B: Hunt (28,off Farrell).
3B: Bearnarth (1,off Zachary).
HBP: Hunt (13,by Zachary).
Team LOB: 6.

BASERUNNING -
SB: Coleman (5,2nd base off Umbricht/Bateman).

Houston Colt .45s	AB	R	H	RBI	BB	SO	PO	A
Vaughan ss	2	0	0	0	0	2	0	0
Runnels ph	0	0	0	1	0	0	0	0
Farrell p	2	0	0	0	0	1	0	0
Dickson p	1	0	0	0	0	0	0	0
Morgan 2b	2	1	0	0	3	1	1	5
Wynn lf	3	0	1	2	2	1	0	0
Staub 1b	4	1	1	1	1	0	8	1

Aspromonte 3b	4	3	2	1	1	0	4	0
Murrell cf	5	1	1	0	0	2	3	0
Paciorek rf	3	4	3	3	2	0	2	0
Bateman c	3	2	2	3	1	0	6	0
Adlesh ph,c	1	0	0	0	0	0	0	0
Zachary p	1	0	0	0	0	1	0	0
Umbricht p	0	0	0	0	0	0	1	0
Spangler ph	1	0	1	0	0	0	0	0
Lillis ss	2	1	2	2	1	0	2	1
Totals	34	13	13	13	11	8	27	7

FIELDING -
DP: 2. Morgan-Staub, Morgan-Lillis-Staub.
E: Wynn (8), Bateman (23).

BATTING -
3B: Bateman (6,off Bearnarth); Aspromonte (5,off Bauta).
SF: Runnels (4,off Bauta).
Team LOB: 9.

PITCHING

New York Mets	IP	H	R	ER	BB	SO	HR
Bearnarth L(3-8)	3	6	7	7	3	5	0
Bauta	1.1	4	3	3	1	1	0
Stallard	0.2	1	1	1	3	1	0
Powell	3	2	2	2	4	1	0
Totals	8	13	13	13	11	8	0

Houston Colt .45s	IP	H	R	ER	BB	SO	HR
Zachary	3.1	5	4	4	1	3	0
Umbricht W(4-3)	0.2	1	0	0	0	1	0
Farrell	3	2	0	0	1	1	0
Dickson SV(2)	2	1	0	0	0	0	0
Totals	9	9	4	4	2	5	0

Bearnarth faced 5 batters in the 4th inning
WP: Powell (9).
HBP: Zachary (3,Hunt).

Umpires: Paul Pryor, Frank Secory, Frank Walsh, Ken Burkhart

Time of Game: 2:28   **Attendance:** 3899

Starting Lineups:

New York Mets		Houston Colt .45s	
1. Kranepool	rf	Vaughan	ss
2. Carmel	cf	Morgan	2b
3. Hunt	2b	Wynn	lf
4. Harkness	1b	Staub	1b
5. Hickman	3b	Aspromonte	3b
6. Hicks	lf	Murrell	cf
7. Coleman	c	Paciorek	rf
8. Moran	ss	Bateman	c
9. Bearnarth	p	Zachary	p

METS 1ST: Kranepool grounded out (second to first); Carmel

struck out; Hunt was hit by a pitch; Harkness walked [Hunt to
second]; Hickman struck out; 0 R, 0 H, 0 E, 2 LOB. Mets 0, Colt
.45s 0.

COLT .45S 1ST: Vaughan struck out; Morgan popped to third; Wynn
struck out; 0 R, 0 H, 0 E, 0 LOB. Mets 0, Colt .45s 0.

METS 2ND: Hicks made an out to right; Coleman grounded out
(first unassisted); Moran made an out to right; 0 R, 0 H, 0 E, 0
LOB. Mets 0, Colt .45s 0.

COLT .45S 2ND: Staub grounded out (first unassisted); Aspromonte
walked; Murrell was called out on strikes; Paciorek walked
[Aspromonte to second]; **Debut game for John Paciorek;**
Bateman tripled to right [Aspromonte scored, Paciorek scored];
Zachary struck out; 2 R, 1 H, 0 E, 1 LOB. Mets 0, Colt .45s 2.

METS 3RD: Bearnarth tripled to left; Kranepool singled to right
[Bearnarth scored]; Carmel struck out; Hunt lined into a double
play (second to first) [Kranepool out at first]; 1 R, 2 H, 0 E,
0 LOB. Mets 1, Colt .45s 2.

COLT .45S 3RD: Vaughan was called out on strikes; Morgan walked;
Wynn lined into a double play (first unassisted) [Morgan out at
first]; 0 R, 0 H, 0 E, 0 LOB. Mets 1, Colt .45s 2.

METS 4TH: Harkness singled to right; Hickman singled to
shortstop [Harkness to second]; Hicks popped to third; Coleman
singled to center [Harkness scored, Hickman to third]; UMBRICHT
REPLACED ZACHARY (PITCHING); Coleman stole second; Moran struck
out; Bearnarth singled to left [Hickman scored, Coleman scored,
Bearnarth to third (error by Wynn)]; Kranepool grounded out
(first to pitcher); 3 R, 4 H, 1 E, 1 LOB. Mets 4, Colt .45s 2.

COLT .45S 4TH: Staub singled to right; Aspromonte singled to
left [Staub to second]; Murrell singled to third [Staub to
third, Aspromonte to second]; Paciorek singled to left [Staub
scored, Aspromonte scored, Murrell to second]; Bateman singled
to center [Murrell scored, Paciorek to second]; SPANGLER BATTED
FOR UMBRICHT; BAUTA REPLACED BEARNARTH (PITCHING); Spangler
singled to shortstop [Paciorek to third, Bateman to second];
RUNNELS BATTED FOR VAUGHAN; Runnels hit a sacrifice fly to right
[Paciorek scored]; Morgan struck out; Wynn singled to center
[Bateman scored, Spangler to third]; Staub grounded out (pitcher
to first); 5 R, 7 H, 0 E, 2 LOB. Mets 4, Colt .45s 7.

METS 5TH: LILLIS REPLACED SPANGLER (PLAYING SS); FARRELL
REPLACED RUNNELS (PITCHING); Carmel walked; Hunt doubled to
right [Carmel to third]; Harkness struck out; Bateman dropped a
foul fly hit by Hickman; Hickman popped to third in foul
territory; Hicks popped to shortstop; 0 R, 1 H, 1 E, 2 LOB.
Mets 4, Colt .45s 7.

COLT .45S 5TH: CANNIZZARO REPLACED COLEMAN (PLAYING C);
Aspromonte tripled to right; Murrell popped to first in foul
territory; Paciorek singled to left [Aspromonte scored]; Bateman
walked [Paciorek to second]; STALLARD REPLACED BAUTA (PITCHING);
Lillis singled to left [Paciorek scored, Bateman to third (error
by Hicks), Lillis to second]; Farrell was called out on strikes;
Morgan walked; Wynn walked [Bateman scored, Lillis to third,

Morgan to second]; Staub walked [Lillis scored, Morgan to third, Wynn to second]; Aspromonte made an out to right; 4 R, 3 H, 1 E, 3 LOB. Mets 4, Colt .45s 11.

METS 6TH: Cannizzaro popped to first; FERNANDEZ BATTED FOR MORAN; Fernandez popped to catcher in foul territory; THOMAS BATTED FOR STALLARD; Thomas made an out to center; 0 R, 0 H, 0 E, 0 LOB. Mets 4, Colt .45s 11.

COLT .45S 6TH: FERNANDEZ STAYED IN GAME (PLAYING SS); POWELL REPLACED THOMAS (PITCHING); Murrell struck out; Paciorek walked; Powell threw a wild pitch [Paciorek to second]; Bateman grounded out (third to first); Lillis singled to center [Paciorek scored, Lillis to second (error by Carmel)]; Farrell grounded out (pitcher to first); 1 R, 1 H, 1 E, 1 LOB. Mets 4, Colt .45s 12.

METS 7TH: Kranepool popped to third; Carmel made an out to center; Hunt singled to center; Harkness grounded out (second to first); 0 R, 1 H, 0 E, 1 LOB. Mets 4, Colt .45s 12.

COLT .45S 7TH: Morgan walked; Wynn walked [Morgan to second]; Staub forced Wynn (second to shortstop) [Morgan to third]; Aspromonte forced Staub (shortstop to second) [Morgan scored]; Murrell forced Aspromonte (shortstop to second); 1 R, 0 H, 0 E, 1 LOB. Mets 4, Colt .45s 13.

METS 8TH: DICKSON REPLACED FARRELL (PITCHING); Hickman popped to third; Hicks grounded out (first unassisted); Cannizzaro made an out to center; 0 R, 0 H, 0 E, 0 LOB. Mets 4, Colt .45s 13.

COLT .45S 8TH: SCHREIBER REPLACED HICKMAN (PLAYING 3B); Paciorek singled to left; ADLESH BATTED FOR BATEMAN; Adlesh grounded into a double play (pitcher to second to first) [Paciorek out at second]; Lillis walked; Dickson popped to third in foul territory; 0 R, 1 H, 0 E, 1 LOB. Mets 4, Colt .45s 13.

METS 9TH: ADLESH STAYED IN GAME (PLAYING C); Fernandez grounded out (second to first); SMITH BATTED FOR POWELL; Smith singled to center; Kranepool grounded into a double play (second to shortstop to first) [Smith out at second]; 0 R, 1 H, 0 E, 0 LOB. Mets 4, Colt .45s 13.

Final Totals	R	H	E	LOB
Mets	4	9	2	6
Colt .45s	13	13	2	9

CHAPTER SEVEN

Saturday September 2, 1972
San Diego Padres at Chicago Cubs

Mr. *Almost* Perfect

WHEN MILT PAPPAS PITCHED HIS first game in the major leagues, I was three years old. When he pitched his final game in the major leagues, I was nineteen. He was one of the guys I grew up with as a baseball fan. I was then and am now a huge fan of Milt Pappas. As I wrote this book, I got to speak with Milt, which is something I would have loved to do when I was growing up.

In his autobiography, *Out At Home*, Milt Pappas describes himself as 'brash'. After speaking with him, I couldn't agree more. Don't get me wrong, he was a heck of a nice guy. He was very friendly and helpful. When I addressed him as 'Mr. Pappas', he said, "Call me Milt, please."

It was fun speaking with him and he was very interesting to listen to. He held nothing back and wasn't shy about his opinions. He is a 'what you see is what you get' kind of guy. Ask him something, he'll answer it. You'll have no doubt about the way he feels about whatever you're asking.

This is the way Milt Pappas conducted himself as a major league baseball player. Pitching through the sixties, baseball was experiencing great change. The catalyst of the changes was the Major League Players Association. The union became stronger and stronger as the decade progressed and Milt Pappas was one of the reasons why. He was very active in the union and a player representative on more than one team on which he played. He made no apologies to anyone for his activities, even when it affected his standing with his employers.

He was one of the guys who planted the seeds for the incredible benefits players of today have in the major leagues; however; Pappas received very few benefits for himself.

Milt Pappas was a very good pitcher. He won 209 games in the major leagues. When he won his 200th game, he became the first pitcher in major league history to win his 200th without ever having a twenty-win season. Since that time, four pitchers, Jerry Reuss, Charlie Hough, Dennis Martinez and Frank Tanana have joined that 'club'.

Pappas just missed being part of another rare club. Of his 209 wins, 110 were in the American League and ninety-nine were in the National League. One more win in the senior circuit and he would have been one of very few pitchers to win at least 100 games in each league.

Milt Pappas was a very good hitting pitcher. In his career, he hit twenty home runs. Quite a feat for a pitcher. Most pitchers never hit one! Some hit one or two, but Milt clubbed twenty. As a member of the Baltimore Orioles, he hit two home runs in one game against the Minnesota Twins in August 1961. That day, he also shut out the Twins, 3-0.

On September 2, 1972, Milt Pappas, now a member of the Cubs, came close to joining an exclusive club. In a game he pitched against the San Diego Padres, Milt came within one pitch of hurling a perfect game. Not just a 'no-hitter' but also a 'perfect game', one in which not one Padre would reach first base.

In the 140 ± years that major league baseball has existed, there have been only seventeen perfect games. Milt came so close on this date. After retiring twenty-six Padres in a row, Milt stood on the Wrigley Field mound facing Larry Stahl, a pinch hitter. Milt worked the count to one ball and two strikes. Just one more strike and Milt would be one of the very few pitchers able to say he pitched a perfect game. The home plate umpire was Bruce Froemming. In his book *Out at Home*, Milt describes what happened.

"The count was one and two. One pitch more. Just one pitch, just one. Make it a strike. Make him hit my pitch. One more out and I'd be in the record books. A perfect game. A no-hitter. By me, Milt Pappas. Just one more pitch and - what? -Immortality? Yeah! Immortality. In the record books forever. A perfect game...Focused? Yes, I was."

"I looked in for the signal. Randy Hundley, my catcher called for a slider, my best pitch that day. I wound up and made the delivery. It was right there where I wanted it. Knee-high on the black...Stahl just stood there. Froemming pointed outside and low and called it a ball. DAMN! Another signal came from Hundley. He wanted another slider. I agreed and I threw a good one...Froemming pointed outside and low again...Hundley called for another pitch. A slider. I nodded as I felt the ball in my hand. I gave it a solid grip, my best. I wound up, kicked my leg, left arm out front, right arm back, then forward. I released and watched it all the say into Hundley's glove. It was nearly perfect again. At the knee on the black. Stahl just stood there. I grimaced for the call and Froemming pointed to first base."

Larry Stahl then trotted down to first base, the first and last base runner for the Padres that day. Milt had a few choice words for the home plate umpire. Gary Jestadt was the next batter and Milt got him to pop out to the second baseman for the final out of the day. Milt had pitched a 'no-hitter', but it was bittersweet, having come so close to a 'perfect game'. His teammates crowded around him to congratulate him. Pappas feels if it weren't for this, he might have gone after Froemming.

A third of a century later, I spoke to Milt Pappas. He hasn't changed his position about this one bit. I asked him if he thought he got strike three.

"Yes. Actually, the last three pitches I threw were (strikes). I had him one ball and two strikes and one pitch away from a perfect game. Unfortunately, Mr. Froemming called the last three pitches balls."

"Consequently, that took care of the perfect game, thanks to this idiot (Froemming). He's not on my Christmas card list by the way. It just didn't make any sense for him to do what he did with what was on the line. Of course one of his famous comments was, 'Name me one umpire that called a perfect game' and I kept telling him, well, let me tell you the other eight at that time could go through the rest of their lives whether they're sitting in the bar, or at home, or at a function, or anywhere saying I called a perfect game. I said because of what you did, you jackass, you can't say that."

Bruce Froemming is still active as a major league umpire as I write this (2006). During the 2006 season, he was honored for umpiring his 5000th game. Some feel that Bruce could be one of the few umpires enshrined in the Hall of Fame. He is still asked about this game, as he was in the August 28-September 10, 2006 edition of *Baseball America*. He was asked by Alan Schwartz if ball four was a close pitch.

"In the Pappas situation, he had the batter, Larry Stahl, the 27th hitter, 0-2 and proceeded to walk him. I didn't walk him - he walked him. You're saying the pitch was close. There's no such thing. It's either a ball or it's a strike. The judgment is, was it on the plate or was it off the plate? A fan says 'it's close'. I'm not a fan. I'm the arbitrator. It's a ball or a strike. I'm not always right, but I try to be."

It's interesting that Bruce Froemming could be in the Hall of Fame, but Milt Pappas probably won't be. In fact, Milt never even made it to the Hall of Fame ballot. He still is bitter about that.

"I had a better percentage record than Drysdale. For me not to even get on the ballot when I was eligible for the Hall of Fame was just totally ridiculous."

"It's gotten to the point where the whole thing is ridiculous the way it's handled today anyway. My feeling has always been that the Hall of Fame is to put people in, not keep them out. You'd never know that with what they're doing. When you've got guys like Jim Rice, and Andre Dawson, Goose Gossage and Lee Smith that don't get in; but Bruce Sutter gets in, there's something wrong...I don't understand it."

"My whole qualm has been since that debacle with me and the Hall of Fame, I said if that's the case then why the hell don't you set up criteria for the Hall of Fame. Whether you win 200 games, 250 games, or 300 games or you hit .280 lifetime or .290 or .300, or five, six, or seven hundred home runs, or 400 saves for a relief pitcher. Set up criteria. Instead, they leave it in the hands of people who never even saw the people play for God's sake. It's sad."

I feel strongly that Milt Pappas belongs in the Hall of Fame. I say that and some fans think I'm crazy, but consider this. Milt Pappas won 209 games in the major leagues, exactly the same amount of games as Don Drysdale. He lost 164, two games less than Drysdale. He had a slightly better lifetime record than Don Drysdale, yet Drysdale is in the Hall of Fame, and Pappas can't get a vote.

Don Drysdale spent his whole career with the Dodgers, a perennial contender. Milt Pappas played on mediocre teams. So, the question is; who had more talent?

Pappas played with the Orioles before they were contenders. He played with the Cincinnati Reds before they became the 'Big Red Machine' then the Atlanta Braves before they had their great years. He finished his career with the Chicago Cubs, *need I say more...*

While Drysdale had several post season appearances, Pappas had only one. In 1969, he played for the Braves, who lost to the New York 'Miracle' Mets in the National League playoffs.

I fully realize the Hall of Fame has standards that need to be maintained. That said, not one standard would be sacrificed if Milt Pappas entered the Hall of Fame.

Milt Pappas had a rocky career. He was a battler all the way, he never played for a great team yet he won over 200 games.

I'd like to say that after his career ended, life settled down for Milt and he had a relatively peaceful existence since then. Unfortunately, that is not so.

In the 1980's, Milt was involved in an unspeakable tragedy. On September 11, 1982, Milt's wife Carole left their suburban Chicago home to do errands and go to the dentist. She left in the morning, which was her routine. Normally, she came home around two o'clock in the afternoon. On this September day, she did not. Milt never saw her alive again. She never came home that day and for five years, she remained a 'missing person'. In 1987, Carole Pappas' body was discovered in her automobile at the bottom of a pond in Wheaton, Illinois.

Today, Milt Pappas lives in Wheaton. He has been a successful sales rep in his post-baseball career. In the last few years, he's gotten into broadcasting for an independent minor league team, the Cook County Cheetahs of the Frontier League and acted as their assistant pitching coach.

In his book, he sums up his life.

"Maybe I've had more than my share of triumphs, but I think I've paid for them with more than my share of tragedies."

September 2, 1972, a no-hitter. Was it a triumph or tragedy?

Chicago Cubs 8, San Diego Padres 0

Game Played on Saturday, September 2, 1972 (D) at Wrigley Field

```
SD  N    0  0  0    0  0  0    0  0  0  -  0  0  1
CHI N    2  0  2    0  0  0    0  4  x  -  8 13  0
```

BATTING

San Diego Padres	AB	R	H	RBI	BB	SO	PO	A
Hernandez ss	3	0	0	0	0	1	3	4
Jestadt ph	1	0	0	0	0	0	0	0
Roberts 3b	3	0	0	0	0	1	1	3
Lee lf	3	0	0	0	0	0	0	0
Colbert 1b	3	0	0	0	0	0	8	0
Gaston rf	3	0	0	0	0	2	1	0
Thomas 2b	3	0	0	0	0	0	5	4
Jeter cf	3	0	0	0	0	0	2	0
Kendall c	3	0	0	0	0	0	4	0
Caldwell p	2	0	0	0	0	2	0	1
Severinsen p	0	0	0	0	0	0	0	0
Stahl ph	0	0	0	0	1	0	0	0
Totals	27	0	0	0	1	6	24	12

FIELDING -
DP: 3. Hernandez-Thomas-Colbert, Roberts-Thomas-Colbert, Hernandez-Colbert
E: Hernandez (18).

Chicago Cubs	AB	R	H	RBI	BB	SO	PO	A
Kessinger ss	5	1	2	3	0	0	2	4
Cardenal rf	4	1	2	1	1	0	0	0
Williams lf	4	1	2	0	0	0	3	0
Santo 3b	3	1	0	0	0	0	0	2
Hickman 1b	4	1	3	1	0	0	11	1
Fanzone 2b	3	1	0	1	1	0	2	1
Hundley c	4	1	2	0	0	0	6	0
North cf	4	1	2	1	0	1	1	0
Pappas p	4	0	0	0	0	3	2	2
Totals	35	8	13	7	2	4	27	10

BATTING -
2B: Hickman (12,off Caldwell); Kessinger (16,off Caldwell).
HBP: Santo (4,by Caldwell).
IBB: Fanzone (5,by Caldwell).
Team LOB: 6.

PITCHING

San Diego Padres	IP	H	R	ER	BB	SO	HR

Caldwell L(6-8)	7.2	13	8	6	2	4	0
Severinsen	0.1	0	0	0	0	0	0
Totals	8	13	8	6	2	4	0

| Chicago Cubs | **IP** | **H** | **R** | **ER** | **BB** | **SO** | **HR** |
| Pappas W(12-7) | 9 | 0 | 0 | 0 | 1 | 6 | 0 |

HBP: Caldwell (3,Santo).
IBB: Caldwell (12,Fanzone).

Umpires: Bruce Froemming, Augie Donatelli, Stan Landes, Satch Davidson

Time of Game: 2:03   **Attendance:** 11144

Starting Lineups:

San Diego Padres		Chicago Cubs	
1. Hernandez	ss	Kessinger	ss
2. Roberts	3b	Cardenal	rf
3. Lee	lf	Williams	lf
4. Colbert	1b	Santo	3b
5. Gaston	rf	Hickman	1b
6. Thomas	2b	Fanzone	2b
7. Jeter	cf	Hundley	c
8. Kendall	c	North	cf
9. Caldwell	p	Pappas	p

PADRES 1ST: Hernandez made an out to center; Roberts lined to pitcher; Lee grounded out (second to first); 0 R, 0 H, 0 E, 0 LOB. Padres 0, Cubs 0.

CUBS 1ST: Kessinger reached on an error by Hernandez [Kessinger to second]; Cardenal singled to center [Kessinger scored (unearned)]; Williams singled to second [Cardenal to second]; Santo forced Williams (shortstop unassisted) [Cardenal to third]; Hickman singled to shortstop [Santo to second]; Fanzone forced Hickman (shortstop to second) [Cardenal scored (unearned), Santo to third]; Hundley grounded out (pitcher to first); 2 R, 3 H, 1 E, 2 LOB. Padres 0, Cubs 2.

PADRES 2ND: Colbert made an out to left; Gaston struck out; Thomas lined to shortstop; 0 R, 0 H, 0 E, 0 LOB. Padres 0, Cubs 2.

CUBS 2ND: North singled to shortstop; On a bunt Pappas popped to first in foul territory; Kessinger singled to third [North to second]; Cardenal grounded into a double play (shortstop to second to first) [Kessinger out at second]; 0 R, 2 H, 0 E, 1 LOB. Padres 0, Cubs 2.

PADRES 3RD: Jeter grounded out (third to first); Kendall lined to shortstop; Caldwell struck out; 0 R, 0 H, 0 E, 0 LOB. Padres 0, Cubs 2.

CUBS 3RD: Williams singled to right; Santo was hit by a pitch [Williams to second]; Hickman singled to right [Williams scored, Santo to third]; Fanzone grounded into a double play (third to second to first) [Santo scored, Hickman out at second]; Hundley grounded out (third to first); 2 R, 2 H, 0 E, 0 LOB. Padres 0,

Cubs 4.

PADRES 4TH: Hernandez struck out; Roberts made an out to second; Lee grounded out (first unassisted); 0 R, 0 H, 0 E, 0 LOB. Padres 0, Cubs 4.

CUBS 4TH: North struck out; Pappas struck out; Kessinger made an out to center; 0 R, 0 H, 0 E, 0 LOB. Padres 0, Cubs 4.

PADRES 5TH: Colbert grounded out (shortstop to first); Gaston grounded out (shortstop to first); Thomas flied to left in foul territory; 0 R, 0 H, 0 E, 0 LOB. Padres 0, Cubs 4.

CUBS 5TH: Cardenal singled to left; Williams made an out to shortstop; Santo forced Cardenal (shortstop to second); Hickman forced Santo (third to second); 0 R, 1 H, 0 E, 1 LOB. Padres 0, Cubs 4.

PADRES 6TH: Jeter grounded out (pitcher to first); Kendall grounded out (third to first); On a bunt Caldwell struck out; 0 R, 0 H, 0 E, 0 LOB. Padres 0, Cubs 4.

CUBS 6TH: Fanzone popped to third in foul territory; Hundley singled to right; North lined into a double play (shortstop to first) [Hundley out at first]; 0 R, 1 H, 0 E, 0 LOB. Padres 0, Cubs 4.

PADRES 7TH: Hernandez popped to first; Roberts was called out on strikes; Lee grounded out (first to pitcher); 0 R, 0 H, 0 E, 0 LOB. Padres 0, Cubs 4.

CUBS 7TH: Pappas struck out; Kessinger made an out to center; Cardenal walked; Williams grounded out (second to first); 0 R, 0 H, 0 E, 1 LOB. Padres 0, Cubs 4.

PADRES 8TH: Colbert grounded out (shortstop to first); Gaston struck out; Thomas grounded out (pitcher to first); 0 R, 0 H, 0 E, 0 LOB. Padres 0, Cubs 4.

CUBS 8TH: Santo grounded out (second to first); Hickman doubled to left; Fanzone was walked intentionally; Hundley singled to third [Hickman to third, Fanzone to second]; North singled to third [Hickman scored, Fanzone to third, Hundley to second]; Pappas struck out; Kessinger doubled to left [Fanzone scored, Hundley scored, North scored]; SEVERINSEN REPLACED CALDWELL (PITCHING); Cardenal lined to right; 4 R, 4 H, 0 E, 1 LOB. Padres 0, Cubs 8.

PADRES 9TH: Jeter lined to left; Kendall grounded out (shortstop to first); STAHL BATTED FOR SEVERINSEN; Stahl walked; JESTADT BATTED FOR HERNANDEZ; Jestadt made an out to second; 0 R, 0 H, 0 E, 1 LOB. Padres 0, Cubs 8.

Final Totals	R	H	E	LOB
Padres	0	0	1	1
Cubs	8	13	0	6

CHAPTER EIGHT

Friday August 18, 1967
California Angels at Boston Red Sox

The Night the Music Died

IT WAS A BEAUTIFUL NIGHT in Boston. Life in New England was grand that summer. I was thirteen years old and the summer of 1967 was one of the most exciting times ever for any Boston Red Sox fan.

We've covered the Billy Rohr one-hitter in a prior chapter. Now, let's fast-forward to a night in August 1967 and entering the final part of the season. The Red Sox were in a fierce pennant race, fighting it out with four other teams. The Minnesota Twins, Chicago White Sox, Detroit Tigers and the California Angels were in the race for the pennant.

When August 18, 1967 began, the fifth place team, the Angels were only four and one-half games out of first place. The fourth place Red Sox record on this date was 62-54; the Angels were 62-56.

On this Friday night, the Angels were in Boston. The starting pitcher for the Angels was Jack Hamilton. Hamilton was a journeyman right-handed pitcher in the middle of his best major league season. He'd made it to the starting rotation for the Angels, entering this game with a record on the year of six wins and two losses. The Red Sox would counter with another journeyman pitcher, Gary Bell. Gary's record entering this game was seven wins, ten losses. It was a bit ironic that Gary Bell was the pitcher this evening and I'll tell you why shortly...

There was a huge crowd, over 31,000 in attendance that evening. However, large crowds were not unusual. Every night was either a sell out or a near sell out. The Red Sox were one very exciting team that year and they earned the nickname 'Cardiac Kids'. They were young and at twenty-seven, Carl Yastrzemski was considered one of the veterans of the team. Yastrzemski was on his way to a Triple Crown year. He would eventually end the season as the American League leader in home runs, runs batted in and batting average. He actually tied with Harmon Killebrew for the home run title. He is, to date (2006) the last player to win the Triple Crown.

Playing right field for the Red Sox was Tony Conigliaro. At twenty-two years old, Tony was another veteran amazingly playing in his fourth major league season.

I loved Tony Conigliaro. I was only thirteen that summer and a New England kid, 100% Italian-American. Those of us who lived through the sixties will remember what a big deal ethnicity was back then. I went to an Italian school, in the Italian side of town. All the Italian kids had a hero - Tony Conigliaro. Tony was one of us, an Italian-American, New England kid. He was living our dream, playing right field for the Boston Red Sox.

Tony was born in Revere, Massachusetts on January 7, 1945. He grew up in the Boston area and attended St. Mary's High School in Lynn, excelling in baseball. In 1963, he graduated from high school and immediately signed his first professional baseball contract with the Red Sox. He was sent to their minor league team in Wellsville, NY. Having missed the first part of the season because he was still in high school, he played the rest of 1963 with this team in the Class A New York-Pennsylvania League. He went on a tear. He hit .363 with twenty-four home runs, forty-two doubles and seventy-four runs batted in; all this in only eighty-three games. At 18-years-old, he became the Most Valuable Player in that league.

When the season ended, he returned to Massachusetts for a brief visit with his family. After his short visit, he went to Florida to play winter ball. He was anxiously waiting for his first spring training. Everyone figured he would be sent to a higher level minor league team in 1964 and continue his development.

He went to the Red Sox spring training camp in Scottsdale, Arizona and got a lot of attention very quickly. When he took batting practice, everyone stopped and watched. Ted Williams was a hitting coach for the Red Sox in spring training and worked with Tony.

The manager of the Red Sox that year was Johnny Pesky. He was impressed with Conigliaro. There was a spring training game scheduled against the Cleveland Indians. One of the Indian pitchers that day was none other than Gary Bell. Bell was Tony's teammate in 1967 and pitched on August 18, 1967, the subject in this chapter.

Tony got into the game as a defensive replacement in the seventh inning. In the eighth inning he batted against Bell and on the second pitch, he crushed it. He hit a 430-foot home run that took forever to land. Larry Claflin, a sports columnist for the Boston Record measured it and calculated it had traveled 572 feet in the air.

Back home in Massachusetts, I heard about this blast. This was the first time I ever heard about Tony Conigliaro. I was impressed and so was everyone else. The sports writers started writing about this kid and his maturity on the field impressed everyone.

David Cataneo's book *Tony C - The Triumph and Tragedy of Tony Conigliaro* is excellent. In the book, Tony's father, Sal Conigliaro is quoted.

"I have never seen Tony hit a ball that far."

He hadn't made the team yet, but fan mail started pouring in for the teenager.

Johnny Pesky, the manager was completely sold. He told the front office he wanted him. He told Mike 'Pinky' Higgins, the general manager,

"Let's give him a chance. Let's give him a month or six weeks and if he doesn't do it, we'll send him out."

Pesky got to keep him and nineteen-year-old Tony Conigliaro was in the major leagues - a New England kid for the Boston Red Sox.

Tony always had a flair for the dramatic. The Sox opened the season in New York. In his first major league game, he faced future Hall of Famer, Whitey Ford. Tony accused him of throwing a 'spitter' and complained about it to the umpire.

Tony went one for four that day, the Red Sox won, and the next day the Red Sox were to play the Chicago White Sox in Boston. That would be Tony Conigliaro's Fenway Park debut.

David Cataneo's book, *Tony C,* describes what happened when Tony made his first plate appearance in Fenway Park.

"There were two outs and the bases were empty when he strode to the plate for his first Fenway Park at-bat in the second inning. The public address announcer mispronounced his name and the fans gave him a nice stretch of applause. The Conigliaros stood and clapped, checking behind them to sit back down when they heard the crack of that bat and a roar. Tony smacked the first pitch from Joel Horlen way over the left-field wall. As he ran between first and second, Tony saw the ball leave the ballpark and gave his head a quick nearly imperceptible shake. Even he didn't believe himself sometimes - the first pitch he saw at Fenway Park and he hit it for a home run!"

The television camera followed him into the dugout, so folks watching could see his great handsome smile as he was congratulated by his teammates."

Keep in mind, twelve months prior to this moment, Tony was still in high school. A year prior, he was running to English class; now he was running around the bases at Fenway Park.

That was the beginning for Tony Conigliaro. He was very popular and nicknamed 'Conig' or 'Tony C'. He was injury prone, but he ended up hitting twenty-four home runs in 1964 in only 111 games and named the Red Sox 'Rookie of the Year'.

Things started to soar for 'Conig'. He was a handsome young guy and very popular with the ladies. He always loved singing and made a few records. Although he was no Sinatra, he had a couple hit records in the Boston area. His biggest hit was 'Little Red Scooter'. In a few years, he would appear on a national television singing 'Something' by the Beatles.

Tony set many records for youth. On June 3, 1964 in a game against the California Angels, he hit a grand slam home run against his future teammate, Dan Osinski, becoming the youngest player ever to hit a grand slam.

In 1965, at the age of twenty, he became the youngest player to lead the league in home runs, a total of thirty-two. He was younger than Williams, Mantle, Yaz, Killebrew, all the greats.

On it went. He had another big year in 1966. Avoiding injury, he played 150 games and hit another twenty-eight home runs, driving in ninety-three runs.

Tony was living large at the age of twenty-one; a rock'n'roll slugger with the Red Sox. He had his own apartment near Fenway Park, which he shared with pitcher Billy Rohr. According to Billy, they were party animals.

"At the start of the '67 season, Tony C. and I lived together in an apartment at Kenmore Square. Remarkably, we both lived through that and could possibly provide material for another book. It would have to be packaged in plain brown paper and sold in the 'back room'. Tony and I were great friends."

Tony C. was having his best year in 1967. Along the way, he hit his one hundredth major league home run making him the youngest American Leaguer to do that. Naturally, he started dating a movie star. Whenever the Sox were in California, he'd meet up with Mamie Van Doren.

On the night of August 18, 1967, Tony Conigliaro had the world by the tail. He was only twenty-two still seemingly at the beginning of a great baseball career and only a few weeks prior, played right field for the American League in the All-Star game. No one could have known, on this night, fate would change the course of Tony C's life forever. What a difference a pitch makes.

In the fourth inning of the game, Tony C came to the plate to face the hard throws of Jack Hamilton. Hamilton was known to throw a mean spitball. He never denied it. The first pitch to Tony got away from him and hit Tony C right on the left eye and cheekbone; one of the most horrible injuries to ever occur on a baseball field. Rico

Petrocelli was on deck at the time. I asked him about this moment and he told me it was awful.

When Tony was hit, Rico ran to the plate. He said it sounded like a 'squash' when the ball hit his head. All the force of the pitch went right into Tony.

Rico said, "The ball just dropped on home plate, usually they bounce away. His head just blew up."

Tony never lost consciousness. He was rushed to the hospital and treated, but the damage was done. It was the beginning of the end for Tony C. Jose Tartabull, the veteran major leaguer pinch ran for Tony and then replaced him in right field.

When a batter is hit in the head by a pitched ball, it is never considered a minor incident. There's always some degree of damage. A very good friend of mine, Art Johnson, was in attendance that night in Fenway Park. He had a perspective that no one else had.

Art Johnson was a major league pitcher in the 40's with the Boston Braves. He led the Braves in strikeouts in 1941. That same year, Art was pitching for the Braves in a game against the St. Louis Cardinals. He beaned Terry Moore, the Cardinals outfielder. This beaning was serious and Moore lost consciousness. He was rushed to the hospital. Although he didn't miss a season as Conigliaro did, the injury did affect his play and the rest of his life.

When Conigliaro played, Art Johnson was retired from the game and living in Holden, Massachusetts. He took his wife and son to Fenway Park as a birthday present for his son the night Tony C. was hit.

I asked him what he remembered about the incident.

"We had front row box seats. We heard the ball hit his temple. We heard the crack when it hit, because it didn't bounce off anything, it didn't glance off a helmet or anything. It just hit him right square in the temple. I turned to my wife and I said, 'Did you hear that'? Both my wife and son heard it. The worst thing I ever experienced in my life was to hear that crack, the ball against the bone … awful. You just knew there was some heavy damage done."

"Of course they drove the ambulance onto the field. Tony was prone at home plate and they took him away in the ambulance."

Art was there as a fan, but he is the only guy there who saw it from another perspective. I asked him to compare this moment to the moment when he hit Terry Moore. I was interested in how he thought Hamilton felt. What does it feel like when you hit a batter in the head?

"It scares you. Because you know, you weren't throwing at him. I hollered the minute I let the ball go. I knew it was going to come awful close and I hollered, 'look out'! He froze. He absolutely froze in place. He never ducked he just froze. He never tried to get out of the way. I don't know why he froze, but he did. I had two strikes on him. I was trying to brush him back, but I certainly wasn't throwing at him."

"I met him some years later in St. Petersburg, Florida in 1990 and he said he was still getting migraine headaches."

I asked Art if he thought Conigliaro just froze as Moore did.

"He froze. He didn't move. If he had moved, he would have turned his head and got hit at the back of the head. But, he froze, there's no question about it."

Some people say to this day that Jack Hamilton intentionally hit Conigliaro. I had the opportunity to speak with him. I found Jack to be a real gentleman, very soft spoken. I asked him about the game.

"I was ahead (the score was 2-0), and he was at bat and I had no reason to hit him, I think I had two outs, and I had a lead and I had no reason to hit him at all."

I asked Jack if Conigliaro froze.

"Yes, he just froze. It was just a fastball right up into the ear. I remember Yastrzemski standing up on the top of the dugout waving his bat like 'I'll kill you, you know what I mean?' I tried to go to the hospital that night but I couldn't get in."

Jack said that he tried many times to get in touch with Conigliaro but never got the chance. Tony C. wouldn't see him. I asked Jack what he would have said to Conigliaro if he did get to see him.

"Well, definitely I'd say I'm sorry, that's the biggest thing I'd say. I respected him. I did. He was a good ballplayer, a good hitter."

After speaking to Jack, I absolutely conclude that he did not throw at Tony C. He was a hard thrower, but very wild. This one just got away from him. You know when you talk to someone if they're sincere or not. I am absolutely certain that this very soft-spoken gentleman would never intentionally try to hurt anyone.

Tony C was a young, handsome player; the youngest player in American League history to hit one hundred home runs. He would never hit two hundred. He came back to play and had a couple of pretty good years, but he was never the same, his vision was badly affected by the beaning. He was out the rest of 1967, missing the World Series. In 1968, it was obvious he couldn't hit the ball as he did the prior year, so he tried to come back as a pitcher in spring training. This didn't work out. He didn't play at all in 1968.

In 1969, he came back, hit twenty home runs and won the American League's Comeback Player of the Year award.

1970 was his most productive season when he pounded out thirty-six home runs for the Sox, playing outfield with his brother, Billy Conigliaro. Billy hit eighteen home runs.

Tony had a problem with one area of the grandstands in straight away center field. The Red Sox stopped allowing people to sit in that section and to this day, that section is referred to as 'Conig's Corner'. To this day, it's still not generally used.

Tony went as far as he could go. In the winter following 1970, Tony was traded. Amazingly, he was traded to the California Angels! He played half a year in 1971, hit only four home runs, but couldn't see anymore. The damage to his vision was too much. In mid season, Tony C retired from the game. He was only twenty-six years old.

While he was in California, he was considered for the role of Michael Corleone in 'The Godfather'. While he had good looks, Tony was no actor.

He sat out three seasons, and in 1975 attempted a comeback. At thirty years old, he returned to the Red Sox, played half a year, but it didn't work out. He played his last major league game on June 12, 1975 against the Chicago White Sox. He went zero for three and that was all. He went back to the minors for a few weeks, but that didn't work out either.

With baseball behind him, Tony became a sports announcer in San Francisco. He was doing very well, when in 1982 he came home to Massachusetts to audition for a Red Sox broadcasting job that had opened up. He had high hopes. After his audition, his brother Billy drove him to the airport so he could return to California. While en route to the airport, Tony had a massive heart attack. He suffered severe brain damage, lost his speech and his mobility and became wheelchair bound.

He became a thirty-seven-year-old invalid. For the next eight years, Tony was housebound at his family's home in Nahant, Massachusetts.

Tony C. passed away on February 24, 1990 at the age of forty-five. His life, like his career was way too short. His former teammate and roommate, Billy Rohr, put it this way,

"Tony and I were great friends and what a sad ending to a shooting-star career/life."

You just never know. On August 18, 1967, one wild pitch changed the course of the Red Sox season and the life of Anthony Richard 'Tony' Conigliaro.

Boston Red Sox 3, California Angels 2

Game Played on Friday, August 18, 1967 (N) at Fenway Park

```
CAL A    0  0  0    0  0  0    1  0  1  -   2  4  1
BOS A    0  0  0    2  0  1    0  0  x  -   3  6  0
```

BATTING

California Angels	AB	R	H	RBI	BB	SO	PO	A
Cardenal cf	4	0	0	0	0	2	3	1
Fregosi ss	4	0	0	0	0	1	1	3
Hall rf	4	2	2	2	0	0	0	0
Mincher 1b	4	0	1	0	0	0	8	1
Reichardt lf	3	0	0	0	0	1	3	0
Rodgers c	2	0	0	0	1	0	5	1
Knoop 2b	3	0	1	0	0	0	1	3
Werhas 3b	2	0	0	0	0	1	2	0
Repoz ph	1	0	0	0	0	0	0	0
Held 3b	0	0	0	0	0	0	0	0
Hamilton p	1	0	0	0	0	0	1	0
Satriano ph	1	0	0	0	0	0	0	0
Kelso p	0	0	0	0	0	0	0	0
Coates p	0	0	0	0	0	0	0	0
Morton ph	1	0	0	0	0	0	0	0
Cimino p	0	0	0	0	0	0	0	0
Totals	30	2	4	2	1	5	24	9

FIELDING -
DP: 1. Rodgers-Knoop.
E: Fregosi (18).

BATTING -
HR: Hall 2 (15,7th inning off Bell 0 on 1 out,9th inning off Bell 0 on 2 out)
Team LOB: 2.

Boston Red Sox	AB	R	H	RBI	BB	SO	PO	A
Andrews 2b	3	0	0	0	1	0	2	3
Adair 3b	3	0	1	0	1	0	1	0
Yastrzemski lf	3	0	0	0	1	1	0	0
Scott 1b	4	0	1	0	0	1	9	0
Smith cf	4	0	0	0	0	1	4	0
Conigliaro rf	1	0	1	0	0	0	2	0
Tartabull pr,rf	1	1	0	0	1	0	0	0
Petrocelli ss	3	2	1	1	1	2	2	6
Howard c	3	0	0	0	0	0	6	0
Bell p	3	0	2	1	0	0	1	0
Totals	28	3	6	2	5	5	27	9

FIELDING -

DP: 1. Andrews-Petrocelli-Scott.

BATTING -
2B: Bell (2,off Hamilton).
3B: Petrocelli (1,off Hamilton).
HBP: Conigliaro (5,by Hamilton).
IBB: Yastrzemski (7,by Hamilton).
Team LOB: 7.

BASERUNNING -
CS: Adair (5,2nd base by Coates/Rodgers).

PITCHING

California Angels	IP	H	R	ER	BB	SO	HR
Hamilton L(6-3)	5	4	2	1	3	2	0
Kelso	0.2	1	1	1	2	0	0
Coates	1.1	1	0	0	0	1	0
Cimino	1	0	0	0	0	2	0
Totals	8	6	3	2	5	5	0

Boston Red Sox	IP	H	R	ER	BB	SO	HR
Bell W(8-10)	9	4	2	2	1	5	2

HBP: Hamilton (1,Conigliaro).
IBB: Hamilton (3,Yastrzemski).

Umpires: Bill Valentine, Bill Kinnamon, Larry Napp, Frank Umont

Time of Game: 2:16   **Attendance:** 31027

Starting Lineups:

California Angels		Boston Red Sox	
1. Cardenal	cf	Andrews	2b
2. Fregosi	ss	Adair	3b
3. Hall	rf	Yastrzemski	lf
4. Mincher	1b	Scott	1b
5. Reichardt	lf	Smith	cf
6. Rodgers	c	Conigliaro	rf
7. Knoop	2b	Petrocelli	ss
8. Werhas	3b	Howard	c
9. Hamilton	p	Bell	p

ANGELS 1ST: Cardenal struck out; Fregosi struck out; Hall grounded out (shortstop to first); 0 R, 0 H, 0 E, 0 LOB. Angels 0, Red Sox 0.

RED SOX 1ST: Andrews walked; Adair grounded out (second to first) [Andrews to second]; Yastrzemski struck out; Scott grounded out (second to first); 0 R, 0 H, 0 E, 1 LOB. Angels 0, Red Sox 0.

ANGELS 2ND: Mincher made an out to center; Reichardt made an out to right; Rodgers made an out to third; 0 R, 0 H, 0 E, 0 LOB. Angels 0, Red Sox 0.

RED SOX 2ND: Smith made an out to left; Conigliaro singled to center; Petrocelli struck out; Howard grounded out (second to first); 0 R, 1 H, 0 E, 1 LOB. Angels 0, Red Sox 0.

ANGELS 3RD: Knoop made an out to center; Werhas made an out to center; Hamilton grounded out (shortstop to first); 0 R, 0 H, 0 E, 0 LOB. Angels 0, Red Sox 0.

RED SOX 3RD: Bell made an out to center; Andrews grounded out (shortstop to first); Adair walked; Yastrzemski grounded out (first unassisted); 0 R, 0 H, 0 E, 1 LOB. Angels 0, Red Sox 0.

ANGELS 4TH: Cardenal made an out to catcher; Fregosi made an out to right; Hall lined to second; 0 R, 0 H, 0 E, 0 LOB. Angels 0, Red Sox 0.

RED SOX 4TH: Scott singled to center [Scott out at second (center to shortstop)]; Smith made an out to center; Conigliaro was hit by a pitch; TARTABULL RAN FOR CONIGLIARO; Petrocelli tripled to center [Tartabull scored, Petrocelli scored (unearned) (error by Fregosi)]; Howard grounded out (shortstop to first); 2 R, 2 H, 1 E, 0 LOB. Angels 0, Red Sox 2.

ANGELS 5TH: TARTABULL STAYED IN GAME (PLAYING RF); Mincher grounded out (first unassisted); Reichardt grounded out (shortstop to first); Rodgers walked; Knoop forced Rodgers (shortstop to second); 0 R, 0 H, 0 E, 1 LOB. Angels 0, Red Sox 2.

RED SOX 5TH: Bell doubled to center; Andrews grounded out (shortstop to first); Adair grounded out (first to pitcher) [Bell to third]; Yastrzemski was walked intentionally; Scott made an out to center; 0 R, 1 H, 0 E, 2 LOB. Angels 0, Red Sox 2.

ANGELS 6TH: Werhas struck out; SATRIANO BATTED FOR HAMILTON; Satriano made an out to shortstop; Cardenal struck out; 0 R, 0 H, 0 E, 0 LOB. Angels 0, Red Sox 2.

RED SOX 6TH: KELSO REPLACED SATRIANO (PITCHING); Smith made an out to left; Tartabull walked; Petrocelli walked [Tartabull to second]; Howard forced Tartabull (third unassisted) [Petrocelli to second]; Bell singled to center [Petrocelli scored, Howard to second]; COATES REPLACED KELSO (PITCHING); Andrews made an out to left; 1 R, 1 H, 0 E, 2 LOB. Angels 0, Red Sox 3.

ANGELS 7TH: Fregosi grounded out (second to first); Hall homered; Mincher singled to center; Reichardt struck out; Rodgers made an out to center; 1 R, 2 H, 0 E, 1 LOB. Angels 1, Red Sox 3.

RED SOX 7TH: Adair singled to center; Yastrzemski made an out to third; Scott struck out while Adair was caught stealing second (catcher to second); 0 R, 1 H, 0 E, 0 LOB. Angels 1, Red Sox 3.

ANGELS 8TH: Knoop singled to center; REPOZ BATTED FOR WERHAS; Repoz made an out to first; MORTON BATTED FOR COATES; Morton grounded into a double play (second to shortstop to first) [Knoop out at second]; 0 R, 1 H, 0 E, 0 LOB. Angels 1, Red Sox 3.

RED SOX 8TH: HELD REPLACED REPOZ (PLAYING 3B); CIMINO REPLACED
MORTON (PITCHING); Smith struck out; Tartabull grounded out
(first unassisted); Petrocelli struck out; 0 R, 0 H, 0 E, 0 LOB.
Angels 1, Red Sox 3.

ANGELS 9TH: Cardenal grounded out (shortstop to first); Fregosi
grounded out (second to first); Hall homered; Mincher lined to
pitcher; 1 R, 1 H, 0 E, 0 LOB. Angels 2, Red Sox 3.

Final Totals	R	H	E	LOB
Angels	2	4	1	2
Red Sox	3	6	0	7

CHAPTER NINE

October 2, 1965
Philadelphia Phillies at New York Mets

What Happened? Absolutely Nothing

I'VE STRUGGLED OVER HOW TO write about this game. This game is completely different from any other covered in this book. The game was unique for sure. There has never been another one like it and believe me, it will be a long time before it happens again, if ever.

The first eight games covered in this book have something in common; something happened. SOMETHING! At the very least, there was a final score!

On October 2, 1965, the Phillies and Mets faced each other for a doubleheader at Shea Stadium on the day before the last day of the season. They played the first game and it was a good one. Jim Bunning (who would later become a United States Senator from Kentucky) of the Phillies two hit the Mets for his nineteenth win of the season.

Then they played the second game. They played and played and played! This is the game that never ended - to this day. After nine innings, the score was tied, 0-0. They kept playing. They played an additional nine innings. Keep in mind; this was the second game of a doubleheader. After eighteen innings, the game ended in a tie, 0-

0. It was the longest 0-0 game in history. This is the game in which NOTHING of any significance happened, not even the smallest effect on the standings.

When the game began, the Mets had a record of 50 wins and 110 losses. At the end of the game, they had a record of 50 wins and 110 losses. The Phillies were 83-76 going in and 83-76 at the end. No change whatsoever.

The Phillies had six hits, the Mets had nine. They had just enough hits to avoid a low hit game. The Phillies were six for fifty-nine, a batting average of .102. The Mets were nine for sixty-one, a batting average of .148. Combined, they were fifteen for one hundred twenty, a batting average of .125. In eighteen innings, there were only four extra base hits, all doubles. All runners were left stranded. There were three stolen bases, only one double play and one error.

Two guys did benefit by this game. The two starting pitchers, Chris Short for the Phillies and Rob Gardner for the Mets.

Chris Short's earned run average going into the game was 2.96. After the game, it was 2.82. That's a big reduction for one game. He pitched fifteen scoreless innings.

Rob Gardner's earned run average going in was 6.92. After this game, it came all the way down to 3.21 He also pitched fifteen scoreless innings.

John Herrnstein played in this game for the Phillies. I had the opportunity to speak to him.

"They had to call the game because of the curfew. It was all day at the ballpark and all night too. It was like, 'please, somebody score a run!' We were out of it. It's not as if this game was meaningful to either team in the standings as far as the race. It was one of those games when nobody could score a run."

The game reached the curfew and was finally called. The next day, Sunday, October 3, the Mets and Phillies played another double-header to end the season. The Phillies won the first game, 3-1. The second game once again went into extra innings. This one went thirteen innings and again, the Phillies won 3-1 ending the season. In two days, these two teams played a total of forty-nine innings.

The Phillies won the other three games. The Phillies ended the season in sixth place with a record of 85-76. The Mets once again ended up dead last with a record of 50-112.

End of season. End of story...there's not much more to say. What else can you say about NOTHING!

New York Mets 0, Philadelphia Phillies 0 (2)

Game Played on Saturday, October 2, 1965 (N) at Shea Stadium

PHI N	0	0	0	0	0	0	0	0	0	0	0	0	0	0	0	0	0	0	-		
NY N	0	0	0	0	0	0	0	0	0	0	0	0	0	0	0	0	0	0	-		

BATTING

Philadelphia Phillies	AB	R	H	RBI	BB	SO	PO	A
Phillips cf	6	0	1	0	0	1	5	0
Callison ph,rf	1	0	0	0	0	0	0	0
Rojas 2b	6	0	1	0	1	0	2	3
Allen 3b	7	0	2	0	0	2	2	2
Stuart 1b	7	0	1	0	0	1	15	0
Amaro ss	0	0	0	0	0	0	0	0
Johnson lf	6	0	0	0	0	1	3	0
Briggs ph,cf	1	0	0	0	0	0	1	0
Gonzalez rf,cf,lf	5	0	1	0	2	0	2	0
Wine ss	5	0	0	0	0	1	1	8
Herrnstein ph,1b	1	0	0	0	0	0	2	0
Corrales c	6	0	0	0	0	0	19	1
Sorrell ph	1	0	0	0	0	0	0	0
Baldschun p	0	0	0	0	0	0	0	1
Short p	5	0	0	0	0	1	0	1
Covington ph	1	0	0	0	0	0	0	0
Wagner p	0	0	0	0	0	0	0	0
Dalrymple ph,c	1	0	0	0	0	0	2	0
Totals	59	0	6	0	3	7	54	16

FIELDING -
DP: 1. Rojas-Wine-Stuart.

BATTING -
2B: Gonzalez (19,off Gardner).
SH: Wine (4,off Gardner).
Team LOB: 9.

BASERUNNING -
SB: Rojas (5,2nd base off Gardner/Goossen).
CS: Gonzalez (4,2nd base by Sutherland/Cannizzaro).

New York Mets	AB	R	H	RBI	BB	SO	PO	A
Hunt 2b	8	0	2	0	0	0	6	5
Christopher rf,lf	7	0	2	0	1	3	2	0
Smith 3b	8	0	1	0	0	2	0	4
Hickman 1b	6	0	2	0	1	0	20	0
Swoboda lf	1	0	0	0	0	1	1	0
Napoleon lf	5	0	0	0	0	3	6	0
Lewis ph,rf	0	0	0	0	0	0	0	0

Goossen c	4	0	1	0	0	0	8	0
Selma pr	0	0	0	0	0	0	0	0
Klaus ss	1	0	0	0	2	0	2	5
Jones cf	7	0	1	0	0	2	5	0
Harrelson ss	3	0	0	0	0	2	1	3
McMillan ph	1	0	0	0	0	1	0	0
Cannizzaro c	2	0	0	0	0	1	2	1
Stephenson ph,c	1	0	0	0	0	0	1	0
Gardner p	5	0	0	0	0	4	0	3
Schaffer ph	1	0	0	0	0	1	0	0
Sutherland p	0	0	0	0	0	0	0	0
Kranepool ph	1	0	0	0	0	1	0	0
Ribant p	0	0	0	0	0	0	0	0
Totals	61	0	9	0	4	21	54	21

FIELDING -
E: Goossen (1), Harrelson (3).

BATTING -
2B: Hunt (12,off Short); Christopher (18,off Short); Hickman (17,off Short).
HBP: Lewis (3,by Wagner).
IBB: Hickman (3,by Short).
Team LOB: 12.

BASERUNNING -
SB: Hickman (3,2nd base off Short/Corrales); Hunt (2,2nd base off Short/Corral
CS: Lewis (7,2nd base by Wagner/Corrales).

PITCHING

Philadelphia Phillies	IP	H	R	ER	BB	SO	HR
Short	15	9	0	0	3	18	0
Wagner	2	0	0	0	1	1	0
Baldschun	1	0	0	0	0	2	0
Totals	18	9	0	0	4	21	0

New York Mets	IP	H	R	ER	BB	SO	HR
Gardner	15	5	0	0	2	7	0
Sutherland	2	1	0	0	1	0	0
Ribant	1	0	0	0	0	0	0
Totals	18	6	0	0	3	7	0

HBP: Wagner (2,Lewis).
IBB: Short (8,Hickman).

Umpires: Lee Weyer, John Kibler, Frank Secory, Ken Burkhart

Time of Game: 4:29 **Attendance:** 10371

Starting Lineups:

Philadelphia Phillies		New York Mets	
1. Phillips	cf	Hunt	2b
2. Rojas	2b	Christopher	rf
3. Allen	3b	Smith	3b
4. Stuart	1b	Hickman	1b
5. Johnson	lf	Swoboda	lf

6. Gonzalez	rf	Goossen	c
7. Wine	ss	Jones	cf
8. Corrales	c	Harrelson	ss
9. Short	p	Gardner	p

PHILLIES 1ST: Phillips singled to left; Rojas walked [Phillips to second]; Allen flied to right [Phillips to third, Rojas to second]; Stuart struck out; Johnson flied to left; 0 R, 1 H, 0 E, 2 LOB. Phillies 0, Mets 0.

METS 1ST: Hunt flied to center; Christopher walked; On a bunt Smith singled to third [Christopher to second]; Hickman flied to center [Christopher to third]; Swoboda was called out on strikes; **Swoboda ejected for arguing called third strike;** 0 R, 1 H, 0 E, 2 LOB. Phillies 0, Mets 0.

PHILLIES 2ND: NAPOLEON REPLACED SWOBODA (PLAYING LF); Gonzalez grounded out (pitcher to first); Wine was called out on strikes; Corrales popped to first in foul territory; 0 R, 0 H, 0 E, 0 LOB. Phillies 0, Mets 0.

METS 2ND: Goossen popped to second; Jones grounded out (first unassisted); Harrelson struck out; 0 R, 0 H, 0 E, 0 LOB. Phillies 0, Mets 0.

PHILLIES 3RD: Short flied to center; Phillips reached on an error by Harrelson; Rojas forced Phillips (third to second); Rojas stole second [Rojas to third (error by Goossen)]; Allen struck out; 0 R, 0 H, 2 E, 1 LOB. Phillies 0, Mets 0.

METS 3RD: Gardner struck out; Hunt doubled to center; Christopher doubled to center [Hunt to third]; Smith struck out; Hickman was walked intentionally; Napoleon was called out on strikes; 0 R, 2 H, 0 E, 3 LOB. Phillies 0, Mets 0.

PHILLIES 4TH: Stuart grounded out (shortstop to first); Johnson was called out on strikes; Gonzalez lined to shortstop; 0 R, 0 H, 0 E, 0 LOB. Phillies 0, Mets 0.

METS 4TH: Goossen grounded out (shortstop to first); Jones struck out; Harrelson grounded out (pitcher to first); 0 R, 0 H, 0 E, 0 LOB. Phillies 0, Mets 0.

PHILLIES 5TH: Wine grounded out (third to first); Corrales popped to first in foul territory; Short struck out; 0 R, 0 H, 0 E, 0 LOB. Phillies 0, Mets 0.

METS 5TH: Gardner struck out; Hunt flied to left; Christopher was called out on strikes; 0 R, 0 H, 0 E, 0 LOB. Phillies 0, Mets 0.

PHILLIES 6TH: Phillips lined to left; Rojas popped to catcher in foul territory; Allen singled to shortstop; Stuart forced Allen (shortstop to second); 0 R, 1 H, 0 E, 1 LOB. Phillies 0, Mets 0.

METS 6TH: Smith flied to right; Hickman doubled to left; Napoleon struck out; Goossen lined to left; 0 R, 1 H, 0 E, 1 LOB. Phillies 0, Mets 0.

PHILLIES 7TH: Johnson lined to center; Gonzalez grounded out (second to first); Wine grounded out (first unassisted); 0 R, 0 H, 0 E, 0 LOB. Phillies 0, Mets 0.

METS 7TH: Jones struck out; Harrelson struck out; Gardner struck out; 0 R, 0 H, 0 E, 0 LOB. Phillies 0, Mets 0.

PHILLIES 8TH: Corrales grounded out (second to first); Short grounded out (shortstop to first); Phillips struck out; 0 R, 0 H, 0 E, 0 LOB. Phillies 0, Mets 0.

METS 8TH: Hunt grounded out (second to first); Christopher flied to center; Smith grounded out (third to first); 0 R, 0 H, 0 E, 0 LOB. Phillies 0, Mets 0.

PHILLIES 9TH: Rojas popped to second; Allen struck out; Stuart singled to right; Johnson flied to center; 0 R, 1 H, 0 E, 1 LOB. Phillies 0, Mets 0.

METS 9TH: Hickman grounded out (shortstop to first); Napoleon grounded out (shortstop to first); Goossen singled to center; SELMA RAN FOR GOOSSEN; Jones singled to first [Selma to second]; MCMILLAN BATTED FOR HARRELSON; McMillan struck out; 0 R, 2 H, 0 E, 2 LOB. Phillies 0, Mets 0.

PHILLIES 10TH: CANNIZZARO REPLACED MCMILLAN (PLAYING C); KLAUS REPLACED SELMA (PLAYING SS); Gonzalez walked; Wine out on a sacrifice bunt (pitcher to second) [Gonzalez to second]; Corrales grounded out (shortstop to first); On a bunt Short grounded out (pitcher to first); 0 R, 0 H, 0 E, 1 LOB. Phillies 0, Mets 0.

METS 10TH: Gardner was called out on strikes; Hunt popped to first in foul territory; Christopher grounded out (shortstop to first); 0 R, 0 H, 0 E, 0 LOB. Phillies 0, Mets 0.

PHILLIES 11TH: On a bunt Phillips grounded out (third to first); Rojas flied to left; Allen singled to right; Stuart popped to second; 0 R, 1 H, 0 E, 1 LOB. Phillies 0, Mets 0.

METS 11TH: Smith lined to left; Hickman singled to left; Napoleon struck out; Hickman stole second; Klaus walked; Jones flied to center; 0 R, 1 H, 0 E, 2 LOB. Phillies 0, Mets 0.

PHILLIES 12TH: Johnson flied to left; Gonzalez flied to left in foul territory; Wine grounded out (shortstop to first); 0 R, 0 H, 0 E, 0 LOB. Phillies 0, Mets 0.

METS 12TH: Cannizzaro was called out on strikes; Gardner grounded out (shortstop to first); Hunt grounded out (third to first); 0 R, 0 H, 0 E, 0 LOB. Phillies 0, Mets 0.

PHILLIES 13TH: Corrales flied to left; Short lined to right; Phillips grounded out (third to first); 0 R, 0 H, 0 E, 0 LOB. Phillies 0, Mets 0.

METS 13TH: Christopher singled to left; Smith grounded into a double play (second to shortstop to first) [Christopher out at second]; Hickman flied to center; 0 R, 1 H, 0 E, 0 LOB. Phillies 0, Mets 0.

PHILLIES 14TH: Rojas grounded out (shortstop to first); Allen flied to center; Stuart popped to catcher in foul territory; 0 R, 0 H, 0 E, 0 LOB. Phillies 0, Mets 0.

METS 14TH: Napoleon grounded out (shortstop to first); Klaus popped to third; Jones flied to right in foul territory; 0 R, 0 H, 0 E, 0 LOB. Phillies 0, Mets 0.

PHILLIES 15TH: Johnson grounded out (shortstop to first); Gonzalez doubled to right; Wine flied to center [Gonzalez to third]; Corrales popped to catcher in foul territory; 0 R, 1 H, 0 E, 1 LOB. Phillies 0, Mets 0.

METS 15TH: Cannizzaro grounded out (second to first); SCHAFFER BATTED FOR GARDNER; Schaffer struck out; Hunt singled to center; Hunt stole second; Christopher struck out; 0 R, 1 H, 0 E, 1 LOB. Phillies 0, Mets 0.

PHILLIES 16TH: SUTHERLAND REPLACED SCHAFFER (PITCHING); COVINGTON BATTED FOR SHORT; Covington flied to left; CALLISON BATTED FOR PHILLIPS; Callison popped to shortstop; Rojas singled to left; Allen grounded out (shortstop to first); 0 R, 1 H, 0 E, 1 LOB. Phillies 0, Mets 0.

METS 16TH: WAGNER REPLACED COVINGTON (PITCHING); CALLISON STAYED IN GAME (PLAYING RF); GONZALEZ CHANGED POSITIONS (PLAYING CF); Smith lined to third; Hickman grounded out (shortstop to first); LEWIS BATTED FOR NAPOLEON; Lewis was hit by a pitch; Lewis was caught stealing second (catcher to second); 0 R, 0 H, 0 E, 0 LOB. Phillies 0, Mets 0.

PHILLIES 17TH: LEWIS STAYED IN GAME (PLAYING RF); CHRISTOPHER CHANGED POSITIONS (PLAYING LF); Stuart grounded out (second to first); BRIGGS BATTED FOR JOHNSON; Briggs grounded out (second to first); Gonzalez walked; HERRNSTEIN BATTED FOR WINE; Gonzalez was caught stealing second (catcher to shortstop); 0 R, 0 H, 0 E, 0 LOB. Phillies 0, Mets 0.

METS 17TH: BRIGGS STAYED IN GAME (PLAYING CF); HERRNSTEIN STAYED IN GAME (PLAYING 1B); GONZALEZ CHANGED POSITIONS (PLAYING LF); AMARO REPLACED STUART (PLAYING SS); Klaus walked; On a bunt Jones popped to first in foul territory; STEPHENSON BATTED FOR CANNIZZARO; Stephenson flied to center; KRANEPOOL BATTED FOR SUTHERLAND; Kranepool struck out; 0 R, 0 H, 0 E, 1 LOB. Phillies 0, Mets 0.

PHILLIES 18TH: RIBANT REPLACED KRANEPOOL (PITCHING); STEPHENSON STAYED IN GAME (PLAYING C); Herrnstein grounded out (second to first); SORRELL BATTED FOR CORRALES; Sorrell popped to second; DALRYMPLE BATTED FOR WAGNER; Dalrymple popped to catcher in foul territory; 0 R, 0 H, 0 E, 0 LOB. Phillies 0, Mets 0.

METS 18TH: DALRYMPLE STAYED IN GAME (PLAYING C); BALDSCHUN REPLACED SORRELL (PITCHING); Hunt grounded out (pitcher to first); Christopher struck out; Smith struck out; **Game called because of curfew;** 0 R, 0 H, 0 E, 0 LOB. Phillies 0, Mets 0.

Final Totals	R	H	E	LOB
Phillies	0	6	0	9
Mets	0	9	2	12

CHAPTER TEN

April 11, 1966
Cleveland Indians at Washington Senators

Another Broken Barrier

OPENING DAY IS ALWAYS FUN. Back in the 60's when there was an American League team in Washington DC, opening day was historically the "Presidential Opener." That meant the President of the United States would show up and throw out the first ball. This tradition was started by President William Howard Taft and continued all the way into the seventies until the Washington Senators moved to Texas and became the Texas Rangers.

This year, however, we were in the middle of the Viet Nam War and President Lyndon Johnson opted to send Vice-President Hubert Humphrey to the ballpark to kick off the baseball season. The Vice-President showed and threw out the first ball. Everything went without much fanfare beyond that.

The forty-four thousand plus fans saw a good game in which the visiting Cleveland Indians defeated the hometown Senators by a score of 5-2. There was some drama. It was a 2-1 game with the Senators on top going into the ninth. The Indians came up with four runs to take the lead and eventually, the game.

There were no Hall of Fame players in this game. There were a couple "name" players. Rocky Colavito was the cleanup hitter for the

Indians and longtime veteran catcher Del Crandall was catching. Colavito had three singles in five at-bats, while Crandall went zero for two.

A relatively routine, nondescript game if you look at the box score; but history was made this day. Probably not many patrons appreciated that fact at the time.

In 1947, Jackie Robinson broke the color barrier when he became the first African-American player of the twentieth century. Here we are, now nineteen years later and another barrier was broken on this day; not by a player, but by the third base umpire.

Making his debut in the major leagues was Emmett Ashford, the first African-American umpire in the history of the major leagues.

Emmett Ashford was born on November 23, 1914 in Los Angeles, California. In 1951, following a stint in the military, Emmett worked as a postal employee. He got his chance to enter professional baseball as an umpire. He was thirty-six years old.

Despite a major pay cut, Emmett went into baseball. It was in the Class C Southwest International League where he became the first African-American umpire in professional baseball. He received a bit of notoriety about this, some articles in newspapers and magazines here and there, but didn't make a lot of money, as was the reality for starting umpires. Considering his age, it wasn't likely that Emmett would make it to the major leagues, but he was a good umpire.

In 1954, he got his chance at umpiring in the Pacific Coast League, an AAA league, one step below the majors. He umpired at this level through 1965. In the last few years, he became the Umpire Chief of the PCL.

Time was of the essence for Emmett Ashford.

At 51, he would have to make the major leagues in order to get five years in for his pension, the mandatory retirement age being fifty-five. That's exactly what happened in the 1966 season. Emmett was named an American League umpire.

I saw Emmett Ashford umpire. In a prior chapter, I covered Billy Rohr's one-hitter and mentioned, a week after that, Billy Rohr beat the Yankees in Boston on a Friday night. I was there, sitting behind the first base dugout and Emmett was the first base umpire. I'll never forget what happened.

The umpires were meeting the managers at home plate before the game. When the meeting was through, the umpires trotted to their positions. As Emmett trotted to first base, he got a thunderous ovation from the fans.

Emmett was indeed a pioneer, and you may question the long time that he spent in the minor leagues and wonder if race was a factor. We'll never know for sure, but one thing we do know is, Emmett didn't face a lot of hatred in his first year, as did Jackie Robinson. There was a reason for it. Emmett Ashford was extremely colorful. While he was in the Pacific Coast League, he was so colorful; he would often take place in promotions. Promoters would tailor promotions to fit the umpiring schedule and wait for Emmett to be in town to do some marketing.

Emmett umpired a total of 810 major league games between 1966 and 1970. In 1967, he was an umpire in baseball's All-Star game. In the 1970 World Series, Emmett Ashford ended his major league career on the field.

When Jackie Robinson came into the game, he and the guy that signed him, Branch Rickey, agreed that in order for this to work, Jackie would not fight back; at least not at the beginning. He had to ignore any racism whether it came from the fans or the other team. It's long been said; Jackie had the right personality to carry this off. In my opinion, the same is true here.

The difference between the first player and the first umpire is; the umpire is in a position of authority and required to judge the performance of the players. He needs to call balls and strikes, handle arguments and throw players out of the game. Emmett was so colorful, that when he tossed someone, he got an ovation. That definitely helped. If the first African-American umpire were a nasty guy, it would have been quite different.

I had a conversation with Art Frantz. Mr. Frantz is a former major league umpire as well and for a time he umpired on the same crew as Emmett Ashford. He couldn't say enough good things about Emmett.

"He was the first black umpire in the big leagues. Emmett was a good guy, a good umpire. He was a class guy and a credit to his race. The fans loved him because he was a showboat as well as a gentleman."

Although he didn't want to and felt he could still umpire with the best of them, Emmett was forced to retire in 1970. He had reached the mandatory age of fifty-five.

His first post-baseball job was in Public Relations for the Hamm Brewing Co. This was a short run, as he would soon be hired by baseball commissioner Bowie Kuhn. Kuhn offered him a position in public relations work for major league baseball on the west coast. Emmett held this job for the rest of his working life. He also returned to the field. In 1971, baseball had the Alaska Summer Program and Emmett worked as an umpire and supervised the other developing umpires. This program lasted for several years in the 1970's.

In 1971, *The Sporting News* covered a special event in Emmett's life, his fifty-seventh birthday. There was a huge party and in the December 11, 1971 edition of *The Sporting News* it is stated,

"The guests had come from far and near, negro, white, and oriental. Just plain friends, captains of industry, high powered attorneys and influential members of the media had turned out to wish Ashford a happy birthday."

His wife of many years, Margaret Ashford said, "I wish all the bigots and militants could see this the way it really is."

On August 18, 1972, Emmett returned to organized baseball for one day, umpiring the Pacific Coast league game between Hawaii and Tacoma. Also in 1972, he umpired a California Angels old timer's game.

In 1975, Frank Robinson became the first black manager in the major leagues when he took the reins of the Cleveland Indians. I have no doubt the road Robinson took to get there was paved, at least in part, by Emmett Ashford.

Emmett had only one regret. He regrets not making the major leagues sooner than he did.

"It took a long time, sure, but it took the covered wagons a while to get across the plains, too."

Emmett Ashford passed away on March 1, 1980 at the age of 65. He was fittingly buried in Cooperstown, New York, the home of the Baseball Hall of Fame.

Although he stood only 5'8", he was a very big man. He became one of the most respected umpires of his day and it all started on April 11, 1966.

Cleveland Indians 5, Washington Senators 2

Game Played on Monday, April 11, 1966 (D) at D.C. Stadium

CLE A	0	0	1	0	0	0	0	0	4	-	5	11	1
WAS A	0	0	0	0	0	2	0	0	0	-	2	4	1

BATTING

Cleveland Indians	AB	R	H	RBI	BB	SO	PO	A
Davalillo cf	4	2	1	2	1	2	3	0
Alvis 3b	5	0	3	2	0	0	1	2
Wagner lf	4	0	0	1	0	0	0	0
Azcue c	0	0	0	0	0	0	0	0
Colavito rf	5	0	3	0	0	0	1	0
Siebert p	0	0	0	0	0	0	0	0
Hinton 1b,lf	4	0	0	0	0	2	7	0
Gonzalez 2b	4	0	2	0	0	0	3	3
Brown ss	3	0	0	0	1	1	0	3
Howser pr,ss	0	1	0	0	0	0	1	0
Crandall c	2	0	0	0	1	0	10	1
Landis ph,rf	1	1	1	0	0	0	0	0
McDowell p	3	0	1	0	0	0	0	1
Salmon ph,1b	0	1	0	0	1	0	1	0
Totals	35	5	11	5	4	5	27	10

FIELDING -
DP: 1. Brown-Gonzalez-Hinton.
E: Gonzalez (1).

BATTING -
2B: Landis (1,off Richert).
SH: Hinton (1,off Richert).
SF: Wagner (1,off Richert).
IBB: Crandall (1,by Richert); Salmon (1,by Kline).
Team LOB: 9.

BASERUNNING -
SB: Gonzalez (1,2nd base off Richert/Camilli).
CS: Alvis (1,2nd base by Richert/Camilli).

Washington Senators	AB	R	H	RBI	BB	SO	PO	A
Valentine rf,lf	4	0	1	0	0	1	2	0
Brinkman ss	3	0	0	0	0	1	3	1
McMullen 3b	2	1	1	0	2	0	1	0
Howard lf	4	1	1	2	0	1	2	0
Kirkland rf	0	0	0	0	0	0	0	0
Lock cf	3	0	0	0	1	2	5	0
Hamlin 2b	3	0	0	0	1	1	3	1
Camilli c	2	0	0	0	0	1	6	2

King ph	1	0	0	0	0	0	0	0
Cunningham 1b	4	0	1	0	0	0	5	0
Richert p	3	0	0	0	0	2	0	3
Kline p	0	0	0	0	0	0	0	0
McCormick p	0	0	0	0	0	0	0	0
Totals	29	2	4	2	4	9	27	7

FIELDING -
E: Valentine (1).

BATTING -
HR: Howard (1,6th inning off McDowell 1 on 1 out).
SH: Brinkman (1,off McDowell).
HBP: Camilli (1,by McDowell).
Team LOB: 6.

BASERUNNING -
CS: Lock (1,2nd base by McDowell/Crandall).

PITCHING

Cleveland Indians	IP	H	R	ER	BB	SO	HR
McDowell W(1-0)	8	4	2	2	4	9	1
Siebert SV(1)	1	0	0	0	0	0	0
Totals	9	4	2	2	4	9	1

Washington Senators	IP	H	R	ER	BB	SO	HR
Richert L(0-1)	8.1	8	3	3	3	5	0
Kline	0	2	2	2	1	0	0
McCormick	0.2	1	0	0	0	0	0
Totals	9	11	5	5	4	5	0

HBP: McDowell (1,Camilli).
IBB: Richert (1,Crandall); Kline (1,Salmon).

Umpires: Johnny Stevens, Bob Stewart, Bill Haller, Emmett Ashford

Time of Game: 2:50   **Attendance:** 44468

Starting Lineups:

	Cleveland Indians		Washington Senators	
1.	Davalillo	cf	Valentine	rf
2.	Alvis	3b	Brinkman	ss
3.	Wagner	lf	McMullen	3b
4.	Colavito	rf	Howard	lf
5.	Hinton	1b	Lock	cf
6.	Gonzalez	2b	Hamlin	2b
7.	Brown	ss	Camilli	c
8.	Crandall	c	Cunningham	1b
9.	McDowell	p	Richert	p

INDIANS 1ST: **VP Humphrey threw out the ceremonial pitch;**
Davalillo grounded out (pitcher to first); Alvis singled to
left; Wagner made an out to center; Colavito made an out to
right; 0 R, 1 H, 0 E, 1 LOB. Indians 0, Senators 0.

SENATORS 1ST: Valentine lined to second; Brinkman struck out; McMullen popped to catcher in foul territory; 0 R, 0 H, 0 E, 0 LOB. Indians 0, Senators 0.

INDIANS 2ND: Hinton struck out; Gonzalez singled to shortstop; Gonzalez stole second; Brown struck out; Crandall was walked intentionally; McDowell grounded out (shortstop to first); 0 R, 1 H, 0 E, 2 LOB. Indians 0, Senators 0.

SENATORS 2ND: Howard struck out; Lock was called out on strikes; Hamlin struck out; 0 R, 0 H, 0 E, 0 LOB. Indians 0, Senators 0.

INDIANS 3RD: Davalillo walked; Alvis singled to right [Davalillo to third]; Alvis was caught stealing second (catcher to second); Wagner hit a sacrifice fly to center [Davalillo scored]; Colavito made an out to right; 1 R, 1 H, 0 E, 0 LOB. Indians 1, Senators 0.

SENATORS 3RD: Camilli struck out; Cunningham popped to third in foul territory; Richert was called out on strikes; 0 R, 0 H, 0 E, 0 LOB. Indians 1, Senators 0.

INDIANS 4TH: Hinton was called out on strikes; Gonzalez singled to right; Brown made an out to center; Crandall made an out to shortstop; 0 R, 1 H, 0 E, 1 LOB. Indians 1, Senators 0.

SENATORS 4TH: Valentine singled to center; Brinkman out on a sacrifice bunt (pitcher to second) [Valentine to second]; McMullen walked; Howard grounded into a double play (shortstop to second to first) [McMullen out at second]; 0 R, 1 H, 0 E, 1 LOB. Indians 1, Senators 0.

INDIANS 5TH: McDowell singled to center; Davalillo was called out on strikes; Alvis popped to catcher in foul territory; Wagner grounded out (pitcher to first); 0 R, 1 H, 0 E, 1 LOB. Indians 1, Senators 0.

SENATORS 5TH: Lock grounded out (third to first); Hamlin walked; Camilli was hit by a pitch [Hamlin to second]; Cunningham singled to left [Hamlin to third, Camilli to second]; Richert struck out; Valentine struck out; 0 R, 1 H, 0 E, 3 LOB. Indians 1, Senators 0.

INDIANS 6TH: Colavito singled to left; Hinton out on a sacrifice bunt (catcher to second) [Colavito to second]; Gonzalez made an out to second; Brown lined to third; 0 R, 1 H, 0 E, 1 LOB. Indians 1, Senators 0.

SENATORS 6TH: Brinkman made an out to center; McMullen singled to shortstop; Howard homered [McMullen scored]; Lock walked; Lock was caught stealing second (catcher to shortstop to first); Hamlin made an out to center; 2 R, 2 H, 0 E, 0 LOB. Indians 1, Senators 2.

INDIANS 7TH: Crandall made an out to left; McDowell popped to shortstop in foul territory; Davalillo struck out; 0 R, 0 H, 0 E, 0 LOB. Indians 1, Senators 2.

SENATORS 7TH: Camilli grounded out (third to first); Cunningham grounded out (second to first); Richert reached on an error by

Gonzalez; Valentine made an out to right; 0 R, 0 H, 1 E, 1 LOB. Indians 1, Senators 2.

INDIANS 8TH: Alvis made an out to left; Wagner grounded out (second to first); Colavito singled to right; Hinton made an out to center; 0 R, 1 H, 0 E, 1 LOB. Indians 1, Senators 2.

SENATORS 8TH: Brinkman grounded out (shortstop to first); McMullen walked; Howard made an out to center; Lock struck out; 0 R, 0 H, 0 E, 1 LOB. Indians 1, Senators 2.

INDIANS 9TH: KIRKLAND REPLACED HOWARD (PLAYING RF); VALENTINE CHANGED POSITIONS (PLAYING LF); Gonzalez grounded out (pitcher to first); Brown walked; HOWSER RAN FOR BROWN; LANDIS BATTED FOR CRANDALL; Landis doubled to left [Howser to third]; SALMON BATTED FOR MCDOWELL; KLINE REPLACED RICHERT (PITCHING); Salmon was walked intentionally; Davalillo singled to left [Howser scored, Landis scored, Salmon to third, Davalillo to second (error by Valentine)]; Alvis singled to center [Salmon scored, Davalillo scored]; MCCORMICK REPLACED KLINE (PITCHING); Wagner made an out to shortstop; Colavito singled to right [Alvis to second]; Hinton made an out to center; 4 R, 4 H, 1 E, 2 LOB. Indians 5, Senators 2.

SENATORS 9TH: AZCUE REPLACED WAGNER (PLAYING C); SIEBERT REPLACED COLAVITO (PITCHING); HINTON CHANGED POSITIONS (PLAYING LF); HOWSER STAYED IN GAME (PLAYING SS); LANDIS STAYED IN GAME (PLAYING RF); SALMON STAYED IN GAME (PLAYING 1B); Hamlin made an out to left; KING BATTED FOR CAMILLI; King made an out to shortstop; Cunningham grounded out (second to first); 0 R, 0 H, 0 E, 0 LOB. Indians 5, Senators 2.

Final Totals	R	H	E	LOB
Indians	5	11	1	9
Senators	2	4	1	6

CHAPTER ELEVEN

October 3, 1947
New York Yankees at Brooklyn Dodgers

Heartbreaker

IN A PRIOR CHAPTER, WE covered Billy Rohr's loss of a no-hitter with two out in the ninth. Later, we covered Milt Pappas' loss of a perfect game with two out in the ninth. The game that we're covering in this chapter is another loss of a no-hitter with two out in the ninth. As was the case with the prior two, this one has a story of its own.

This game gook place during the World Series of 1947. It was a subway series, the Yankees against the Dodgers. There is a lot of folklore associated with the rivalry between these two teams. In total there were seven World Series played between these two teams before the Dodgers left Brooklyn and moved to Los Angeles in 1958. The Yankees won six of them and the Dodgers won one, in 1955.

The 1947 World Series was the second fall classic played between these two teams. Baseball was still in its post war phase, with the World War II veterans having completed their second season back from the war.

This World Series began on Tuesday September 30, 1947 at Yankee Stadium. The Yankees sent a rookie to the mound, Spec Shea. He had an excellent rookie season with fourteen wins against five losses and in the opener; he defeated the Dodgers twenty-one-year-old twenty-one game winner, Ralph Branca. In game two, the next day, also at Yankee Stadium, the Yankees Allie Reynolds, a nineteen game winner during the season, pitched a complete game win and defeated the Dodgers and their pitcher, Vic Lombardi. With no need for travel time, the next game took place the next day, Thursday, October 2, as the series moved to Brooklyn and their immortal stadium, Ebbets Field. In this game, the Dodgers beat up on Yankee starter Bobo Newsome for six runs in less than two innings. The Dodgers starter, Joe Hatten was also hit hard. He gave up two runs in the third, fourth, and fifth innings. Ralph Branca relieved, and gave up two more and then Hugh Casey finished the game. Even though Hatten left the game with a lead that the Yankees never overtook, because he pitched less than the required five innings, the win was awarded to Casey. Sadly, Casey would pass away less than four years later at the age of thirty-seven.

Then came game four. Here we are, at Ebbets Field on Friday, October 3. The Yankees are ahead in the series two games to one and need to get past this game to go back to their game one starter, Spec Shea. They are hoping to get there up in the series three games to one. Taking the mound for the Bronx Bombers was thirty-year-old pitcher Bill Bevens. Although Bevens had two pretty good years in 1945 and 1946 when he won twenty nine games against twenty two losses, he didn't have such a good year in 1947. He won only seven games during the regular season and lost thirteen. His overall major league record at this point was forty wins against thirty-six losses. The loss of that travel day left the other three starters unavailable for this game. Had there been a travel day, I think it's safe to assume that Spec Shea would have started game four with three days rest. However, there was no way he could go with only two days rest. With no one else available, Manager Bucky Harris sent Bill Bevens to the mound for the Yankees.

There were over thirty-three thousand people in attendance this day. Not one of them expected a historic game for this one. However, it was. This game was arguably the biggest heartbreaker in the history of the World Series.

Bill Bevens normally had very good control. In his career, he averaged less than four walks per nine innings. On this day, he was quite wild. He became the first pitcher ever to hit double figures for bases on balls in a World Series game. He remains the only pitcher in history to walk ten in a game. At the same time, though, for the first eight innings, he kept the Dodgers hitless.

Up to this point, no one had ever pitched a no-hitter in the World Series. It wouldn't have been a shutout as the Dodgers scored a run on no hit in the fifth. Entering the ninth, the Yankees had a lead of 2-1, and Bevens was three outs away from pitching the first ever World Series no-hitter. The first batter up was Bruce Edwards, the Dodgers catcher. He flied out to center field. Two outs to go. Carl Furillo then walked, the ninth base on balls given up by Bevens that day. The next batter was Spider Jorgensen and he fouled out to the Yankee first baseman George McQuinn. One out to go. Brooklyn Manager Burt Shotton then sent little Al Gionfriddo in to run for Furillo. Pinch hitter Pete Reiser was next and while he was at bat, Gionfriddo stole second. Sending Gionfriddo was gutsy. He gets caught stealing, the game is over. Gionfriddo made it to second safely. Bucky Harris then had Bevens intentionally walk Reiser to set up a force play at any base. This was the tenth walk of the day given up by Bevens. Eddie Miksis then came in to run for Reiser. No one knew it at the time, but Reiser had a very bad ankle. Had Harris known that, he probably would have pitched to him rather than intentionally walk him. The next batter up was to be the lead off batter, second baseman Eddie Stanky. Shotton chose to pinch hit Cookie Lavagetto for him. Cookie used to be a regular third baseman, but played sparingly now. This World Series would be the end of Cookie's career as a player. He would remain in the game as a coach and Manager. On this occasion, he established himself as one of the game's greatest spoilers. Lavagetto doubled off the Ebbets Field right field wall, scoring the fleet footed Gionfriddo and Miksis, giving the Dodgers the win 3-2.

Bill Bevens was one out away from pitching the first ever World Series no-hitter, and on one pitch, he lost It all. He lost the no-hitter and the game. Instead of getting credit for a World Series win and the first no-hitter, Bevens ended up with a loss and a record for the most bases on balls issued in one World Series game. This record still stands today. As I said, a heartbreaker.

Bill Bevens would pitch once more in this series, and pitch well. In game seven, with the series tied at three games each, Spec Shea started for the Yankees but didn't make it out of the second inning. Bevens came in and pitched two and two-thirds of scoreless ball, setting up the stage for Joe Page to come in and get the win for the Yankees, who with this win became world champions once again. This was it for Bevens. Injures prevented him from pitching again at the major league level. He retired to his native Oregon where he lived the rest of this life. He passed away in 1991.

Brooklyn Dodgers 3, New York Yankees 2

World Series Game 4 Played on Friday, October 3, 1947 (D) at Ebbets Field

```
NY  A    1  0  0    1  0  0    0  0  0  -  2  8  1
BRO N    0  0  0    0  1  0    0  0  2  -  3  1  3
```

BATTING

New York Yankees	AB	R	H	RBI	BB	SO	PO	A
Stirnweiss 2b	4	1	2	0	1	2	2	1
Henrich rf	5	0	1	0	0	1	2	0
Berra c	4	0	0	0	0	0	6	1
DiMaggio cf	2	0	0	1	2	0	3	0
McQuinn 1b	4	0	1	0	0	1	7	0
Johnson 3b	4	1	1	0	0	0	3	2
Lindell lf	3	0	2	1	1	0	2	0
Rizzuto ss	4	0	1	0	0	0	1	2
Bevens p	3	0	0	0	0	1	0	1
Totals	33	2	8	2	4	5	26	7

FIELDING -
E: Berra (2).

BATTING -
2B: Lindell (3,off Gregg).
3B: Johnson (2,off Gregg).
SH: Bevens (1,off Behrman).
Team LOB: 9.

BASERUNNING -
SB: Rizzuto (1,2nd base off Gregg/Edwards).

Brooklyn Dodgers	AB	R	H	RBI	BB	SO	PO	A
Stanky 2b	1	0	0	0	2	0	2	3
Lavagetto ph	1	0	1	2	0	0	0	0
Reese ss	4	0	0	1	0	0	3	5
Robinson 1b	4	0	0	0	0	1	11	1
Walker rf	2	0	0	0	2	0	0	1
Hermanski lf	4	0	0	0	0	0	2	0
Edwards c	4	0	0	0	0	3	7	1
Furillo cf	3	0	0	0	1	0	2	0
Gionfriddo pr	0	1	0	0	0	0	0	0
Jorgensen 3b	2	1	0	0	2	0	0	1
Taylor p	0	0	0	0	0	0	0	0
Gregg p	1	0	0	0	1	1	0	1
Vaughan ph	0	0	0	0	1	0	0	0
Behrman p	0	0	0	0	0	0	0	1
Casey p	0	0	0	0	0	0	0	1
Reiser ph	0	0	0	0	1	0	0	0

```
Miksis pr         0   1   0   0      0   0      0   0
Totals           26   3   1   3     10   5     27  15
```

FIELDING -
DP: 3. Reese-Stanky-Robinson, Gregg-Reese-Robinson, Casey-Edwards-Robinson.
E: Reese (1), Edwards (1), Jorgensen (1).

BATTING -
2B: Lavagetto (1,off Bevens).
SH: Stanky (1,off Bevens).
IBB: Reiser (1,by Bevens).
Team LOB: 8.

BASERUNNING -
SB: Reese (3,2nd base off Bevens/Berra); Gionfriddo (1,2nd base off Bevens/Berra).

PITCHING

New York Yankees	IP	H	R	ER	BB	SO	HR
Bevens L(0-1)	8.2	1	3	3	10	5	0

Brooklyn Dodgers	IP	H	R	ER	BB	SO	HR
Taylor	0	2	1	0	1	0	0
Gregg	7	4	1	1	3	5	0
Behrman	1.1	2	0	0	0	0	0
Casey W(2-0)	0.2	0	0	0	0	0	0
Totals	9	8	2	1	4	5	0

Taylor faced 4 batters in the 1st inning
WP: Bevens (1).
IBB: Bevens (1,Reiser).

Umpires: Larry Goetz, Bill McGowan, Babe Pinelli, Eddie Rommel, Jim Boyer, George Ma

Time of Game: 2:20   **Attendance:** 33443

Starting Lineups:

New York Yankees		Brooklyn Dodgers	
1. Stirnweiss	2b	Stanky	2b
2. Henrich	rf	Reese	ss
3. Berra	c	Robinson	1b
4. DiMaggio	cf	Walker	rf
5. McQuinn	1b	Hermanski	lf
6. Johnson	3b	Edwards	c
7. Lindell	lf	Furillo	cf
8. Rizzuto	ss	Jorgensen	3b
9. Bevens	p	Taylor	p

YANKEES 1ST: Stirnweiss singled to left; Henrich singled to
center [Stirnweiss to second]; Berra reached on a fielder's
choice [Stirnweiss to third, Henrich to second (error by Reese;
assist by Robinson)]; DiMaggio walked [Stirnweiss scored
(unearned), Henrich to third, Berra to second]; GREGG REPLACED
TAYLOR (PITCHING); McQuinn popped to shortstop; Johnson grounded
into a double play (shortstop to second to first) [DiMaggio out
at second]; 1 R, 2 H, 1 E, 2 LOB. Yankees 1, Dodgers 0.

DODGERS 1ST: Stanky walked; Reese grounded out (second to first) [Stanky to second]; Robinson grounded out (third to first); Walker walked; Hermanski popped to third in foul territory; 0 R, 0 H, 0 E, 2 LOB. Yankees 1, Dodgers 0.

YANKEES 2ND: Lindell grounded out (shortstop to first); Rizzuto singled to left; Rizzuto stole second; Bevens made an out to center; Stirnweiss struck out; 0 R, 1 H, 0 E, 1 LOB. Yankees 1, Dodgers 0.

DODGERS 2ND: Edwards struck out; Furillo grounded out (shortstop to first); Jorgensen walked; Gregg struck out; 0 R, 0 H, 0 E, 1 LOB. Yankees 1, Dodgers 0.

YANKEES 3RD: Henrich struck out; Berra grounded out (first unassisted); DiMaggio walked; McQuinn singled to catcher [DiMaggio out at home (right to catcher), McQuinn to second (error by Edwards)]; 0 R, 1 H, 1 E, 1 LOB. Yankees 1, Dodgers 0.

DODGERS 3RD: Stanky walked; Reese made an out to left; Bevens threw a wild pitch [Stanky to second]; Robinson made an out to left; Walker popped to third in foul territory; 0 R, 0 H, 0 E, 1 LOB. Yankees 1, Dodgers 0.

YANKEES 4TH: Johnson tripled to center; Lindell doubled to right [Johnson scored]; Rizzuto grounded out (first unassisted) [Lindell to third]; Bevens grounded out (shortstop to first); Stirnweiss was called out on strikes; 1 R, 2 H, 0 E, 1 LOB. Yankees 2, Dodgers 0.

DODGERS 4TH: Hermanski made an out to center; Edwards was called out on strikes; Furillo popped to catcher in foul territory; 0 R, 0 H, 0 E, 0 LOB. Yankees 2, Dodgers 0.

YANKEES 5TH: Henrich grounded out (shortstop to first); Berra grounded out (second to first); DiMaggio popped to second; 0 R, 0 H, 0 E, 0 LOB. Yankees 2, Dodgers 0.

DODGERS 5TH: Jorgensen walked; Gregg walked [Jorgensen to second]; Stanky out on a sacrifice bunt (catcher to second) [Jorgensen to third, Gregg to second]; Reese reached on a fielder's choice [Jorgensen scored, Gregg out at third (shortstop to third)]; Reese stole second [Reese to third (error by Berra)]; Robinson struck out; 1 R, 0 H, 1 E, 1 LOB. Yankees 2, Dodgers 1.

YANKEES 6TH: McQuinn was called out on strikes; Johnson made an out to left; Lindell walked; Rizzuto made an out to center; 0 R, 0 H, 0 E, 1 LOB. Yankees 2, Dodgers 1.

DODGERS 6TH: Walker walked; Hermanski popped to second; Edwards struck out; Furillo made an out to right; 0 R, 0 H, 0 E, 1 LOB. Yankees 2, Dodgers 1.

YANKEES 7TH: Bevens struck out; Stirnweiss walked; Henrich grounded into a double play (pitcher to shortstop to first) [Stirnweiss out at second]; 0 R, 0 H, 0 E, 0 LOB. Yankees 2, Dodgers 1.

DODGERS 7TH: Jorgensen lined to center; VAUGHAN BATTED FOR
GREGG; Vaughan walked; Stanky popped to shortstop; Reese
grounded out (first unassisted); 0 R, 0 H, 0 E, 1 LOB. Yankees
2, Dodgers 1.

YANKEES 8TH: BEHRMAN REPLACED VAUGHAN (PITCHING); Berra grounded
out (second to first); DiMaggio reached on an error by Jorgensen
[DiMaggio to first]; McQuinn made an out to left; Johnson
grounded out (third to first); 0 R, 0 H, 1 E, 1 LOB. Yankees 2,
Dodgers 1.

DODGERS 8TH: Robinson grounded out (third to first); Walker
grounded out (pitcher to first); Hermanski made an out to right;
0 R, 0 H, 0 E, 0 LOB. Yankees 2, Dodgers 1.

YANKEES 9TH: Lindell singled to right; Rizzuto forced Lindell
(pitcher to shortstop); Bevens reached on a fielder's choice on
a sacrifice bunt [Rizzuto to second]; Stirnweiss singled to
center [Rizzuto to third, Bevens to second]; CASEY REPLACED
BEHRMAN (PITCHING); Henrich grounded into a double play (pitcher
to catcher to first) [Rizzuto out at home]; 0 R, 2 H, 0 E, 2
LOB. Yankees 2, Dodgers 1.

DODGERS 9TH: Edwards flied to center; Furillo walked; Jorgensen
popped to first in foul territory; GIONFRIDDO RAN FOR FURILLO;
REISER BATTED FOR CASEY; Gionfriddo stole second; Reiser was
walked intentionally; MIKSIS RAN FOR REISER; LAVAGETTO BATTED
FOR STANKY; Lavagetto doubled to right [Gionfriddo scored,
Miksis scored]; 2 R, 1 H, 0 E, 1 LOB. Yankees 2, Dodgers 3.

Final Totals	R	H	E	LOB
Yankees	2	8	1	9
Dodgers	3	1	3	8

CHAPTER TWELVE

July 3, 1966
Atlanta Braves at San Francisco Giants

Tony Cloninger Makes History

THE HALL OF FAME IS full of great hitters, many former National Leaguers. To name a few, Ernie Banks, Mel Ott, Hank Aaron, Stan Musial, Frank Robinson, Willie Mays. These guys hit a lot of home runs, thousands when you combine them, including their fair share of grand slams. However, none of these guys hit two grand slams in one game. Until 1966, no National League batter ever did that and it's very interesting who the first one was.

Tony Cloninger was a major league pitcher from 1961-1972. He was a very good pitcher, no Hall of Famer, but a guy who won 113 games in the major leagues, surely something to be proud of. He pitched for the Braves in Milwaukee and Atlanta, the Cincinnati Reds and the St. Louis Cardinals.

Tony had a value that went beyond the pitcher's mound. Tony Cloninger was a very good hitting pitcher. We see fewer and fewer of these guys nowadays because of the designated hitter, but I remember the days when the pitcher batting was a routine matter of course. Tony was the kind of pitcher the manager didn't need to pinch hit for if he was pitching well. Tony was often used as a pinch hitter on the days he didn't pitch.

When July 3, 1966 began, the San Francisco Giants were in first place in the National League; three games in front of the Pittsburgh Pirates. They had forty-nine wins against twenty-nine losses. The Atlanta Braves were in eighth place, a full fifteen games behind with a record of thirty-five wins and forty-five losses. It was a good crowd at Candlestick Park, over 27,000.

Tony Cloninger entered the game with a record of eight wins and seven losses. The year before, 1965, was a banner year for Tony. He won twenty-four games against eleven losses. He didn't have as big a year in 1966, but he did end up with fourteen wins against eleven losses. Between 1964-1966, Tony won fifty-seven games.

On July 3, 1966, Tony Cloninger became the first National Leaguer to hit two grand slams in one game. He is, to this day, the only pitcher ever to accomplish such a feat. In addition to that, he holds the record for driving in nine runs as a pitcher. Amazingly, this was not Cloninger's first multi home run game. Two and a half weeks before, on June 16, Tony hit two home runs and drove in five runs as he pitched the Braves to a 17-1 win against the Mets. Tony ended the 1966 season with five home runs and twenty-three runs batted in.

In April 2006, forty years after the Braves started playing in Atlanta, I spoke to Frank Bolling about this game. Frank was the second baseman for the Braves that day. He went two for five in that game, scored two runs and drove in two. He batted sixth in the order and had good things to say about this game and Tony Cloninger.

"That game was in San Francisco. That's quite a feat, especially for a pitcher. I was just with him a few days ago in Atlanta. We had a fortieth anniversary of the first game the Braves played in Atlanta."

"They brought a bunch of us back and Tony was there. He pitched thirteen innings in that game and got beat. I do remember Tony hitting those grand slams...it was a rare thing and he was a pretty good hitter for a pitcher. He had lot of power. He hit those home runs in succession. He was a big strong kid and he could swing the bat good."

Another teammate, John Herrnstein had many memories of this game.

"He pitched and won that game. He was the reason we won it. Not only for his pitching, but because of his hitting. Tony had such a terrific day that day. He was such a strong guy. He was just a powerfully built guy. Very strong. A very likeable nice person, too. I remember him from our minor league days. He signed about the same time I did. I played against him in the old Three I League. I was at Des Moines and he was at Cedar Rapids. He and Denis Menke were on that team together as young ballplayers, rookies just getting started. I played against him then. I hit against him. He could throw hard."

Tony Cloninger ended his career in 1972 and became a minor league pitching coach. He worked for many teams and then became a major league coach with the New York Yankees and the Boston Red Sox. In the late 1980's Tony worked as a minor league pitching coach for the Albany Yankees of the Eastern League; a AA team for the New York Yankees.

I spoke to Paul Keating, the owner of that team at the time. I asked him about his memories of Tony Cloninger.

"Tony Cloninger is one of the humblest, nicest guys I have ever met in baseball. An absolute gentleman, moral standards so much higher than anyone else in the game, an absolute gentleman. Never even a swear word out of the guy. He was quite a guy."

I asked Paul how he handled the young pitchers in the minor leagues.

"Excellent! That's what he specialized in. All the young pitchers went out there and he didn't brag or say anything about what he was doing. He just went down in the bullpen everyday with his pitch counter and charts, working with the young pitchers. I never heard a young pitcher complain at all about Tony Cloninger."

A few years ago, Tony was working with the Boston Red Sox as their pitching coach. He is one of the guys who built the pitching staff that ultimately won the World Series in 2004. Unfortunately, he wasn't in the dugout when that happened. Prior to that, Tony was diagnosed with colon cancer and, although he still works for the Red

Sox in some capacity, he spends most of his time home fighting this disease.

Everyone who knows him wishes him well. Everyone I talked to about Tony says the same thing about him. He is just a very nice guy.

A nice guy who was a pretty good major league pitcher and a pretty decent hitter. He date in history; July 3, 1966.

Atlanta Braves 17, San Francisco Giants 3

Game Played on Sunday, July 3, 1966 (D) at Candlestick Park

```
ATL N    7  1  0    5  1  0    0  1  2  -  17 20  1
SF  N    0  0  0    1  1  0    0  1  0  -   3  7  3
```

BATTING

Atlanta Braves	AB	R	H	RBI	BB	SO	PO	A
Alou 1b	3	0	0	0	1	0	3	1
de la Hoz 3b	2	0	0	0	0	0	1	0
Jones cf	6	1	3	0	0	2	2	0
Aaron rf	4	2	1	1	0	0	2	0
Geiger rf	2	1	1	1	0	1	2	0
Carty lf	4	3	3	1	1	0	1	0
Herrnstein lf	1	0	0	0	0	0	0	0
Torre c	6	2	3	3	0	0	6	0
Bolling 2b	5	2	2	2	0	0	1	4
Woodward ss	6	2	4	0	0	1	2	4
Menke 3b,1b	3	2	0	0	2	0	6	1
Cloninger p	5	2	3	9	0	0	1	0
Totals	47	17	20	17	4	4	27	10

FIELDING -
DP: 1. Woodward-Bolling-Alou.
E: Cloninger (7).

BATTING -
2B: Woodward 2 (11,off Priddy,off Sadecki); Jones (7,off Sadecki); Geiger (4, Sadecki).
HR: Torre (19,1st inning off Gibbon 2 on 2 out); Cloninger 2 (4,1st inning off Priddy 3 on 2 out,4th inning off Sadecki 3 on 2 out); Carty (3,2nd inning off Priddy 0 on 2 out); Aaron (25,5th inning off Sadecki 0 on 0 out).
SF: Bolling (1,off Sadecki).
Team LOB: 8.

San Francisco Giants	AB	R	H	RBI	BB	SO	PO	A
Alou rf	4	0	1	0	0	0	1	0
Haller c,1b	3	1	1	1	1	0	8	0
Mays cf	1	1	0	0	1	0	1	0
Landrum cf	2	0	0	0	0	1	2	0
McCovey 1b	1	0	0	0	0	1	2	0
Dietz c	3	0	0	0	0	1	4	0
Hart 3b	3	0	1	0	0	0	1	1
Virgil 3b	1	0	0	0	0	1	0	1
Gabrielson lf	4	0	1	1	0	0	2	0
Davenport ss	1	0	0	0	0	0	1	2
Mason 2b	3	0	0	0	0	0	2	3

Lanier 2b,ss	4	0	2	0	0	0	3	4
Gibbon p	0	0	0	0	0	0	0	0
Priddy p	0	0	0	0	0	0	0	0
Sadecki p	3	1	1	1	0	1	0	0
Peterson ph	1	0	0	0	0	0	0	0
Totals	34	3	7	3	2	5	27	11

FIELDING -
DP: 1. Virgil-Mason-Haller.
E: Hart (15), Gabrielson (1), Lanier (11).

BATTING -
HR: Sadecki (2,5th inning off Cloninger 0 on 0 out); Haller (16,8th inning off Cloninger 0 on 0 out).
Team LOB: 6.

PITCHING

Atlanta Braves	IP	H	R	ER	BB	SO	HR
Cloninger W(9-7)	9	7	3	3	2	5	2

San Francisco Giants	IP	H	R	ER	BB	SO	HR
Gibbon L(3-5)	0.2	5	5	5	0	0	1
Priddy	2	4	3	3	2	0	2
Sadecki	6.1	11	9	5	2	4	2
Totals	9	20	17	13	4	4	5

WP: Cloninger (13), Sadecki (5).

Umpires: Doug Harvey, Harry Wendelstedt, Shag Crawford, Ed Vargo

Time of Game: 2:42   **Attendance:** 27002

Starting Lineups:

Atlanta Braves		San Francisco Giants	
1. Alou	1b	Alou	rf
2. Jones	cf	Haller	c
3. Aaron	rf	Mays	cf
4. Carty	lf	McCovey	1b
5. Torre	c	Hart	3b
6. Bolling	2b	Gabrielson	lf
7. Woodward	ss	Davenport	ss
8. Menke	3b	Lanier	2b
9. Cloninger	p	Gibbon	p

BRAVES 1ST: Alou made an out to second; Jones singled; Aaron forced Jones (second to shortstop); Carty singled to right [Aaron to third]; Torre homered [Aaron scored, Carty scored]; Bolling singled; Woodward singled to right [Bolling to third]; PRIDDY REPLACED GIBBON (PITCHING); Menke walked [Woodward to second]; Cloninger homered [Bolling scored, Woodward scored, Menke scored]; Alou grounded out (shortstop to first); 7 R, 6 H, 0 E, 0 LOB. Braves 7, Giants 0.

GIANTS 1ST: Alou grounded out (second to first); Haller walked; Mays grounded into a double play (shortstop to second to first) [Haller out at second]; 0 R, 0 H, 0 E, 0 LOB. Braves 7, Giants

0.

BRAVES 2ND: Jones made an out to second; Aaron made an out to center; Carty homered; Torre singled to center; Bolling made an out to first; 1 R, 2 H, 0 E, 1 LOB. Braves 8, Giants 0.

GIANTS 2ND: McCovey struck out; Hart popped to first in foul territory; Gabrielson made an out to shortstop; 0 R, 0 H, 0 E, 0 LOB. Braves 8, Giants 0.

BRAVES 3RD: DIETZ REPLACED MCCOVEY (PLAYING C); HALLER CHANGED POSITIONS (PLAYING 1B); Woodward doubled to right; Menke made an out to first; Cloninger grounded out (shortstop to first); Alou walked; SADECKI REPLACED PRIDDY (PITCHING); Jones was called out on strikes; 0 R, 1 H, 0 E, 2 LOB. Braves 8, Giants 0.

GIANTS 3RD: Davenport made an out to right; Lanier reached on an error by Cloninger; Sadecki struck out; Alou singled to center [Lanier to third]; Haller made an out to third; 0 R, 1 H, 1 E, 2 LOB. Braves 8, Giants 0.

BRAVES 4TH: MASON REPLACED DAVENPORT (PLAYING 2B); LANIER CHANGED POSITIONS (PLAYING SS); Aaron grounded out (second to first); Carty walked; Torre reached on an error by Hart [Carty to second]; Bolling singled to left [Carty scored, Torre to second]; Woodward made an out to shortstop; Menke walked [Torre to third, Bolling to second]; Cloninger homered (unearned) [Torre scored (unearned), Bolling scored (unearned), Menke scored (unearned)]; Alou reached on an error by Lanier; Jones struck out; 5 R, 2 H, 2 E, 1 LOB. Braves 13, Giants 0.

GIANTS 4TH: DE LA HOZ REPLACED ALOU (PLAYING 3B); MENKE CHANGED POSITIONS (PLAYING 1B); Mays walked; Dietz was called out on strikes; Cloninger threw a wild pitch [Mays to second]; Hart singled [Mays to third]; Gabrielson singled to right [Mays scored, Hart to second]; Mason made an out to right; Lanier made an out to left; 1 R, 2 H, 0 E, 2 LOB. Braves 13, Giants 1.

BRAVES 5TH: LANDRUM REPLACED MAYS (PLAYING CF); Aaron homered; Carty singled to right; Torre made an out to center; Bolling forced Carty (shortstop to second); Woodward singled to left [Bolling to second]; Menke forced Bolling (third unassisted); 1 R, 3 H, 0 E, 2 LOB. Braves 14, Giants 1.

GIANTS 5TH: GEIGER REPLACED AARON (PLAYING RF); Sadecki homered; Alou made an out to center; Haller popped to catcher in foul territory; Landrum made an out to right; 1 R, 1 H, 0 E, 0 LOB. Braves 14, Giants 2.

BRAVES 6TH: Cloninger made an out to left; de la Hoz grounded out (third to first); Jones singled to left [Jones to second (error by Gabrielson)]; Geiger struck out; 0 R, 1 H, 1 E, 1 LOB. Braves 14, Giants 2.

GIANTS 6TH: Dietz grounded out (shortstop to first); Hart grounded out (shortstop to first); Gabrielson grounded out (second to first); 0 R, 0 H, 0 E, 0 LOB. Braves 14, Giants 2.

BRAVES 7TH: VIRGIL REPLACED HART (PLAYING 3B); Carty grounded out (shortstop to first); Torre made an out to center; Bolling grounded out (second to first); 0 R, 0 H, 0 E, 0 LOB.   Braves 14, Giants 2.

GIANTS 7TH: HERRNSTEIN REPLACED CARTY (PLAYING LF); Mason made an out to center; Lanier singled to center; Sadecki popped to third in foul territory; Alou made an out to right; 0 R, 1 H, 0 E, 1 LOB.   Braves 14, Giants 2.

BRAVES 8TH: Woodward doubled to left; Menke grounded out (shortstop to first); Sadecki threw a wild pitch [Woodward to third]; Cloninger singled to left [Woodward scored]; de la Hoz grounded into a double play (third to second to first) [Cloninger out at second]; 1 R, 2 H, 0 E, 0 LOB.   Braves 15, Giants 2.

GIANTS 8TH: Haller homered; Landrum struck out; Dietz grounded out (shortstop to first); Virgil struck out; 1 R, 1 H, 0 E, 0 LOB.   Braves 15, Giants 3.

BRAVES 9TH: Jones doubled to center; Geiger doubled to right [Jones scored]; Herrnstein made an out to left; Torre singled to right [Geiger to third]; Bolling hit a sacrifice fly to right [Geiger scored]; Woodward was called out on strikes; 2 R, 3 H, 0 E, 1 LOB.   Braves 17, Giants 3.

GIANTS 9TH: Gabrielson grounded out (first to pitcher); Mason made an out to shortstop; Lanier singled to left; PETERSON BATTED FOR SADECKI; Peterson grounded out (second to first); 0 R, 1 H, 0 E, 1 LOB.   Braves 17, Giants 3.

Final Totals	R	H	E	LOB
Braves	17	20	1	8
Giants	3	7	3	6

CHAPTER THIRTEEN

September 28, 1995
Cincinnati Reds at Montreal Expos

Switch Pitcher?

THERE HAVE BEEN MANY SWITCH hitters in the history of the major leagues and there always will be. It is quite a skill. Mickey Mantle was a switch-hitter. He batted lefty against righties and righty against lefties.

How about a pitcher that pitches both right-handed and left-handed? There haven't been many of those.

Greg Harris was a major league pitcher for 15 years from 1981 to 1995. He pitched for the Mets, Reds, Expos (twice), Padres, Rangers, Phillies, Red Sox, and Yankees, eight different teams. He was both a starter and reliever. In his career, he won seventy-four games, lost ninety and retired with an earned run average of 3.69.

His most productive years were from 1989 to 1994, the years he spent with the Boston Red Sox. During that time, he had his best year in 1990 winning thirteen and losing nine as a starter. Three years later, in 1993, he pitched strictly in relief and led the American League pitchers by pitching in eighty games.

Greg Harris had a very special talent. It was one he wanted badly to use in his career, but the powers that be wouldn't let him use it.

Greg Harris is listed in the record book as a right-handed pitcher. One guy disagrees - Greg Harris himself. He (Harris) was ambidextrous. He could do things with both his right hand as well as his left hand, including pitching. If he had his way, he would have done this regularly. He would have pitched righty to righties and lefty to lefties.

He made his intentions clear to the Red Sox when he was with them. He had a special glove made that could be used with either hand. That's the glove he used when he played. Lou Gorman, the Red Sox general manager wouldn't allow him to pitch both ways. He said it would 'make a mockery' of the game.

Harris said, "Boston is so conservative. People are afraid to try anything." Gorman would allow him to pitch only as a right-hander.

It would make sense to me that if you could do this and could get guys out doing this, then why not do so? Why wouldn't the major league team exploit the talent of the pitcher if he were able to do this? Just think if your left arm got hurt, then rest it and pitch with your right, and vice versa. If you're using both arms, you should have twice the life. It's like getting two pitchers in one. A manager could make a pitching change without changing pitchers!

Lou Gorman said things like this should be done in the minors or in exhibition games but not a game that has meaning in the standings. I guarantee you Bill Veeck and Charlie Finley would disagree. They would allow this in a minute.

Harris had a tailor made ambidextrous glove, which he used on the field. He never had any problems fielding with it.

Greg Harris was born on November 2, 1955 in Lynwood, California. He attended Long Beach City College before his baseball career began. He worked his way through the minors and made it to the majors in 1981 with the Mets. He appeared in sixteen games, fourteen as a starter. In the 1982 season, he was traded to Cincinnati and stayed there through 1983 pitching mostly in relief.

He split 1984 between the Montreal Expos and the San Diego Padres, again as a relief pitcher. In 1985, it was on to the Texas Rangers and through 1986; he was one of the best relief pitchers in the American League. He appeared in 131 games during the two years, all as a relief pitcher.

In 1987, still with the Rangers, he went back to starting. In 1988 and half of 1989, he was back in the National League with the Phillies and back to relieving. By mid 1989, he went to Boston to begin his five year run with the Red Sox. In his days with the Sox, he spent time as a starter and a reliever. He won a total of thirty-nine games and saved another sixteen. He ended 1994 with a three-game stint as a New York Yankee reliever and went back to Montreal for one more year, working out of the bullpen with the Expos.

On September 28, 1995, the Expos allowed Greg to make use of his ambidextrous talent. He faced four batters, the first one he pitched right handed, the next two left handed and the fourth right handed. Hard-hitting left handed hitting outfielder Reggie Sanders led off the inning and grounded out with Harris pitching right handed. Harris then switched to left-handed pitching and faced lifetime .304 hitter Hal Morris, a left-handed batter. Morris drew a walk. Continuing to pitch southpaw, Harris faced Ed Taubensee, another lefty batter and a good hitting catcher. Taubensee bounded a ball in front of the plate and catcher Joe Siddal picked it up and threw to first baseman David Segui for the out. Morris went to second. Switching back to pitching right handed, Harris faced right-handed hitter Bret Boone who hit a come backer to Harris. Harris threw to first to retire Boone and end the inning.

This was the first and last time any pitcher pitched ambidextrously in the major leagues in the twentieth century. It was done once in 1888 in the American Association (which was then considered a major league) by Elton "Ice Box" Chamberlain. It was also done in a minor league game in the Florida State League on August 13, 1962. Bert Campaneris, usually a shortstop, pitched in relief for Daytona Beach against Fort Lauderdale.

As it turned out, this was the second to last appearance for Greg Harris in the major leagues. The next night he pitched again against Cincinnati. He pitched only right handed and threw two scoreless innings. It was the 703rd and last game of Greg Harris' career.

He waited and waited for his chance to prove he could do it. He finally got the chance on September 28, 1995.

Cincinnati Reds 9, Montreal Expos 7

Game Played on Thursday, September 28, 1995 (N) at Stade Olympique

CIN N	0	1	0	3	0	0	2	3	0	-	9	8	0
MON N	0	0	2	0	1	0	0	0	4	-	7	10	3

BATTING

Cincinnati Reds	AB	R	H	RBI	BB	SO	PO	A
Howard cf	4	1	1	0	0	1	0	1
Walton lf	1	1	1	3	0	0	2	0
Larkin ss	4	1	1	1	0	0	3	2
D. Lewis cf	1	0	0	0	0	0	0	0
Gant lf	2	1	0	1	1	1	0	0
Jackson p	0	0	0	0	0	0	0	0
Harris ph	1	0	0	0	0	0	0	0
Pugh p	0	0	0	0	0	0	0	0
McElroy p	0	0	0	0	0	0	0	0
Brantley p	0	0	0	0	0	0	0	0
R. Sanders rf	5	0	0	0	0	3	1	0
Morris 1b	4	0	2	0	1	0	4	2
Santiago c	0	1	0	0	0	0	2	0
Taubensee c	3	1	1	1	1	0	8	0
Boone 2b	5	1	1	0	0	1	5	0
Branson 3b	2	1	1	2	2	1	2	2
Schourek p	3	0	0	0	0	1	0	1
Duncan ss	1	1	0	0	0	0	0	0
Totals	36	9	8	8	5	8	27	8

FIELDING -
DP: 1. Branson-Schourek-Branson-Morris.
PB: Santiago (6).

BATTING -
2B: Branson (18,off Martinez); Howard (15,off Martinez).
HR: Walton (8,8th inning off Fraser 2 on 1 out).
SF: Gant (5,off Heredia).
HBP: Santiago (4,by Martinez).
Team LOB: 7.

BASERUNNING -
SB: Gant (23,2nd base off Martinez/Laker).

Montreal Expos	AB	R	H	RBI	BB	SO	PO	A
R. White cf	4	1	3	1	0	1	3	0
Fraser p	0	0	0	0	0	0	0	0
Harris p	0	0	0	0	0	0	0	1
Andrews ph	1	1	1	4	0	0	0	0
Segui 1b	4	0	1	2	1	0	8	1

Benitez rf	5	0	1	0	0	2	3	0
Berry 3b	4	0	0	0	0	1	0	1
Cordero lf	3	0	0	0	0	2	1	0
Lansing 2b	4	0	1	0	0	0	1	3
Grudzielanek ss	4	1	1	0	0	1	2	2
Laker c	2	0	1	0	0	1	4	0
Siddall pr,c	1	2	0	0	1	0	4	1
Martinez p	1	1	0	0	0	0	1	0
Heredia p	0	0	0	0	0	0	0	0
Floyd ph,cf	1	0	0	0	0	1	0	0
Silvestri ph	1	1	1	0	0	0	0	0
Totals	35	7	10	7	2	9	27	9

FIELDING -
E: R. White (4), Segui (3), Lansing (6).

BATTING -
2B: Benitez (2,off Schourek); R. White 2 (33,off Schourek 2); Segui (24,off Schourek); Laker (8,off Schourek); Grudzielanek (12,off Pugh).
HR: Andrews (8,9th inning off McElroy 3 on 2 out).
HBP: Martinez (2,by Schourek); Cordero (9,by Schourek).
Team LOB: 5.

BASERUNNING -
CS: Lansing (4,2nd base by Schourek/Taubensee).

PITCHING

Cincinnati Reds	IP	H	R	ER	BB	SO	HR
Schourek W(18-7)	6	7	3	3	0	6	0
Jackson	1	0	0	0	0	2	0
Pugh	1.2	1	2	2	1	1	0
McElroy	0	2	2	2	0	0	1
Brantley SV(28)	0.1	0	0	0	1	0	0
Totals	9	10	7	7	2	9	1

Montreal Expos	IP	H	R	ER	BB	SO	HR
Martinez L(14-10)	6	6	6	5	3	7	0
Heredia	1	1	0	0	0	1	0
Fraser	1	1	3	2	1	0	1
Harris	1	0	0	0	1	0	0
Totals	9	8	9	7	5	8	1

Martinez faced 2 batters in the 7th inning
HBP: Schourek 2 (8,Martinez,Cordero); Martinez (11,Santiago).

Umpires: Gerry Davis, Mike Winters, Terry Tata, Eric Gregg

Time of Game: 3:01   **Attendance:** 14581

Starting Lineups:

Cincinnati Reds		Montreal Expos	
1. Howard	cf	R. White	cf
2. Larkin	ss	Segui	1b
3. Gant	lf	Benitez	rf
4. R. Sanders	rf	Berry	3b

5. Morris	1b	Cordero	lf
6. Santiago	c	Lansing	2b
7. Boone	2b	Grudzielanek	ss
8. Branson	3b	Laker	c
9. Schourek	p	Martinez	p

REDS 1ST: Howard grounded out (second to first); Larkin flied to right; Gant struck out; 0 R, 0 H, 0 E, 0 LOB. Reds 0, Expos 0.

EXPOS 1ST: R. White singled to left; Segui hit into a double play [R. White out at first (third to first)]; Benitez doubled to left; Santiago allowed a passed ball [Benitez to third]; Berry grounded out (shortstop to first); 0 R, 2 H, 0 E, 1 LOB. Reds 0, Expos 0.

REDS 2ND: R. Sanders flied to center; Morris lined to shortstop; Santiago was hit by a pitch; Boone reached on an error by R. White [Santiago scored (unearned), Boone to second]; Branson struck out; 1 R, 0 H, 1 E, 1 LOB. Reds 1, Expos 0.

EXPOS 2ND: Cordero struck out; Lansing popped to shortstop; Grudzielanek was called out on strikes; 0 R, 0 H, 0 E, 0 LOB. Reds 1, Expos 0.

REDS 3RD: Schourek grounded out (first to pitcher); Howard struck out; Larkin flied to right; 0 R, 0 H, 0 E, 0 LOB. Reds 1, Expos 0.

EXPOS 3RD: TAUBENSEE REPLACED SANTIAGO (PLAYING C); Laker was called out on strikes; Martinez was hit by a pitch; R. White doubled to right [Martinez to third]; Segui doubled to left [Martinez scored, R. White scored]; Benitez struck out; Berry flied to right; 2 R, 2 H, 0 E, 1 LOB. Reds 1, Expos 2.

REDS 4TH: Gant walked; Gant stole second; R. Sanders struck out; Morris flied to right; Taubensee singled to left [Gant scored]; Boone singled to left [Taubensee to second]; Branson doubled to right [Taubensee scored, Boone scored]; Schourek grounded out (second to first); 3 R, 3 H, 0 E, 1 LOB. Reds 4, Expos 2.

EXPOS 4TH: Cordero was hit by a pitch; Lansing reached on a fielder's choice [Cordero out at second (shortstop to center to second)]; Lansing was picked off and caught stealing second (pitcher to first to shortstop); Grudzielanek popped to second; 0 R, 0 H, 0 E, 0 LOB. Reds 4, Expos 2.

REDS 5TH: Howard lined to center; Larkin grounded out (third to first); Gant popped to second; 0 R, 0 H, 0 E, 0 LOB. Reds 4, Expos 2.

EXPOS 5TH: Laker doubled to center; SIDDALL RAN FOR LAKER; On a bunt Martinez grounded out (first to second); R. White doubled to shortstop [Siddall scored]; Segui grounded out (first unassisted) [R. White to third]; Benitez was called out on strikes; 1 R, 2 H, 0 E, 1 LOB. Reds 4, Expos 3.

REDS 6TH: SIDDALL STAYED IN GAME (PLAYING C); R. Sanders struck out; Morris singled to right; Taubensee walked [Morris to second]; Boone struck out; Branson walked [Morris to third, Taubensee to second]; Schourek struck out; 0 R, 1 H, 0 E, 3 LOB.

Reds 4, Expos 3.

EXPOS 6TH: Berry popped to shortstop; Cordero struck out;
Lansing singled to left; Grudzielanek popped to second; 0 R, 1
H, 0 E, 1 LOB. Reds 4, Expos 3.

REDS 7TH: Howard doubled to left; Larkin singled to center
[Howard scored, Larkin to third (error by Segui)]; HEREDIA
REPLACED MARTINEZ (PITCHING); Gant out on a sacrifice fly to
center [Larkin scored]; R. Sanders was called out on strikes;
Morris singled to right; Taubensee flied to left; 2 R, 3 H, 1 E,
1 LOB. Reds 6, Expos 3.

EXPOS 7TH: JACKSON REPLACED GANT (PITCHING); WALTON REPLACED
HOWARD (PLAYING LF); D. LEWIS REPLACED LARKIN (PLAYING CF);
DUNCAN REPLACED SCHOUREK (PLAYING SS); Siddall flied to left;
FLOYD BATTED FOR HEREDIA; Floyd struck out; R. White struck out;
0 R, 0 H, 0 E, 0 LOB. Reds 6, Expos 3.

REDS 8TH: FLOYD STAYED IN GAME (PLAYING CF); FRASER REPLACED R.
WHITE (PITCHING); Boone grounded out (shortstop to first);
Branson walked; Duncan reached on an error by Lansing [Branson
to second]; Walton homered [Branson scored, Duncan scored
(unearned)]; D. Lewis grounded out (second to first); HARRIS
BATTED FOR JACKSON; Harris popped to shortstop; 3 R, 1 H, 1 E, 0
LOB. Reds 9, Expos 3.

EXPOS 8TH: PUGH REPLACED HARRIS (PITCHING); Segui lined to left;
Benitez popped to third; Berry struck out; 0 R, 0 H, 0 E, 0 LOB.
Reds 9, Expos 3.

REDS 9TH: HARRIS REPLACED FRASER (PITCHING). Harris Pitching Right
Handed, R. Sanders grounded out (shortstop to first). With Harris pitching left handed,
Morris walked. With Harris pitching left handed, Taubensee grounded out (catcher to
first), Morris to second; With Harris pitching right handed, Boone grounded out (pitcher
to first). 0 R, 0H, 0E, 1 LOB. Reds 9, Expos 3

EXPOS 9TH: Cordero popped to second; Lansing popped to catcher;
Grudzielanek doubled to right; Siddall walked; MCELROY REPLACED
PUGH (PITCHING); SILVESTRI BATTED FOR FLOYD; Silvestri singled
to right [Grudzielanek to third, Siddall to second]; ANDREWS
BATTED FOR HARRIS; Andrews homered [Grudzielanek scored, Siddall
scored, Silvestri scored]; BRANTLEY REPLACED MCELROY (PITCHING);
Segui walked; Benitez grounded out (third to first); 4 R, 3 H, 0
E, 1 LOB. Reds 9, Expos 7.

Final Totals	R	H	E	LOB
Reds	9	8	0	7
Expos	7	10	3	5

Read Me

CHAPTER FOURTEEN

August 25, 1968
Detroit Tigers at New York Yankees

Now Pitching...Rocky Colavito

ROCCO DOMENICO COLAVITO, BETTER KNOWN as Rocky, was an excellent major league outfielder from 1955 through 1968. He was a very powerful batter hitting 374 home runs in his career. He never played with fabulous teams, so he never got the chance to showcase his ability in the World Series. He did play in nine all-star games and hit three home runs in them. He was a home run champion once; an RBI champion once and at one point in his career, went five consecutive seasons playing in at least 160 games.

It's always fun when a position player comes into the game to pitch. It doesn't happen often, but it usually makes a boring one-sided game interesting. I remember one time; Jose Canseco pitched for the Texas Rangers. It was a game against the Boston Red Sox in Boston. After seven and a half innings, the Red Sox were ahead 12-1. Rather than use a regular relief pitcher in a hopeless role for only one inning, Manager Kevin Kennedy let Canseco pitch the last of the eighth. He didn't do too well, giving up another three runs, hurting his arm in the process, keeping him from playing the outfield for a while because of it.

Ted Williams pitched a game one time in 1940. A position player coming in to pitch is a very rare occurrence, but when it does happen, it is usually in a game that is hopelessly one-sided and your team has no chance of coming back.

In August of 1968, Rocky Colavito was a thirty-five -year-old bench player with the New York Yankees, playing in his last major league season. He had a background as a pitcher and actually pitched once before in the major leagues. It was almost exactly ten years prior, on August 13, 1958 when Rocky was a slugging Cleveland Indian outfielder. This game was also against the Tigers and Rocky pitched three scoreless innings.

What sets this game apart from all the others, is, even though Rocky came into the game with his team behind (5-0 after three and one third innings), Rocky ended up the winning pitcher. The Yankees pulled out a come-from-behind victory and Rocky Colavito ended up becoming only the second player in history (Babe Ruth is the other) to have won both a home run championship as a batter and a major league win as a pitcher.

It happened at a time when the Yankees' pitching staff was very thin, and there were a bunch of doubleheaders scheduled. Manager Ralph Houk approached Colavito with the idea of pitching him, if needed. Pro that he was, Rocky answered the call.

"Ralph told me Saturday that I might have to do some pitching because of the heavy doubleheader schedule," Rocky told *The Sporting News* in their September 7, 1968 edition. In fact, this game was the first of a doubleheader. It was in Yankee Stadium and the starting pitcher was the veteran Steve Barber. He got hit hard. The Tigers scored two runs in the top of the first and another two in the top of the third. In the fourth, with one out, Barber walked the pitcher Pat Dobson, then threw a wild pitch and Dobson went to second.

All this was going on while Rocky warmed up in the bullpen. The next batter, Mickey Stanley singled, scoring Dobson, and then Dick Tracewski singled sending Stanley to second. With two on, one out, and the Yankees trailing by five in the fourth inning, Rocky Colavito came into the game to pitch. The Tiger's rally was over.

The first batter he faced was future Hall of Famer Al Kaline. Kaline grounded out to short. Powerful Willie Horton was the next batter and flied out to left to end the inning. In the last of the fourth, the Yankees scraped out a run on three singles.

Rocky pitched the fifth and sixth innings, allowing no runs and only one hit, a double to Al Kaline. After five and one half innings, the Tigers led by a score of 5-1 and in the last of the sixth, the Yankees rallied for five runs. Rocky was one of the batters and it was fitting that he would be the guy to score the go-ahead-run, making himself the pitcher of record.

After six innings, the Yankees led six to five. In the top of the seventh, Dooley Womack came in to pitch for the Yankees There were boos in the crowd. The fans wanted to see more of Colavito on the mound. Womack did his job, pitching a scoreless seventh.

In the eighth, veteran Lindy McDaniel came in to pitch two scoreless innings. Game over, Yankees won, 6-5, with Rocky Colavito the winning pitcher.

He was excited. "Sure it has to be a big thrill after a career in the outfield. Don't forget, I was signed as a pitcher-outfielder and the Yanks wanted me mostly to pitch, while Cleveland wanted me as an outfielder...when I came in, Ralph just told me to throw strikes. I used mostly fast balls with a few curves and sliders. I had a better slider in the bullpen than on the mound."

The catcher that day was Jake Gibbs. I asked him to tell me what his memories were of this game. He chuckled at the memories.

"Rocky always had the good arm and he was always kind of messing around. He had the good strong arm and we did kind of run short (of pitchers), we did have doubleheaders and I don't know all of what happened during the game, but I remember when Rocky came in."

Jake was surprised when Rocky had his own ideas about how to pitch.

"He shook me off quite a few times," Jake laughed.

"Here's a guy that's been playing right field and I've been catching and I know the hitters and I called a lot of fast balls because I didn't know what kind of curve ball he had. I was basically just calling for fast balls, you know put the ball in play and maybe we'll catch it. But he wanted to throw some sliders every now and then!"

I asked Jake if Rocky had good stuff that day.

"Yes, not bad, you know he had a great arm from the outfield. He didn't give up any runs in two and two thirds! That's a helluva relief job!"

I reminded him that Rocky walked two and struck out one.

"Hey, that ain't bad, is it? He had a great arm and he surprised me that he was able to get his slider over. It worked real good. We just went fast ball, slider, fast ball, and slider."

I asked Jake what kind of guy Rocky was to have around.

"Rocky was a prince of a guy! He was a great teammate."

It had to be a particular thrill for Rocky being a native New Yorker. He was born on August 10, 1933 in New York City. He grew up to be a fabulous baseball player who could pitch, hit, and play the outfield. He had a fabulous body and grew to 6'3", 190 lbs., long, lean and strong with huge biceps. When he got a hold of one, he could hit the ball for miles.

He signed with the Cleveland Indians in 1951 and worked his way through the minors until he came up to the majors to stay in September 1955. From 1956-1959 he banged out 129 home runs for the Indians, including a league leading forty-two in 1959. On June 10, 1959, Colavito hit four home runs in one game, tying a record with several others that has never been broken. He hit those four home runs on successive at-bats.

At this point, Rocky Colavito was a twenty-six-year-old superstar. He was by far the most popular Indian; indeed, he was the team's top draw. The fans loved him. They were counting on him to be a power-hitting outfielder for many years to come.

Rocky went to spring training in 1960 with the Indians and had a pretty good spring. He was set to come north to play another season when something shocking happened. During the final spring training game on April 10, 1960, Rocky was traded to the Detroit Tigers. SHOCK! He was traded by the Indians General Manager Frank Lane for the Tigers' Harvey Kuenn. Kuenn had led the

American League in batting in 1959 with a .353 batting average, but he hit only nine home runs and drove in only seventy-one runs. The American League's home run champion was traded for the American League's batting champion straight up. It was one of the most controversial trades of all time. The fans were furious. They hung Frank Lane in effigy. They would have lynched him if they could have.

The Tiger fans were thrilled to get Colavito. It was particularly hard on Kuenn. The fans in Cleveland blamed him for the trade and gave him a hard time all season. He lasted only one year in Cleveland. He was then traded to the San Francisco Giants.

The Cleveland fans always blamed Lane for this trade and said this caused thirty years of mediocrity. Just as the Boston Red Sox fans had the "Curse of the Bambino," the Indian fans have "The Curse of Rocky Colavito."

Rocky ended up playing four years for the Tigers and pounded out 139 home runs in those four years. He had a lifetime total of 268. In 1961, he had has finest season in Detroit banging out forty-five home runs driving in 140.

After the 1963 season, Rocky was traded again, this time to the Kansas City Athletics. He lasted only one year in Kansas City, but did well hitting thirty-four home runs and driving in 102.

In February 1965, to the great joy of all the Cleveland fans, Rocky was traded back to the Cleveland Indians. He had another great year hitting twenty-six home runs and leading the league in RBI's with 108. He also set a record as a fielder. He played in all 162 games in right field without an error all season.

In 1966, he hit another thirty home runs with the Tribe but then his productivity started to go. In 1967, he found himself not playing everyday for the first time in his career. He didn't like this arrangement and let the Indian management know it. They traded him to the Chicago White Sox in July. He finished the season there. In 1968, he started the year with the Los Angeles Dodgers but was released in July. He was then signed by the Yankees where he played the rest of the season and ended his career.

In his two games as a pitcher, Rocky pitched a total of five and two thirds innings, allowed only one hit, no runs, and had an earned run average of 0.00 and a winning percentage of 1.000.

To this day, Rocky remains the most beloved Indian of all time. Rocky is not in the Hall of Fame, but some think he should be. If he were in the Hall of Fame, no standard would be compromised.

Bob Morgan, former sportscaster, remembers Colavito.

"He had a ferocious arm...They loved him in Cleveland, and they hated Harvey Kuenn when he came over too...He was a good ballplayer too, not just a good hitter. He was like Canseco without steroids. A big guy, a muscular guy, he used to put the bat way up over his back and down...and he had a rifle of an arm as good as anyone I've ever seen including Dewey Evans or any of them. He had a great arm."

In his retirement years, Rocky values his privacy and guards it very closely. He came back to baseball for a time. He was a major league hitting coach for a few years, but now is completely retired and living a quiet life in Pennsylvania. As of this writing (2006) he is seventy-two years old.

Rocky Colavito... Pitcher. Has a ring to it, doesn't it?

New York Yankees 6, Detroit Tigers 5 (1)

Game Played on Sunday, August 25, 1968 (D) at Yankee Stadium

```
DET A   2  0  2   1  0  0   0  0  0  -   5 10 0
NY  A   0  0  0   1  0  5   0  0  x  -   6 10 2
```

BATTING

Detroit Tigers	AB	R	H	RBI	BB	SO	PO	A
Stanley cf	5	1	2	1	0	0	2	0
Tracewski ss	3	2	2	0	1	1	2	1
Brown ph	1	0	1	0	0	0	0	0
McMahon p	0	0	0	0	0	0	0	0
Kaline rf	5	1	3	1	0	0	2	0
Horton lf	4	0	1	2	1	1	1	0
Freehan 1b,c	4	0	1	0	1	0	12	0
Wert 3b	4	0	0	0	1	1	1	1
Price c	3	0	0	0	1	0	0	0
Oyler ss	0	0	0	0	0	0	0	0
Northrup ph	1	0	0	0	0	0	0	0
Matchick 2b	4	0	0	0	0	0	3	3
Dobson p	2	1	0	0	1	0	0	1
Patterson p	0	0	0	0	0	0	0	0
Cash ph,1b	1	0	0	0	0	0	1	0
Totals	37	5	10	4	6	3	24	6

FIELDING -
DP: 1. Matchick-Freehan.

BATTING -
2B: Horton (17,off Barber); Kaline (11,off Colavito); Brown (5,off McDaniel
Team LOB: 11.

New York Yankees	AB	R	H	RBI	BB	SO	PO	A
Clarke 2b	5	0	1	0	0	0	0	5
Gibbs c	4	0	1	1	0	0	4	0
Mantle 1b	4	0	0	0	0	0	11	1
Pepitone cf	4	1	1	0	0	0	0	0
Kosco rf	4	1	2	0	0	0	3	0
Tresh ss	2	1	1	0	2	0	2	4
Robinson lf	3	1	2	4	1	0	2	0
Cox 3b	4	1	1	1	0	1	2	2
Barber p	1	0	1	0	0	0	0	0
Colavito p	1	1	0	0	1	0	0	0
Womack p	0	0	0	0	0	0	1	1
McDaniel p	1	0	0	0	0	1	2	0
Totals	33	6	10	6	4	2	27	13

FIELDING -

DP: 1. Womack-Tresh.
E: Tresh (22), Cox (16).

BATTING -
2B: Kosco 2 (11,off Dobson 2).
HR: Robinson (4,6th inning off Dobson 2 on 2 out); Cox (6,6th inning off Dobs
0 on 2 out).
Team LOB: 7.

PITCHING

Detroit Tigers	IP	H	R	ER	BB	SO	HR
Dobson	5.2	8	5	5	2	0	2
Patterson L(2-3)	1.1	2	1	1	2	0	0
McMahon	1	0	0	0	0	2	0
Totals	8	10	6	6	4	2	2

New York Yankees	IP	H	R	ER	BB	SO	HR
Barber	3.1	7	5	4	3	1	0
Colavito W(1-0)	2.2	1	0	0	2	1	0
Womack	1	1	0	0	1	0	0
McDaniel SV(8)	2	1	0	0	0	1	0
Totals	9	10	5	4	6	3	0

WP: Barber (3).

Umpires: Marty Springstead, Red Flaherty, Bob Stewart, Lou DiMuro

Time of Game: 3:04

Starting Lineups:

Detroit Tigers		New York Yankees	
1. Stanley	cf	Clarke	2b
2. Tracewski	ss	Gibbs	c
3. Kaline	rf	Mantle	1b
4. Horton	lf	Pepitone	cf
5. Freehan	1b	Kosco	rf
6. Wert	3b	Tresh	ss
7. Price	c	Robinson	lf
8. Matchick	2b	Cox	3b
9. Dobson	p	Barber	p

TIGERS 1ST: Stanley singled to center; Tracewski walked [Stanley
to second]; Kaline singled to left [Stanley scored, Tracewski to
third]; Horton walked [Kaline to second]; Freehan reached on a
fielder's choice [Tracewski scored (unearned) (error by Cox),
Kaline out at third (third), Horton to second]; Wert struck out;
Price grounded out (third to first); 2 R, 2 H, 1 E, 2 LOB.
Tigers 2, Yankees 0.

YANKEES 1ST: Clarke grounded out (shortstop to first); Gibbs
grounded out (pitcher to first); Mantle popped to third in foul
territory; 0 R, 0 H, 0 E, 0 LOB. Tigers 2, Yankees 0.

TIGERS 2ND: Matchick grounded out (second to first); Dobson made
an out to right; Stanley grounded out (shortstop to first); 0 R,
0 H, 0 E, 0 LOB. Tigers 2, Yankees 0.

YANKEES 2ND: Pepitone lined to first; Kosco doubled to center; Tresh made an out to second; Robinson walked; Cox made an out to right; 0 R, 1 H, 0 E, 2 LOB. Tigers 2, Yankees 0.

TIGERS 3RD: Tracewski singled to left; Kaline singled to center [Tracewski to third]; Horton doubled to left [Tracewski scored, Kaline scored]; Freehan grounded out (third to first) [Horton to third]; Wert grounded out (shortstop to first); Price made an out to left; 2 R, 3 H, 0 E, 1 LOB. Tigers 4, Yankees 0.

YANKEES 3RD: Barber singled to right; Clarke grounded into a double play (second to first) [Barber out at second]; Gibbs grounded out (first unassisted); 0 R, 1 H, 0 E, 0 LOB. Tigers 4, Yankees 0.

TIGERS 4TH: Matchick grounded out (second to first); Dobson walked; Barber threw a wild pitch [Dobson to second]; Stanley singled to center [Dobson scored]; Tracewski singled to center [Stanley to second]; COLAVITO REPLACED BARBER (PITCHING); Kaline grounded out (shortstop to first) [Stanley to third, Tracewski to second]; Horton made an out to left; 1 R, 2 H, 0 E, 2 LOB. Tigers 5, Yankees 0.

YANKEES 4TH: Mantle made an out to shortstop; Pepitone singled to shortstop; Kosco popped to first in foul territory; Tresh singled [Pepitone to third]; Robinson singled to left [Pepitone scored, Tresh to second]; Cox made an out to shortstop; 1 R, 3 H, 0 E, 2 LOB. Tigers 5, Yankees 1.

TIGERS 5TH: Freehan walked; Wert popped to catcher in foul territory; Price walked [Freehan to second]; Matchick made an out to first; Dobson grounded out (second to first); 0 R, 0 H, 0 E, 2 LOB. Tigers 5, Yankees 1.

YANKEES 5TH: Colavito made an out to center; Clarke made an out to left; Gibbs made an out to center; 0 R, 0 H, 0 E, 0 LOB. Tigers 5, Yankees 1.

TIGERS 6TH: Stanley made an out to right; Tracewski was called out on strikes; Kaline doubled to center; Horton lined to third; 0 R, 1 H, 0 E, 1 LOB. Tigers 5, Yankees 1.

YANKEES 6TH: Mantle grounded out (second to first); Pepitone grounded out (second to first); Kosco doubled to left; **Horton hit in the head**; Tresh walked; Robinson homered [Kosco scored, Tresh scored]; Cox homered; PATTERSON REPLACED DOBSON (PITCHING); Colavito walked; Clarke singled to right [Colavito to second]; Gibbs singled to right [Colavito scored, Clarke to third]; Mantle lined to right; 5 R, 5 H, 0 E, 2 LOB. Tigers 5, Yankees 6.

TIGERS 7TH: WOMACK REPLACED COLAVITO (PITCHING); Freehan singled to left; Wert walked [Freehan to second]; On a bunt Price hit into a double play (pitcher to shortstop) [Freehan out at third]; Matchick forced Wert (second to shortstop); 0 R, 1 H, 0 E, 1 LOB. Tigers 5, Yankees 6.

YANKEES 7TH: Pepitone grounded out (first unassisted); Kosco grounded out (third to first); Tresh walked; Robinson made an out to second; 0 R, 0 H, 0 E, 1 LOB.   Tigers 5, Yankees 6.

TIGERS 8TH: CASH BATTED FOR PATTERSON; MCDANIEL REPLACED WOMACK (PITCHING); Cash grounded out (first to pitcher); Stanley made an out to right; BROWN BATTED FOR TRACEWSKI; Brown doubled to right; Kaline grounded out (second to pitcher); 0 R, 1 H, 0 E, 1 LOB.   Tigers 5, Yankees 6.

YANKEES 8TH: MCMAHON REPLACED BROWN (PITCHING); CASH STAYED IN GAME (PLAYING 1B); FREEHAN CHANGED POSITIONS (PLAYING C); OYLER REPLACED PRICE (PLAYING SS); Cox struck out; McDaniel struck out; Clarke grounded out (first unassisted); 0 R, 0 H, 0 E, 0 LOB.   Tigers 5, Yankees 6.

TIGERS 9TH: Horton struck out; Freehan grounded out (shortstop to first); Wert reached on an error by Tresh; NORTHRUP BATTED FOR OYLER; Northrup grounded out (first unassisted); 0 R, 0 H, 1 E, 1 LOB.   Tigers 5, Yankees 6.

Final Totals	R	H	E	LOB
Tigers	5	10	0	11
Yankees	6	10	2	7

CHAPTER FIFTEEN

September 14, 1978
Atlanta Braves at San Francisco Giants

Jim Bouton Makes it Back

JIM BOUTON IS ONE OF the most interesting baseball personalities of all time. He was a pitcher who, when he was young, had a great fastball. He climbed the minor league ladder rather quickly and made it to the major leagues with the defending world champion New York Yankees in 1962. He had a career that included a twenty-one win season, two World Series wins and a scoreless All-Star appearance.

One of the Yankees' catchers during those years was Jake Gibbs. I had the opportunity to speak with Jake and ask him about his memories of Jim Bouton.

"I caught him for four or five years. He had good stuff; he had a good overhand curve ball and a good fastball. He had a little arm trouble and that kind of bothered him and he lost a little bit off of his fastball."

When he lost his fastball, he went back to the minors and started throwing the knuckleball regularly. The knuckleball got him back into the major leagues as a relief pitcher. He went from the Yankees to the expansion Seattle Pilots and then to the National League with the Houston Astros.

He finished with the Astros in 1970 and then retired, or so we thought at the time.

In 1969, Jim wrote a book that became one of the greatest literary works of the twentieth century. Not just as a baseball book, but as a timepiece. It was called *Ball Four* and it was the first tell all book ever written about baseball.

Jim started the 1969 season with the Seattle Pilots, the only season this team existed. They moved to Milwaukee in 1970 and became the Milwaukee Brewers. Because of *Ball Four*, the memory of the Seattle Pilots will live forever. Otherwise, no one would remember them.

Jim went down to the minors briefly in 1969, came back, pitched in fifty seven games for the Pilots, all but one in relief. He was traded to the Houston Astros for the final month of the season. All those happenings were perfect for the book he wrote, which was in diary form. When the book came out in 1970, the Commissioner of Baseball, Bowie Kuhn was furious. He called Jim for a meeting, spoke his mind and the sales of the book skyrocketed.

Jim played for the Houston Astros in 1970 as a spot starter and reliever and, after a record of four wins, six losses; Jim left the game to pursue other things.

For the next few years, he did several things. His first new venture was as a sportscaster. For six years, he worked for both WABC and WCBS in New York.

He also had a small part in the movie "The Long Goodbye." He originated the bubble gum 'Big League Chew' and did more television, this time as an actor. His book became a situation comedy. *Ball Four* made it to prime time television for a short time and Jim played the lead. His name in the television series was Jim Barton.

Jim Bouton was thirty-seven years old and never stopped pitching. He played amateur ball in New Jersey all the while after he retired with such teams as the Clifton Tigers, the Teaneck Blues, the Englewood Rangers and the Ridgewood-Paramus Barons.

When you think about it, Jim Bouton accomplished a lot in his thirty-seven years, but the best was yet to come.

In 1977, Jim Bouton decided he would like to return to the major leagues. Keep in mind; he hadn't pitched professionally for seven years. He was at an age when most players were retired and this was not just a comeback. When you talk about a player who made a comeback, it usually means from injury. A player may break a bone or hurt his arm, miss a season, then come back. That's not what we're talking about here. Jim Bouton would have to start all over again in the lower minors and work his way up just as he did when he was twenty years old. It's something that was never done before.

At the time, the Chicago White Sox were owned by Bill Veeck, a legendary maverick owner. This crazy idea would be right up his alley. Bill Veeck gave Jim Bouton a chance to start his return in AA ball with Knoxville of the Southern League. It didn't work out too well there. Jim got into ten games, started eight, won none and lost six. His ERA was 5.26. Not giving up, Jim Bouton went to Durango, Mexico and pitched in the AAA Mexican League. He didn't do much better there. Jim got into six games, started five, won one, lost four and had an ERA of 4.97. Time to give up? Not this guy. From Mexico, he went to an independent Class A team in Portland, Oregon-the Portland Mavericks of the Northwest League. This team was owned by the actor Bing Russell-Kurt Russell's father. This is where the old knuckleball started to knuckle again. Jim started nine games, won five, and lost one. A good record, but it was only Class A. Where would Jim go in 1978?

He needed another maverick owner like Bill Veeck to give him another chance. He found Ted Turner, the billionaire owner of the Atlanta Braves. Ted liked the idea of a thirty-nine-year-old guy making a comeback like this. Ted himself was thirty-nine.

Jim started the year as the batting practice pitcher for the AAA Richmond Braves. When the major league Braves came to Richmond to play the AAA team in an exhibition game, Jim Bouton pitched for Richmond and pitched well. Then he got a chance to go to the Braves' AA team in Savannah, Georgia as an active roster player. Jim pitched the rest of the season in Savannah. He won eleven, lost nine but his earned run average was a very good 2.82. This earned him his promotion to the major leagues. He had made it! He referred to it as making it back to 'Emerald City'.

In 2000, Jim wrote about this experience in an updated version of *Ball Four*. He called it *Ball Four - The Final Pitch*.

He writes, "When I walked into Atlanta's Fulton County Stadium, I was floating as if in a dream. How large it was compared to the tiny stadiums I'd been playing in for two years."

"When I got into my uniform with my old No. 56 on it and went out to the field, I could feel my heart pounding under my shirt. What a feeling it was standing on the mound listening to the national anthem, waiting to pitch my first game. I felt like I was standing on top of Mount Everest. I thought to myself, *how lucky I was to experience this twice in the same lifetime.*"

In his first game against the Dodgers, he lost. Then came this game. This game, as far as I'm concerned was the pinnacle of Jim Bouton's career. It was at San Francisco's Candlestick Park, September 14, 1978, eight years, two months and three days after winning his last major league game. Jim Bouton won once more beating the Giants 4-1.

He pitched six innings, struck out two, walked three and allowed only one unearned run. It was his own error that caused the run.

I spoke to Jim about this game. He enjoyed talking about it very much.

"It was a very windy day, and I felt a tremendous amount of pressure on me. Probably more pressure than I've ever felt in my life. I had already pitched against the Dodgers...the Giants were fighting for the pennant that year. I remember that after my game against the Dodgers when they knocked me out in the fourth inning, some people from the Cincinnati Reds and the Giants appealed to the baseball commissioner that it wasn't fair for the Braves to pitch me, somebody who had just come out of the minor leagues and didn't deserve to be in the big leagues, they should pitch me against the Dodgers in a pennant race and it wasn't fair. He should order that the Braves must also pitch me against the Giants and the Cincinnati Reds. So here is my chance and that game I think probably knocked them out of the pennant race...the knuckler was working very well and I would have shut them out if I hadn't thrown a double play ball into center field."

The Giants hitters had a strange reaction to this game.

Bill Madlock who went zero for two said, "Next time I'm going to bring up my little boy to bat against him."

Darrell Evans said, "It was the most humiliating experience of my life." Evans was one for three.

Mike Ivie simply said, "He was terrible." Ivie went zero for three.

Jim thinks their reaction was rather comical.

"These guys who were saying I had nothing...that was utter nonsense because before the games are played, they always take batting practice and there is always some old coach out there lobbing them in and they have no trouble blasting those balls all over the place. As a matter of fact, they like to put on home run shows where the old coach throws in some lollypops and then they pop them out of the park. I wasn't throwing any different that those old coaches except that my ball was moving. How is it possible for a team in a pennant race not hit me unless I had good stuff? I thought their comments were embarrassing to themselves. Here they are in a pennant race, and you got a guy out there who they claim has nothing and they don't do anything with it. Can you imagine today a guy coming along and being inserted in a pennant race in September who hadn't played in the big leagues for eight years, guys are complaining that he doesn't belong there and he beats the Yankees or the Red Sox? Imagine the human cry today on something like that."

Jim feels as though he definitely deserved to be in the big leagues at that point.

"I earned my way into the big leagues; it was not a celebrity walk on. I had one of the best pitching records in all of the minor leagues. I won eleven games in Savannah; it's not easy to win eleven games in double A. Not too many guys win eleven games in double A and if they do, they're in the big leagues pretty soon."

Jim feels as though he pitched well in the next two games he pitched, even though he didn't get the wins.

"Then they pitched me against Cincinnati, and I think I pitched eight innings and Cincinnati beat me 2-1 but it was a five hitter, and (Reds Manager) Sparkey Anderson said 'He deserves to be here.' How many guys pitch a five hit complete game against the Cincinnati Reds during a pennant race? They had Pete Rose and Bench and all those guys. In the Houston game, I could have won that one too. I think I left in the eighth inning. It was a 2-2 tie at that point and I got no decision. I had three good games...I could have won all three."

"I came back after a whole career outside of the game. I don't think anybody ever came back to a major sport after eight years. It was not a celebrity walk on, I was still the author of *Ball Four* and I was anything but a celebrity as far as baseball was concerned. Marty Appel (head of publicity for major league baseball) told me that he recommended to (Commissioner) Bowie Kuhn that baseball pick up this story and follow it because it was the story about a guy who loved baseball so much that he was willing to give up his television career and come back to baseball. He thought it was a story that showed baseball in a very good light. Bowie Kuhn didn't want to do it because he had had a problem with me over *Ball Four*. Baseball ignored my comeback. Imagine today, somebody coming along. Pick any guy who retired eight years ago, stick him in a pennant race against the Yankees and the Red Sox and ask if that would be a story."

In his book, Jim says he won this game with his head as much as with his arm.

"It wasn't my lack of speed that threw them off, as the hitters claimed. All season long, these guys clobber batting practice pitchers (usually old coaches) who throw the ball even slower than I do. No, what mostly did them in was their own conviction that they ought to be knocking this old sportscaster out of the box in the first inning."

"I understood that the duel between pitcher and hitter was a relationship and I was able to use their anger to my advantage. By feeling instead of thinking, my body chose the proper pitch, speed and location. All I had to do was execute. It's like bullfighting, where the bull knows the fighter is out there but he can't quite get a hold of him."

Jim thought about playing a few more years, but didn't. "Being there was not as much fun as getting there. The real experience of baseball was the bus rides, the country ballparks and the chili at 3 AM with a bunch of guys chasing a dream. Making it to the major leagues a second time was going to be the ultimate achievement that would finally do it for me. To do what? I wasn't sure. I only knew that I didn't feel right about myself and it had something to do with acceptance and recognition."

The New York Yankees have a legendary old timers' game every year. Jim Bouton, who made more than a few enemies in baseball, was never invited back to Yankee Stadium for the annual Old Timers' day.

In 1998, Jim's son Michael wrote a letter to Yankee owner George Steinbrenner and asked him to bring Jim back for the 1998 Old Timers' day game. Steinbrenner liked the idea and on July 25, 1998, Jim once again stood on a major league pitcher's mound. On his first pitch, his hat flew off (which used to happen often in his younger years) and the announcer called 'BALL FOUR'! It was just great.

I had a chance to meet Jim Bouton in person in 2005. He was promoting his latest book *Foul Ball* that was about his fight to save Waconnah Park, a legendary minor league baseball field in Pittsfield, Massachusetts.

I so enjoyed meeting him and found him to be very sharp and gregarious.

Jim Bouton is a man who lives his life his way. He has endured some hardship in his life. His daughter, Laurie, was killed in an automobile accident in 1997 at the age of thirty-one.

He is someone to be admired. I know I admire the man very much. Even though he was a twenty-one game winner way back in 1963 and won two games in the World Series, Jim never stood as tall as he did when he came all the way back on September 14, 1978.

Atlanta Braves 4, San Francisco Giants 1

Game Played on Thursday, September 14, 1978 (D) at Candlestick Park

```
ATL N    0  1  0    0  0  0    2  1  0  -   4  7  3
SF  N    0  0  1    0  0  0    0  0  0  -   1  3  3
```

BATTING

Atlanta Braves	AB	R	H	RBI	BB	SO	PO	A
Royster ss	5	0	1	1	0	0	0	2
Office cf	4	0	0	0	1	1	1	0
Matthews rf	5	0	2	0	0	1	5	0
Burroughs lf	3	0	1	0	1	0	2	0
Bonnell pr,lf	0	1	0	0	0	0	0	0
Nolan c	3	1	0	0	1	0	5	0
Murphy 1b	4	2	1	1	0	1	8	1
Hubbard 2b	3	0	1	2	0	1	2	7
Gilbreath 3b	3	0	1	0	1	1	2	0
Bouton p	2	0	0	0	0	0	2	1
Beall ph	0	0	0	0	1	0	0	0
Skok p	1	0	0	0	0	0	0	0
Garber p	0	0	0	0	0	0	0	0
Totals	33	4	7	4	5	5	27	11

FIELDING -
DP: 1. Royster-Hubbard-Murphy.
E: Nolan (4), Gilbreath (6), Bouton (1).

BATTING -
2B: Royster (16,off Halicki); Burroughs (30,off Moffitt).
3B: Gilbreath (3,off Halicki).
SH: Hubbard (3,off Halicki).
IBB: Office (2,by Halicki).
Team LOB: 8.

BASERUNNING -
SB: Matthews (8,2nd base off Halicki/Tamargo); Murphy (11,2nd base off Halicki/Tamarg
Nolan (3,2nd base off Halicki/Tamargo).

San Francisco Giants	AB	R	H	RBI	BB	SO	PO	A
Madlock 2b	3	1	0	0	1	1	0	3
Whitfield lf	4	0	1	0	0	0	2	0
Moffitt p	0	0	0	0	0	0	1	1
Ivie 1b	3	0	0	1	0	2	13	1
Evans 3b	3	0	1	0	1	0	2	2
Cruz cf,lf	3	0	1	0	1	0	3	0
Dwyer rf	4	0	0	0	0	0	0	0
Tamargo c	4	0	0	0	0	0	5	0
Metzger ss	3	0	0	0	1	0	1	2

Halicki p	2	0	0	0	0	0	0	2
Herndon ph,cf	1	0	0	0	0	1	0	0
Totals	30	1	3	1	4	4	27	11

FIELDING -
DP: 1. Halicki-Metzger-Ivie.
E: Dwyer (2), Tamargo (6), Halicki (4).

BATTING -
2B: Cruz (11,off Bouton); Evans (22,off Bouton).
SF: Ivie (3,off Bouton).
Team LOB: 7.

BASERUNNING -
SB: Whitfield 2 (4,2nd base off Bouton/Nolan 2).

PITCHING

Atlanta Braves	IP	H	R	ER	BB	SO	HR
Bouton W(1-1)	6	3	1	0	3	2	0
Skok	2	0	0	0	1	2	0
Garber SV(24)	1	0	0	0	0	0	0
Totals	9	3	1	0	4	4	0

San Francisco Giants	IP	H	R	ER	BB	SO	HR
Halicki L(8-9)	7	5	3	2	4	5	0
Moffitt	2	2	1	1	1	0	0
Totals	9	7	4	3	5	5	0

IBB: Halicki (9,Office).

Umpires: Paul Pryor, Terry Tata, Satch Davidson, Ed Vargo

Time of Game: 2:25   **Attendance:** 3358

Starting Lineups:

Atlanta Braves		San Francisco Giants	
1. Royster	ss	Madlock	2b
2. Office	cf	Whitfield	lf
3. Matthews	rf	Ivie	1b
4. Burroughs	lf	Evans	3b
5. Nolan	c	Cruz	cf
6. Murphy	1b	Dwyer	rf
7. Hubbard	2b	Tamargo	c
8. Gilbreath	3b	Metzger	ss
9. Bouton	p	Halicki	p

BRAVES 1ST: Royster made an out to left; Office grounded out (shortstop to first); Matthews singled; Matthews stole second; Burroughs walked; Nolan grounded out (second to first); 0 R, 1 H, 0 E, 2 LOB. Braves 0, Giants 0.

GIANTS 1ST: Madlock was called out on strikes; Whitfield singled to right; Whitfield stole second; Ivie struck out; Evans made an out to right; 0 R, 1 H, 0 E, 1 LOB. Braves 0, Giants 0.

BRAVES 2ND: Murphy reached on an error by Halicki [Murphy to first]; Murphy stole second [Murphy to third (error by Tamargo)]; Hubbard out on a sacrifice bunt (pitcher to first) [Murphy scored (unearned)]; Gilbreath grounded out (second to first); Bouton made an out to center; 1 R, 0 H, 2 E, 0 LOB. Braves 1, Giants 0.

GIANTS 2ND: Cruz doubled; Dwyer grounded out (second to first) [Cruz to third]; Tamargo grounded out (second to first); Metzger walked; Halicki popped to third in foul territory; 0 R, 1 H, 0 E, 2 LOB. Braves 1, Giants 0.

BRAVES 3RD: Royster grounded out (third to first); Office struck out; Matthews made an out to center; 0 R, 0 H, 0 E, 0 LOB. Braves 1, Giants 0.

GIANTS 3RD: Madlock walked; Whitfield reached on an error by Bouton [Madlock to third, Whitfield to first]; Ivie hit a sacrifice fly to left [Madlock scored (unearned)]; Whitfield stole second [Whitfield to third (error by Nolan)]; Evans grounded out (second to first); Cruz walked; Dwyer made an out to right; 1 R, 0 H, 2 E, 2 LOB. Braves 1, Giants 1.

BRAVES 4TH: Burroughs made an out to center; Nolan grounded out (first unassisted); Murphy was called out on strikes; 0 R, 0 H, 0 E, 0 LOB. Braves 1, Giants 1.

GIANTS 4TH: Tamargo made an out to right; Metzger made an out to center; Halicki made an out to left; 0 R, 0 H, 0 E, 0 LOB. Braves 1, Giants 1.

BRAVES 5TH: Hubbard made an out to left; Gilbreath tripled to right; Bouton grounded out (first unassisted); Royster grounded out (third to first); 0 R, 1 H, 0 E, 1 LOB. Braves 1, Giants 1.

GIANTS 5TH: Madlock made an out to third; Whitfield grounded out (pitcher to first); Ivie reached on an error by Gilbreath [Ivie to first]; Evans doubled to left [Ivie to third]; Cruz popped to catcher in foul territory; 0 R, 1 H, 1 E, 2 LOB. Braves 1, Giants 1.

BRAVES 6TH: Office grounded out (second to first); Matthews singled; Burroughs grounded into a double play (pitcher to shortstop to first) [Matthews out at second]; 0 R, 1 H, 0 E, 0 LOB. Braves 1, Giants 1.

GIANTS 6TH: Dwyer made an out to right; Tamargo grounded out (first to pitcher); Metzger grounded out (second to pitcher); 0 R, 0 H, 0 E, 0 LOB. Braves 1, Giants 1.

BRAVES 7TH: Nolan walked; Nolan stole second; Murphy singled [Nolan scored]; Hubbard struck out; Gilbreath struck out; BEALL BATTED FOR BOUTON; Beall walked [Murphy to second]; Royster doubled [Murphy scored, Beall to third]; Office was walked intentionally; Matthews struck out; 2 R, 2 H, 0 E, 3 LOB. Braves 3, Giants 1.

GIANTS 7TH: SKOK REPLACED BEALL (PITCHING); HERNDON BATTED FOR HALICKI; Herndon struck out; Madlock made an out to second; Whitfield grounded out (second to first); 0 R, 0 H, 0 E, 0 LOB.

Braves 3, Giants 1.

BRAVES 8TH: HERNDON STAYED IN GAME (PLAYING CF); MOFFITT
REPLACED WHITFIELD (PITCHING); CRUZ CHANGED POSITIONS (PLAYING
LF); Burroughs doubled to right [Burroughs to third (error by
Dwyer)]; BONNELL RAN FOR BURROUGHS; Nolan grounded out (first
unassisted); Murphy grounded out (pitcher to first); Hubbard
singled to center [Bonnell scored]; Gilbreath walked [Hubbard to
second]; Skok forced Hubbard (third unassisted); 1 R, 2 H, 1 E,
2 LOB. Braves 4, Giants 1.

GIANTS 8TH: BONNELL STAYED IN GAME (PLAYING LF); Ivie was called
out on strikes; Evans walked; Cruz grounded into a double play
(shortstop to second to first) [Evans out at second]; 0 R, 0 H,
0 E, 0 LOB. Braves 4, Giants 1.

BRAVES 9TH: Royster made an out to first; Office popped to third
in foul territory; Matthews grounded out (first to pitcher); 0
R, 0 H, 0 E, 0 LOB. Braves 4, Giants 1.

GIANTS 9TH: GARBER REPLACED SKOK (PITCHING); Dwyer made an out
to right; Tamargo grounded out (second to first); Metzger
grounded out (shortstop to first); 0 R, 0 H, 0 E, 0 LOB. Braves
4, Giants 1.

Final Totals	R	H	E	LOB
Braves	4	7	3	8
Giants	1	3	3	7

CHAPTER SIXTEEN

May 26, 1959
Pittsburgh Pirates at Milwaukee Braves

Greatest Pitching Performance

ON A TUESDAY IN MAY of 1959, there was a game played in Milwaukee, Wisconsin between the Pittsburgh Pirates and the defending National League champion Milwaukee Braves. As the game began, the Braves were in first place, the Pirates in third, three and one-half games behind. Pitching that day were two thirty-three-year-old veteran pitchers, both proven winners.

Lew Burdette was pitching for the Braves. Burdette had been a twenty game winner in 1958, and in 1957, he was the hero of the World Series, winning three games to help the Braves beat the Yankees and bring a world championship to Milwaukee.

Pitching for the Pirates was Harvey Haddix whose best year was in 1953 when he was with the St. Louis Cardinals. That year Harvey won twenty games, lost only nine and led the league with six shutouts.

As this day began, Burdette was having a great year again. He already had seven wins against only two losses.

Harvey Haddix was only 5'9" and 160 lbs., but he was very rugged. He was raised on the family farm in Ohio. He remained a farmer for the rest of his life, always returning to his own farm in Ohio after the baseball season ended.

He entered pro ball in the late forties and made it to the majors in 1952 with the St. Louis Cardinals. He became very close to Harry 'The Cat' Brecheen, a veteran pitcher who was nearing the end of his career. Because of that friendship, the young Haddix was nicknamed 'Kitten' by his teammates.

One of his roommates with the Cardinals was a pitcher, Paul "Lefty" La Palme. He remembers Harvey.

"He was extremely wiry and very cat like, an excellent fielder. He was a great competitor and a great guy. A great humanitarian. He was such a competitor and just such a great guy to be around. Knowing Harvey made me a better person."

I asked Paul if Harvey was a fast ball or a curve ball pitcher.

"He threw both very very well. And he also had a great change up to go with it."

Harvey Haddix stayed with the Cardinals until early 1956 when he was traded to the Philadelphia Phillies. He stayed in Philadelphia through 1957, then went to the Cincinnati Reds in 1958, and became a Pirate in 1959. He was an exceptionally good fielder, having won several gold glove awards. Haddix was a member of the Pirates starting rotation in 1959 and had a record of four wins and two losses as he walked to the mound at County Stadium in Milwaukee, May 26, 1959 ready to face the Braves.

No one could have known that history was about to be made. Harvey Haddix was about to pitch the entire game for the Pirates, a game that went thirteen innings. Harvey did something no one ever had done before, hasn't done since and it is doubtful anyone will ever do again.

Harvey Haddix pitched twelve perfect innings! Not nine, but twelve. Thirty-six men up and thirty-six men down. He mowed them down, one after another.

Burdette, pitching for the Braves also did well. He pitched the whole game, gave up twelve hits, no walks and allowed no runs.

Harvey wasn't feeling well.

He later said, "I got up at seven o'clock to get to the airport in Pittsburgh in time for the ten o'clock flight to Milwaukee. When we arrived in Milwaukee about noon, I headed straight for my bed in the Schroder Hotel. I slept until four, got up, ate a steak and went to the park on the bus. When I warmed up, I just didn't feel good. I'd been fighting off a slight cold and I just figured to do my best."

With all that going on, he watched his Pirate teammates go three up and three down in the top of the first.

The Pirates then took to the field and Haddix went to his place on the mound. After his warm-up pitches, the first batter he faced was Johnny O'Brien. He quietly got O'Brien to ground out to the shortstop. Eddie Mathews followed with a line drive that went right in the glove of Rocky Nelson at first. Henry Aaron flied out to center. Three up and three down, a quiet perfect inning.

The game kept going on and on with no score. The Pirates occasionally reached base, but could never score. The Braves kept going down, inning after inning, three up and three down.

The Pirates had their best chance in the third inning. With one out, fast running Roman Mejias was the base runner at first. Harvey Haddix himself was up at bat and hit a sizzler back to Burdette. Burdette stopped the ball with his bare hand and the ball rolled behind the mound. Mejias had made it to second but with the ball still rolling around, he broke for third. Johnny Logan, the Braves' shortstop, rushed for the ball, scooped it up and threw a perfect strike to third baseman Eddie Mathews to nail Mejias. Instead of having runners on first and second with one out and a fast runner at second, the Pirates had a runner on first with two out. This proved huge because the next batter up was the leadoff batter, Dick Schofield. He hit a single to right. If Mejias was at second, he could have scored the games first run. After Schofield reached first, the Pirates had runners on first and second with two out, but Bill Virdon followed and flied out to left ending the threat and the inning.

As the game progressed, the reality of a perfect game became more and more evident. After eight innings, the score remained nothing-nothing and the Pirates had another opportunity in the top of the ninth. They had runners on first and third with two outs and Bob Skinner at bat. Running on third was Bill Virdon. He wanted badly to score a run so Haddix could take the mound in the last of the ninth with a lead; but Skinner hit a come backer to the pitcher and was retired, another squandered opportunity.

Even though Haddix was on the visiting team, the fans were supportive of him. With two out in the ninth, the batter was opposing pitcher Lou Burdette. After Burdette struck out to end the inning, the fans of Milwaukee gave Harvey a standing ovation. He had just pitched nine perfect innings.

Between innings, the Pirate players said nothing to Haddix in the dugout about the game. They focused on the batters, trying to encourage them to get on base and score. When Haddix went to the mound, the players were shouting words of encouragement, not mentioning the term 'perfect game'.

At the top of the thirteenth, the Pirates came to bat against Burdette with hopes of scoring the first run of the game. Joe Christopher, batting for the first time in the major leagues, led off by grounding to the pitcher. Harvey Haddix followed and flied out to center. Dick Schofield singled to left but then Bill Virdon grounded out to second to end the inning. Then came the last of the thirteenth. Harvey Haddix still had his perfect game going on but it was about to end. The ending was completely bizarre.

Felix Mantilla was the first batter up. This was the first at-bat of the day for Felix who entered the game in the eleventh inning. Felix hit a ground ball to third and third baseman Don Hoak fielded the ball, threw to first, but threw low and the ball hit first baseman Rocky Nelson's foot. Mantilla had reached first on a error.

He was the Braves' first base runner of the day. Then came the argument. Danny Murtaugh, the Pirates' manager argued that Mantilla had turned toward second after the hit and the Pirates should be allowed a putout. Umpire Frank Dascoli was firm. The fans had an interesting reaction. They didn't cheer, even though their home team player had reached first. The didn't boo either, but you could feel the disappointment of the crowd with that certain 'hum'. The perfect game was gone, but the no-hitter was still alive.

The next batter was the great Eddie Mathews. In a move that would never occur today, Mathews, a power hitter who would eventually hit over five hundred home runs, bunted. He successfully sacrificed Mantilla to second base. Henry Aaron, the eventual home run king came up. Haddix was ordered to intentionally walk Aaron, setting up a possible double play. With runners on first and second, one out, a no-hitter still going, the next batter was Joe Adcock.

Adcock was a powerful, thirty-one-year-old cleanup hitter who would hit 336 home runs in the major leagues. He was a powerfully built guy, 6'4", 220 lbs. In four at-bats this afternoon, Adcock struck out twice and grounded out the other two times. This time, he connected on Haddix' second pitch; a slider up high. This one went deep flying between center fielder Bill Virdon and right fielder Roman Mejias. Virdon made a gallant leap to try to keep the ball in the park, but could not. The ball went just over the fence for a home run; at least that's what it looked like. Mantilla had already scored the winning run, but a base running error by Aaron turned this home run into a double.

Aaron thought the ball had stayed in the park with Mantilla's run ending the game. Aaron had rounded second and then, thinking the game ended with a 1-0 score, Aaron, standing near shortstop, made his way back to the Braves' first base dugout, crossing over the pitchers mound. Adcock kept running as the Pirate players left the field. Now, the umpires had to get to work. How do we handle this one? Aaron never touched third base; much less, home plate.

Milwaukee manager Fred Haney came out with his coaches and brought Aaron and Adcock with him. He had them go to third base and second base respectively and trot home. They did so but the umpires ruled Adcock had passed Aaron on the base path and was therefore out, so his run wouldn't count. His home run would turn into a double. The game would end with a score of 2-0.

The next day the National League President, Warren Giles had to make a ruling. He ruled that since it was not a home run, but a double, then as soon as Mantilla scored, the game was over. Therefore, the final score was 1-0.

In any event, with one swing, Adcock took away the no-hitter, the shutout and the win for Harvey Haddix. Haddix, who had just pitched the best game in the history of baseball, did so with a loss. It really stung. Again, the crowd didn't cheer.

The Sporting News covered this game in their June 3, 1959 edition. They pointed out that Harvey Haddix was disappointed, but more at the loss of the game, not the loss of a no-hitter or perfect game.

"My main idea was to win. I knew we needed this game to stretch our winning streak and try to catch the Braves and as far as I'm concerned, the records don't mean much if we lose. I knew I had a no-hitter because the scoreboard was in full view, but I wasn't so certain about it being a perfect game. I also lost track of the innings since the scoreboard only carried ten innings. I thought perhaps I might have walked a batter in the early innings and nobody on the bench said anything to me. My main aim was to win. It was just another loss but it hurt a little more."

After Adcock's hit, as the Pirates team came off the field, everyone surrounded Haddix. Manager Danny Murtaugh gave his 160 lb. Pitcher a bear hug.

In the locker room, Murtaugh said, "What a shame to lose a game for a fellow like that."

Bill Virdon said, "A pitcher does this once in a lifetime - once in baseball history - and we can't win the game for him. To think, Adcock's ball just barely got over the fence."

Veteran pitcher Bob Friend said it best, "We're happy to be teammates of a man who pitched the greatest game in history. We were breathing with him on every pitch."

Paul La Palme was no longer a teammate of Harvey's when he pitched this game, but he remembers it very well. I asked Paul if keeping the pitcher in the game for thirteen innings was a surprise.

"In those days, everything was so different. That was a pitchers goal. Your goal is to pitch the full ballgame. You never want to come out. Nobody ever talked about the pitch count. They didn't go by pitch counts. They watched you and how you acted. If you got sluggish and you weren't following through which means that your legs are getting tired. Then the pitches are going high. Those are the things they used to look for in my day."

Isn't it interesting that the greatest single game pitching performance of all time was a loss?

Mark Miller is a baseball historian who lives near Harvey's old farm in Ohio. He has only good things to say about Harvey Haddix.

"Harvey was just a wonderful person, just a good old country boy that made it big because he had a pretty good fast ball and a super curve ball. He could throw it hard, but he had a great curve. That's what put him apart from everyone else. He had a curve that was one of those twelve o'clock six o'clocks, it just went straight down. He was a twenty game winner as a rookie."

I wondered if Mark ever heard Harvey speak about this game.

"He did not think that was the most important game that he pitched. He thought being the winning pitcher in game seven of the 1960 World Series was much larger for him and he actually won two games in the 1960 World Series. Everybody remembers Mazeroski but nobody remembers that Harvey was the winning pitcher."

Mark, who knew Harvey and his family, says, "He has two brothers that are living here in Clark County. One younger, one older. Marcia, Harvey's wife still lives here in town. The first time I met him I was about nine years old and I was riding my bike out by his farm and we stopped in. He was actually up on a ladder painting the house, and I had an old ratty Reds hat and he said 'Boy, it looks like you need a new hat'. He went down into his garage and pulled out a bag of Cincinnati Reds hats that he had gotten when he pitched for the Reds. He was just using them to paint in and he threw me a Cincinnati Reds hat that had number 20 on the bill. I didn't think too much about it, but that would have been Frank Robinson's hat. Had I saved that, I'd probably have big bucks now, but I wore it as a kid and wore it out. He was just a common guy around here. You'd see him around town or shopping or anything and if you wanted an autograph he'd sign you an autograph and he'd come out and do little clinics for the kids...He was a great guy."

Mark reminded me that the game was not broadcasted in Pittsburgh that night.

"I believe that was supposed to be broadcasted back in Pittsburgh that night, however (Vice President Richard) Nixon had created one of his faux pas' as Vice President and he was preparing for his run for the White House, and went on national TV that night for a speech. I don't know if it was the Checkers Speech or one of those speeches, and he went on and pre-empted the game so the game was not broadcasted live in Pittsburgh that night."

After his playing career, Harvey Haddix stayed in baseball for many years as pitching coach for many teams. He always spoke with pride about this game, always combining careers of baseball and farming.

I remember when he was the pitching coach for the Boston Red Sox in the seventies. One year I was listening to the game on radio and it was the last game of the season.

Veteran broadcaster Jim 'Possom' Woods reminded Harvey that, "Tomorrow you'll be on your farm in Ohio."

Harvey responded, "No, I'll be there tonight."

One former Brave that remembers this game is Carlton Willey.

"Boy I know one thing. I know both of them (Burdette and Haddix) pitched a heck of a ball game. We were lucky, we scored... Whether you're on the same team or on the other team, you hate to see someone lose a game like that."

Harvey Haddix passed away on January 8, 1994. I doubt there will ever be a game like the one he pitched on May 26, 1959.

Milwaukee Braves 1, Pittsburgh Pirates 0

Game Played on Tuesday, May 26, 1959 (N) at County Stadium

```
PIT N    0  0  0    0  0  0    0  0  0    0  0  0    0  -   0 12  1
MIL N    0  0  0    0  0  0    0  0  0    0  0  0    1  -   1  1  0
```

BATTING

Pittsburgh Pirates	AB	R	H	RBI	BB	SO	PO	A
Schofield ss	6	0	3	0	0	0	2	4
Virdon cf	6	0	1	0	0	0	8	0
Burgess c	5	0	0	0	0	0	8	0
Nelson 1b	5	0	2	0	0	0	15	0
Skinner lf	5	0	1	0	0	0	4	0
Mazeroski 2b	5	0	1	0	0	1	0	0
Hoak 3b	5	0	2	0	0	1	0	6
Mejias rf	3	0	1	0	0	0	1	0
Stuart ph	1	0	0	0	0	0	0	0
Christopher rf	1	0	0	0	0	0	0	0
Haddix p	5	0	1	0	0	0	0	2
Totals	47	0	12	0	0	2	38	12

FIELDING -
E: Hoak (5).

Milwaukee Braves	AB	R	H	RBI	BB	SO	PO	A
O'Brien 2b	3	0	0	0	0	1	2	5
Rice ph	1	0	0	0	0	0	0	0
Mantilla 2b	1	1	0	0	0	0	1	2
Mathews 3b	4	0	0	0	0	1	2	3
Aaron rf	4	0	0	0	1	0	1	0
Adcock 1b	5	0	1	1	0	2	17	3
Covington lf	4	0	0	0	0	0	4	0
Crandall c	4	0	0	0	0	0	2	1
Pafko cf	4	0	0	0	0	1	6	0
Logan ss	4	0	0	0	0	0	3	5
Burdette p	4	0	0	0	0	3	1	4
Totals	38	1	1	1	1	8	39	23

FIELDING -
DP: 3. Adcock-Logan-Adcock, Mathews-O'Brien-Adcock, Adcock-Logan.

BATTING -
2B: Adcock (3,off Haddix).
SH: Mathews (1,off Haddix).
IBB: Aaron (2,by Haddix).
Team LOB: 1.

PITCHING

Pittsburgh Pirates	IP	H	R	ER	BB	SO	HR
Haddix L(4-3)	12.2	1	1	0	1	8	0

Milwaukee Braves	IP	H	R	ER	BB	SO	HR
Burdette W(8-2)	13	12	0	0	0	2	0

IBB: Haddix (5,Aaron).

Umpires: Vinnie Smith, Frank Dascoli, Frank Secory, Hal Dixon

Time of Game: 2:54 **Attendance:** 19194

Starting Lineups:

Pittsburgh Pirates		Milwaukee Braves	
1. Schofield	ss	O'Brien	2b
2. Virdon	cf	Mathews	3b
3. Burgess	c	Aaron	rf
4. Nelson	1b	Adcock	1b
5. Skinner	lf	Covington	lf
6. Mazeroski	2b	Crandall	c
7. Hoak	3b	Pafko	cf
8. Mejias	rf	Logan	ss
9. Haddix	p	Burdette	p

PIRATES 1ST: Schofield popped to third; Virdon grounded out (catcher to first); Burgess made an out to left; 0 R, 0 H, 0 E, 0 LOB. Pirates 0, Braves 0.

BRAVES 1ST: O'Brien grounded out (shortstop to first); Mathews lined to first; Aaron made an out to center; 0 R, 0 H, 0 E, 0 LOB. Pirates 0, Braves 0.

PIRATES 2ND: Nelson singled to center; Skinner grounded into a double play (first to shortstop to first) [Nelson out at second]; Mazeroski struck out; 0 R, 1 H, 0 E, 0 LOB. Pirates 0, Braves 0.

BRAVES 2ND: Adcock struck out; Covington lined to first; Crandall grounded out (third to first); 0 R, 0 H, 0 E, 0 LOB. Pirates 0, Braves 0.

PIRATES 3RD: Hoak singled to second; Mejias forced Hoak (third to second); Haddix singled to pitcher [Mejias out at third (shortstop to third)]; Schofield singled to right [Haddix to third]; Virdon made an out to left; 0 R, 3 H, 0 E, 2 LOB. Pirates 0, Braves 0.

BRAVES 3RD: Pafko made an out to right; Logan lined to shortstop; Burdette was called out on strikes; 0 R, 0 H, 0 E, 0 LOB. Pirates 0, Braves 0.

PIRATES 4TH: Burgess lined to center; Nelson grounded out (second to first); Skinner singled to center; Mazeroski made an out to center; 0 R, 1 H, 0 E, 1 LOB. Pirates 0, Braves 0.

BRAVES 4TH: O'Brien was called out on strikes; Mathews made an out to center; Aaron made an out to center; 0 R, 0 H, 0 E, 0 LOB. Pirates 0, Braves 0.

PIRATES 5TH: Hoak grounded out (shortstop to first); Mejias singled to right; Haddix grounded into a double play (third to second to first) [Mejias out at second]; 0 R, 1 H, 0 E, 0 LOB. Pirates 0, Braves 0.

BRAVES 5TH: Adcock grounded out (third to first); Covington made an out to left; Crandall made an out to left; 0 R, 0 H, 0 E, 0 LOB. Pirates 0, Braves 0.

PIRATES 6TH: Schofield grounded out (second to first); Virdon grounded out (first to pitcher); Burgess made an out to left; 0 R, 0 H, 0 E, 0 LOB. Pirates 0, Braves 0.

BRAVES 6TH: Pafko popped to first; Logan grounded out (shortstop to first); Burdette struck out; 0 R, 0 H, 0 E, 0 LOB. Pirates 0, Braves 0.

PIRATES 7TH: Nelson grounded out (pitcher to first); Skinner made an out to right; Mazeroski made an out to center; 0 R, 0 H, 0 E, 0 LOB. Pirates 0, Braves 0.

BRAVES 7TH: O'Brien grounded out (third to first); Mathews struck out; Aaron grounded out (third to first); 0 R, 0 H, 0 E, 0 LOB. Pirates 0, Braves 0.

PIRATES 8TH: Hoak was called out on strikes; Mejias grounded out (third to first); Haddix grounded out (shortstop to first); 0 R, 0 H, 0 E, 0 LOB. Pirates 0, Braves 0.

BRAVES 8TH: Adcock struck out; Covington made an out to left; Crandall grounded out (third to first); 0 R, 0 H, 0 E, 0 LOB. Pirates 0, Braves 0.

PIRATES 9TH: Schofield grounded out (second to first); Virdon singled to center; Burgess made an out to center; Nelson singled to right [Virdon to third]; Skinner grounded out (pitcher to first); 0 R, 2 H, 0 E, 2 LOB. Pirates 0, Braves 0.

BRAVES 9TH: Pafko struck out; Logan made an out to left; Burdette struck out; 0 R, 0 H, 0 E, 0 LOB. Pirates 0, Braves 0.

PIRATES 10TH: Mazeroski grounded out (second to first); Hoak singled to left; STUART BATTED FOR MEJIAS; Stuart made an out to center; Haddix grounded out (pitcher to first); 0 R, 1 H, 0 E, 1 LOB. Pirates 0, Braves 0.

BRAVES 10TH: CHRISTOPHER REPLACED STUART (PLAYING RF); RICE BATTED FOR O'BRIEN; Rice made an out to center; **Debut game for Joe Christopher;** Mathews made an out to center; Aaron grounded out (shortstop to first); 0 R, 0 H, 0 E, 0 LOB. Pirates 0, Braves 0.

PIRATES 11TH: MANTILLA REPLACED RICE (PLAYING 2B); Schofield singled to left; Virdon forced Schofield (second to shortstop); Burgess grounded into a double play (first to shortstop) [Virdon out at second]; 0 R, 1 H, 0 E, 0 LOB. Pirates 0, Braves 0.

BRAVES 11TH: Adcock grounded out (shortstop to first); Covington lined to center; Crandall made an out to center; 0 R, 0 H, 0 E, 0 LOB. Pirates 0, Braves 0.

PIRATES 12TH: Nelson made an out to left; Skinner lined to first; Mazeroski singled to center; Hoak forced Mazeroski (shortstop to second); 0 R, 1 H, 0 E, 1 LOB. Pirates 0, Braves 0.

BRAVES 12TH: Pafko grounded out (pitcher to first); Logan made an out to center; Burdette grounded out (third to first); 0 R, 0 H, 0 E, 0 LOB. Pirates 0, Braves 0.

PIRATES 13TH: Christopher grounded out (pitcher to first); Haddix made an out to center; Schofield singled to left; Virdon grounded out (second to first); 0 R, 1 H, 0 E, 1 LOB. Pirates 0, Braves 0.

BRAVES 13TH: Mantilla reached on an error by Hoak; Mathews out on a sacrifice bunt (pitcher to first) [Mantilla to second]; Aaron was walked intentionally; Adcock doubled to left [Mantilla scored (unearned), Aaron to third, Adcock out at second (shortstop)]; 1 R, 1 H, 1 E, 1 LOB. Pirates 0, Braves 1.

Final Totals	R	H	E	LOB
Pirates	0	12	1	8
Braves	1	1	0	1

CHAPTER SEVENTEEN

May 11, 1977
Atlanta Braves at Pittsburgh Pirates

Ted Turner, Manager?

BILL VEECK, TOM YAWKEY, PHIL Wrigley, Charlie Finley, George Steinbrenner and on and on. Baseball owners. Guys who own baseball teams. Since Major League Baseball began in 1869, there has always been fascination with the guy or guys that own the teams that compete on the field. The five guys that I mentioned above all have very distinct reputations as owners. Not one of them ever played the game, or ever wore a uniform, but their personalities came through loud and clear in the times their ownership took place. There are so many more, too many to mention.

There have been a few team owners who did at one time wear the uniform. Connie Mack and Charles Comiskey were team owners who had played in the major leagues prior to their ownership. Both of these guys also were managers. Connie Mack owned and managed the Philadelphia Athletics for fifty years, from 1901 to 1950.

Ted Turner was definitely one of the most interesting persons of the twentieth century. He was a television genius. He started out with a television station in Atlanta and ended up with CNN. He became a billionaire, an incredible philanthropist, he was once married to actress Jane Fonda, and he was a very successful yachtsman. He captained his boat **Courageous** to the America's Cup championship in 1977.

In the early seventies, Ted Turner bought the Atlanta Braves baseball team. He put the Braves on coast to coast television every night on his TV station and pretty much was the pioneer of the cable TV/baseball marriage. He was a very hands on owner and wanted to know what was going on himself.

In 1977, the Braves weren't too good. They were managed by Dave Bristol. They didn't start out too badly, on April 22; their record was eight wins, five losses. Then they started to lose. They had lost sixteen in a row and after the games (doubleheader) on May 10 against the Pirates, the Braves' record was eight wins and twenty-one losses.

Ted Turner is not used to this kind of losing streak. He wanted to find out what was wrong with his team. In a bizarre move, he decided to make himself the manager. He told Dave Bristol that he was giving him a ten day leave of absence. Bristol went home, and was bewildered at what was going on.

"I'm going home to Andrews, North Carolina to contemplate, take a little self-inventory. I don't know what I'll do. I think they may be trying to get me to quit."

Ted Turner joined the team in Pittsburgh, donned an Atlanta Braves uniform and informed the team that he was the new Braves manager. When the players arrived at the stadium, they found Ted, in uniform, and with a big chaw of chewing tobacco in his mouth. He did have his lineup cards in his pocket. He explained himself by saying "I want to see if I can find an answer, in the dugout."

One major fault with this whole thing is that Turner didn't know the first thing about being a baseball manager. He didn't know signs or strategy. He had one of his coaches, Vern Benson, take care of that. Ted Turner simply was a cheerleader. Once again, the Braves lost, by a score of 2-1.

I had a very nice conversation with Vern Benson. Vern was a major league player and a long time major league coach. In all, he spent fifty-six years in baseball. I asked him if he remembered this game.

"I remember it very distinctly. He (Turner) said 'I don't know a damn thing about baseball so you run the game.' Fortunately, we lost that game. The commissioner told him that he couldn't manage anymore so I had to take over again the next night. I managed for about a week. We went back to Atlanta and I guess three or four games later, the writers were in the dugout and Turner was in the dugout, and the writers said 'Hey when are you going to bring Bristol back?' Then he (Turner) said 'What for, Vern's the best manager I have.' I went to Cito Gaston, Darrell Chaney, Tom Paciorek, and Andy Messersmith. I knew all of those fellows liked Dave (Bristol). I told them that if you don't say anything, and tell Turner to bring Bristol back, I'm afraid he's going to make a statement that he can't back off of. I was afraid he was going to ask me to take the club the rest of the year, and I didn't want to have anything to do with that. He called Dave in the middle of the ball game and he was back there the next night. So that's the story of me managing in Atlanta."

About Turner, Vern said, "He knew his business. He only started out selling billboards, sign boards and all. Then he took over the TV station. He was a genius in his field, but about baseball he had no clue."

Wayne Minshew, the then Atlanta reporter for *The Sporting News* reported that Turner "simply observed though he signed the official lineup card presented to the umpires before the game."

After the game was over, Ted Turner said, "I had the best seat in the house. I learned that our pitching is coming around. I thought everybody played well in spite of the loss."

He also said, "Managing isn't all that difficult. All you've got to do is score more runs that the other guy."

In all, it was pretty funny. We all laughed at it and I think that might have been the idea. One guy, who wasn't laughing, though, was National League President Chub Feeney. He announced the next day that Turner was in violation of the rules. Major League Rule 20 (a) states that "No manager or player on a club shall directly or indirectly own stock or have any financial interest in the club by which he is employed except under an agreement approved by the commissioner..." Turner had not asked for any such approval and it's doubtful that Commissioner Bowie Kuhn would have given his approval if Turner had asked for it. So the next day, Ted Turner returned to his seat in the stands, and Vern Benson served as the official 'acting manager'. After 17 straight losses, the Braves finally won one, beating the Pirates 6-2. Dave Bristol returned to the Braves the next night and finished the season as the Braves' manager.

Ted Turner continues to this day to be the owner of the Braves. In 1995, with Bobby Cox as manager, the Braves won the World Series, putting Ted Turner on top of the world. A long, long way from where they were, in the doldrums, on May 11, 1977.

Pittsburgh Pirates 2, Atlanta Braves 1

Game Played on Wednesday, May 11, 1977 (N) at Three Rivers Stadium

```
ATL N    0  1  0    0  0  0    0  0  0  -  1  8  0
PIT N    1  0  1    0  0  0    0  0  x  -  2  6  2
```

BATTING

Atlanta Braves	AB	R	H	RBI	BB	SO	PO	A
Royster ss	4	0	1	0	0	1	2	1
Office ph	1	0	0	0	0	1	0	0
Gilbreath 2b	3	0	0	0	0	0	1	1
Moore 3b	4	0	0	0	0	1	2	2
Burroughs rf	3	0	1	0	1	0	1	0
Gaston lf	4	1	0	0	0	0	5	0
Paciorek 1b	4	0	1	0	0	1	6	0
Correll c	4	0	1	0	0	0	4	1
Rockett pr	0	0	0	0	0	0	0	0
Bonnell cf	4	0	3	1	0	0	3	0
Niekro p	2	0	0	0	0	1	0	1
Chaney ph	1	0	1	0	0	0	0	0
Totals	34	1	8	1	1	5	24	6

BATTING -
2B: Bonnell (1,off Candelaria); Chaney (2,off Candelaria).
SH: Gilbreath (2,off Candelaria); Niekro (2,off Candelaria).
Team LOB: 9.

Pittsburgh Pirates	AB	R	H	RBI	BB	SO	PO	A
Moreno cf	4	0	0	0	0	0	3	0
Taveras ss	4	1	0	0	0	1	0	2
Parker rf	3	1	2	1	1	0	3	0
Oliver lf	4	0	1	0	0	0	0	0
Stargell 1b	2	0	1	0	2	0	8	0
Stennett 2b	4	0	1	1	0	1	7	2
Garner 3b	3	0	0	0	1	0	0	4
Dyer c	4	0	1	0	0	1	6	1
Candelaria p	2	0	0	0	1	2	0	1
Gossage p	0	0	0	0	0	0	0	0
Totals	30	2	6	2	5	5	27	10

FIELDING -
E: Moreno (4), Taveras (6).

BATTING -
2B: Stargell (2,off Niekro).
HR: Parker (6,3rd inning off Niekro 0 on 1 out).
IBB: Stargell 2 (3,by Niekro 2).
Team LOB: 9.

BASERUNNING -
CS: Parker (9,3rd base by Niekro/Correll).

PITCHING

Atlanta Braves	IP	H	R	ER	BB	SO	HR
Niekro L(0-7)	8	6	2	2	5	5	1

Pittsburgh Pirates	IP	H	R	ER	BB	SO	HR
Candelaria W(4-0)	8.2	8	1	0	1	4	0
Gossage SV(6)	0.1	0	0	0	0	1	0
Totals	9	8	1	0	1	5	0

WP: Niekro 3 (3).
IBB: Niekro 2 (3,Stargell 2).

Umpires: Jerry Dale, John McSherry, Bill Williams, Bob Engel

Time of Game: 2:15   **Attendance:** 6816

Starting Lineups:

Atlanta Braves		Pittsburgh Pirates	
1. Royster	ss	Moreno	cf
2. Gilbreath	2b	Taveras	ss
3. Moore	3b	Parker	rf
4. Burroughs	rf	Oliver	lf
5. Gaston	lf	Stargell	1b
6. Paciorek	1b	Stennett	2b
7. Correll	c	Garner	3b
8. Bonnell	cf	Dyer	c
9. Niekro	p	Candelaria	p

BRAVES 1ST: Royster singled to center; Gilbreath out on a sacrifice bunt (catcher to second) [Royster to second]; Moore grounded out (first unassisted) [Royster to third]; Burroughs made an out to second; 0 R, 1 H, 0 E, 1 LOB. Braves 0, Pirates 0.

PIRATES 1ST: Moreno grounded out (second to first); Taveras struck out but advanced to first on a wild pitch; Parker singled to center [Taveras to third, Parker to second (on throw to 3b)]; Oliver made an out to third; Stargell was walked intentionally; Stennett singled to third [Taveras scored, Parker to third, Stargell to second]; Garner forced Stennett (shortstop unassisted); 1 R, 2 H, 0 E, 3 LOB. Braves 0, Pirates 1.

BRAVES 2ND: Gaston reached on an error by Taveras [Gaston to first]; Paciorek singled to left [Gaston to second]; Correll popped to catcher in foul territory; Bonnell singled to center [Gaston scored (unearned) (error by Moreno), Paciorek to third, Bonnell to second (error by Moreno)]; Niekro lined to second; Royster popped to second; 1 R, 2 H, 2 E, 2 LOB. Braves 1, Pirates 1.

PIRATES 2ND: Dyer popped to shortstop; Candelaria struck out; Moreno lined to right; 0 R, 0 H, 0 E, 0 LOB. Braves 1, Pirates 1.

BRAVES 3RD: Gilbreath grounded out (second to first); Moore made an out to center; Burroughs grounded out (pitcher to first); 0 R, 0 H, 0 E, 0 LOB. Braves 1, Pirates 1.

PIRATES 3RD: Taveras made an out to center; Parker homered; Oliver singled to left; Stargell grounded out (pitcher to first) [Oliver to second]; Stennett struck out; 1 R, 2 H, 0 E, 1 LOB. Braves 1, Pirates 2.

BRAVES 4TH: Gaston made an out to right; Paciorek grounded out (third to first); Correll grounded out (third to first); 0 R, 0 H, 0 E, 0 LOB. Braves 1, Pirates 2.

PIRATES 4TH: Garner grounded out (third to first); Dyer grounded out (third to first); Candelaria walked; Niekro threw a wild pitch [Candelaria to second]; Moreno made an out to center; 0 R, 0 H, 0 E, 1 LOB. Braves 1, Pirates 2.

BRAVES 5TH: Bonnell doubled to left; Niekro out on a sacrifice bunt (third to second) [Bonnell to third]; Royster struck out; Gilbreath made an out to second; 0 R, 1 H, 0 E, 1 LOB. Braves 1, Pirates 2.

PIRATES 5TH: Taveras made an out to second; Parker lined to first; Oliver lined to left; 0 R, 0 H, 0 E, 0 LOB. Braves 1, Pirates 2.

BRAVES 6TH: Moore struck out; Burroughs singled to third; Gaston made an out to right; Paciorek struck out; 0 R, 1 H, 0 E, 1 LOB. Braves 1, Pirates 2.

PIRATES 6TH: Stargell doubled to right; Stennett grounded out (shortstop to first); Garner walked; Dyer singled to center [Stargell to third, Garner to second]; Candelaria struck out; Moreno made an out to left; 0 R, 2 H, 0 E, 3 LOB. Braves 1, Pirates 2.

BRAVES 7TH: Correll grounded out (shortstop to first); Bonnell singled to shortstop; Niekro struck out; Royster forced Bonnell (shortstop to second); 0 R, 1 H, 0 E, 1 LOB. Braves 1, Pirates 2.

PIRATES 7TH: Taveras made an out to left; Parker walked; Oliver lined to left; Niekro threw a wild pitch [Parker to second]; Stargell was walked intentionally; Parker was caught stealing third (catcher to third); 0 R, 0 H, 0 E, 1 LOB. Braves 1, Pirates 2.

BRAVES 8TH: Gilbreath grounded out (third to first); Moore made an out to right; Burroughs walked; Gaston grounded out (second to first); 0 R, 0 H, 0 E, 1 LOB. Braves 1, Pirates 2.

PIRATES 8TH: Stennett lined to center; Garner made an out to left; Dyer struck out; 0 R, 0 H, 0 E, 0 LOB. Braves 1, Pirates 2.

BRAVES 9TH: Paciorek made an out to center; Correll singled to center; ROCKETT RAN FOR CORRELL; Bonnell made an out to center; CHANEY BATTED FOR NIEKRO; Chaney doubled [Rockett to third];

GOSSAGE REPLACED CANDELARIA (PITCHING); OFFICE BATTED FOR
ROYSTER; Office struck out; 0 R, 2 H, 0 E, 2 LOB. Braves 1,
Pirates 2.

Final Totals	R	H	E	LOB
Braves	1	8	0	9
Pirates	2	6	2	9

CHAPTER EIGHTEEN

June 23, 1971
Philadelphia Phillies at Cincinnati Reds

Greatest Day by a Pitcher

IN A PRIOR CHAPTER, WE covered the Sandy Koufax - Bob Hendley game. Considering the performance of both pitchers, I called that game 'The Greatest Pitched Game'. In another chapter, we covered the Harvey Haddix game when he pitched twelve perfect innings but lost in the thirteenth on an unearned run. That game I considered the 'Greatest Pitching Performance'. Now here's one more.

In this game, we will inject the offensive side of the equation. We will factor in the hitting performance of the pitcher as well as his performance on the mound. This game I consider the 'Greatest All Around Game by a Pitcher'. How's that?

On Wednesday night, June 23, 1971, the Philadelphia Phillies were in Cincinnati to play the Reds at Riverfront Stadium. As the game began, the Phillies were in last place in the National League's Eastern Division with a record of twenty-seven wins and forty losses, placing them fifteen and a half games behind the first place Pittsburgh Pirates. The Reds were the defending National League champions. They were in fourth place in the National League West with a record of thirty-two wins, thirty-eight losses putting them fourteen games behind the first place San Francisco Giants. The attendance was approximately 13,000.

Although the Phillies were off to a bad start, their starter, Rick Wise was off to a great start. His record as the game began was seven wins, four losses - for a last place team. Rick was twenty-five years old and already a seasoned major league veteran. He had won sixty-six games in the major leagues in his career, his first one coming at the age of eighteen. On that occasion, Rick Wise, pitching for the Phillies, started the second game of a doubleheader. He went six innings, allowed no earned runs and beat the Mets. In the first game of that doubleheader, Jim Bunning pitched a perfect game against the Mets.

On this day in 1971, Rick Wise came very close to pitching a perfect game against the Reds. He pitched a no-hitter, missing a perfect game by only one walk in the sixth inning. The final score was 4-0. What makes this game so unique is, Rick Wise along with no-hitting the Reds, also drove in three of the four runs with two home runs! He became the only pitcher ever to hit two dingers while pitching a no-hitter.

Rick Wise was known as a good hitting pitcher. He took great pride in his hitting and worked on it. He knew something other pitchers didn't seem to know; that being, you can help yourself if you can hit.

After the game, Rick was asked how he felt about his two home runs.

"I'm not surprised by them (the homers). I've always taken my rips. It seems like all the balls I've hit lately were extra base hits."

When asked about his pitching performance, he said, "I had good stuff in the no-hitter, but I wasn't as overpowering as I had been other times. I think the key was I was mixing up my pitches and keeping the ball down...there were some fine plays behind me, but most of the tough plays were early in the game."

Rick also helped himself with a great defensive effort. In the sixth, Tommy Helms hit a high grounder that bounced over the mound.

This could have been trouble. If Rick had stayed on the mound, it could have been an infield hit; but Rick had the instinct to back up, drift back to the grassy area between the pitcher's mound and second base, allowing him to field the ball in plenty of time to get the runner out at first.

With two out in the ninth, Rick Wise, one out away from history, had to get past the number one hit maker in the history of the major leagues. Pete Rose, batting left-handed took his place in the batter's box.

Tim McCarver, the Phillies catcher that day said to Rose, "Of all the guys to come up here, it has to be you in this situation."

Rose ran the count to three balls and two strikes. On the next pitch, Rose hit a line drive right to the third baseman, John Vukovich.

Wise spoke of that at-bat. "He just dropped the bat on the ball. He didn't hit the ball hard - sort of a semi line drive - and I knew somebody had a chance to get in front of it. Vuke was right there."

As for the only Reds base runner that day, it was Dave Concepcion drawing a base on balls in the sixth.

"I tried to overpower the ball to Concepcion. I got behind, 3 and 0, then just laid a strike in there but I tried to get too much on it (the next pitch) and it was high. I got a little tired in that inning and that's why Tim came out to talk to me. He told me to relax and take a breather. I did and then Carbo popped up and I got Rose on a curve."

"I didn't use a sweatshirt the rest of the way. I was too hot."

Rick Wise would have another big day on the diamond later in the year. On August 28, in the second game of a doubleheader against the San Francisco Giants, Rick pitched a complete game win against the Giants, beating them seven to three. In this game Rick drove in five of the seven runs, again with two home runs. He tied a record that day with two multi-homer games by a pitcher in a season. In all, Rick would hit fifteen home runs in the major leagues and probably would have hit more, but he spent six years in the American League with the designated hitter having not a single at-bat in those years.

Rick Wise finished the 1971 season with the Phillies and ended up with a 17-14 won loss record. After that year, he was traded to the St. Louis Cardinals for Steve Carlton. He spent two years in St. Louis and was traded to the Boston Red Sox for the 1974 season. He was hurt for most of 1974 but came back to win nineteen games for the Sox in 1975. He played a great part in getting the Red Sox to the World Series.

Rick Wise was involved in some history again in October 1975. He was the winning pitcher (in relief) of game six in the World Series. This is the game that Carlton Fisk hit a home run in the last of the twelfth to win the come-from-behind game against Cincinnati. Rick pitched a scoreless top of the twelfth and went on once again to beat the Reds in a historic game.

Rick pitched for the Red Sox for four years, winning forty-seven games. He was traded to the Cleveland Indians where he pitched for two years. He was traded back to the National League and the San Diego Padres where he pitched for two years.

He began the 1982 season with the Padres, got into one game in April and that was it. The career of Rick Wise was over. He ended up with 188 wins in the major leagues.

After his career, he became a pitching coach for many years in the minor and independent leagues.

Philadelphia Phillies 4, Cincinnati Reds 0

Game Played on Wednesday, June 23, 1971 (N) at Riverfront Stadium

```
PHI N    0 1 0    0 2 0    0 1 0  -  4 7 0
CIN N    0 0 0    0 0 0    0 0 0  -  0 0 0
```

BATTING

Philadelphia Phillies	AB	R	H	RBI	BB	SO	PO	A
Harmon 2b	4	0	0	0	0	0	0	1
Bowa ss	4	0	0	0	0	0	1	6
McCarver c	3	0	2	0	1	0	3	0
Johnson 1b	2	0	0	0	2	0	15	0
Lis lf	2	1	0	0	0	1	0	0
Stone lf	1	0	0	0	0	0	0	0
Montanez cf	4	0	1	0	0	0	5	0
Freed rf	4	1	1	1	0	1	1	0
Vukovich 3b	4	0	1	0	0	1	1	5
Wise p	4	2	2	3	0	0	1	2
Totals	32	4	7	4	3	3	27	14

BATTING -
2B: Montanez (12,off Grimsley); Freed (7,off Grimsley).
HR: Wise 2 (4,5th inning off Grimsley 1 on 1 out,8th inning off Carroll 0 on 0 out).
HBP: Lis (2,by Grimsley).
Team LOB: 5.

BASERUNNING -
CS: McCarver (2,2nd base by Grimsley/Bench).

Cincinnati Reds	AB	R	H	RBI	BB	SO	PO	A
Rose rf	4	0	0	0	0	0	0	0
Foster cf	3	0	0	0	0	1	5	0
May 1b	3	0	0	0	0	1	11	1
Bench c	3	0	0	0	0	0	4	1
Perez 3b	3	0	0	0	0	0	1	3
McRae lf	3	0	0	0	0	0	1	0
Granger p	0	0	0	0	0	0	0	0
Helms 2b	3	0	0	0	0	0	2	2
Concepcion ss	1	0	0	0	1	0	3	8
Stewart ph	1	0	0	0	0	1	0	0
Grimsley p	1	0	0	0	0	0	0	0
Carbo ph	1	0	0	0	0	0	0	0
Carroll p	0	0	0	0	0	0	0	0
Cline lf	1	0	0	0	0	0	0	0
Totals	27	0	0	0	1	3	27	15

FIELDING -

DP: 2. May-Concepcion-May, Bench-Helms-May.

PITCHING

Philadelphia Phillies	IP	H	R	ER	BB	SO	HR
Wise W(8-4)	9	0	0	0	1	3	0

Cincinnati Reds	IP	H	R	ER	BB	SO	HR
Grimsley L(4-3)	6	4	3	3	2	1	1
Carroll	2	2	1	1	1	1	1
Granger	1	1	0	0	0	1	0
Totals	9	7	4	4	3	3	2

HBP: Grimsley (2,Lis).

Umpires: Jerry Dale, Tom Gorman, Chris Pelekoudas, Doug Harvey

Time of Game: 1:53   **Attendance:** 13329

Starting Lineups:

Philadelphia Phillies		Cincinnati Reds	
1. Harmon	2b	Rose	rf
2. Bowa	ss	Foster	cf
3. McCarver	c	May	1b
4. Johnson	1b	Bench	c
5. Lis	lf	Perez	3b
6. Montanez	cf	McRae	lf
7. Freed	rf	Helms	2b
8. Vukovich	3b	Concepcion	ss
9. Wise	p	Grimsley	p

PHILLIES 1ST: Harmon grounded out (third to first); Bowa grounded out (shortstop to first); McCarver walked; Johnson forced McCarver (third to second); 0 R, 0 H, 0 E, 1 LOB. Phillies 0, Reds 0.

REDS 1ST: Rose grounded out (shortstop to first); Foster grounded out (shortstop to first); May struck out; 0 R, 0 H, 0 E, 0 LOB. Phillies 0, Reds 0.

PHILLIES 2ND: Lis was hit by a pitch; Montanez doubled to right [Lis to third]; Freed grounded out (shortstop to first) [Lis scored]; Vukovich popped to first; Wise reached on a fielder's choice [Montanez out at third (shortstop to third)]; 1 R, 1 H, 0 E, 1 LOB. Phillies 1, Reds 0.

REDS 2ND: Bench grounded out (third to first); Perez grounded out (shortstop to first); McRae made an out to center; 0 R, 0 H, 0 E, 0 LOB. Phillies 1, Reds 0.

PHILLIES 3RD: Harmon grounded out (third to first); Bowa made an out to center; McCarver popped to catcher in foul territory; 0 R, 0 H, 0 E, 0 LOB. Phillies 1, Reds 0.

REDS 3RD: Helms grounded out (third to first); Concepcion grounded out (third to first); Grimsley grounded out (pitcher to first); 0 R, 0 H, 0 E, 0 LOB. Phillies 1, Reds 0.

PHILLIES 4TH: Johnson walked; Lis popped to shortstop; Montanez grounded into a double play (first to shortstop to first) [Johnson out at second]; 0 R, 0 H, 0 E, 0 LOB. Phillies 1, Reds 0.

REDS 4TH: Rose lined to center; Foster popped to first in foul territory; May grounded out (shortstop to first); 0 R, 0 H, 0 E, 0 LOB. Phillies 1, Reds 0.

PHILLIES 5TH: Freed doubled to right; Vukovich grounded out (shortstop to first); Wise homered [Freed scored]; Harmon made an out to center; Bowa made an out to center; 2 R, 2 H, 0 E, 0 LOB. Phillies 3, Reds 0.

REDS 5TH: Bench grounded out (third to first); Perez made an out to right; McRae popped to shortstop in foul territory; 0 R, 0 H, 0 E, 0 LOB. Phillies 3, Reds 0.

PHILLIES 6TH: McCarver singled to right; Johnson lined to shortstop; Lis struck out while McCarver was caught stealing second (catcher to second to first); 0 R, 1 H, 0 E, 0 LOB. Phillies 3, Reds 0.

REDS 6TH: Helms grounded out (pitcher to first); Concepcion walked; CARBO BATTED FOR GRIMSLEY; Carbo made an out to center; Rose grounded out (first unassisted); 0 R, 0 H, 0 E, 1 LOB. Phillies 3, Reds 0.

PHILLIES 7TH: CARROLL REPLACED CARBO (PITCHING); Montanez grounded out (second to first); Freed grounded out (shortstop to first); Vukovich struck out; 0 R, 0 H, 0 E, 0 LOB. Phillies 3, Reds 0.

REDS 7TH: STONE REPLACED LIS (PLAYING LF); Foster struck out; May made an out to center; Bench grounded out (shortstop to first); 0 R, 0 H, 0 E, 0 LOB. Phillies 3, Reds 0.

PHILLIES 8TH: Wise homered; Harmon grounded out (shortstop to first); Bowa made an out to center; McCarver singled to center; Johnson walked [McCarver to second]; Stone lined to left; 1 R, 2 H, 0 E, 2 LOB. Phillies 4, Reds 0.

REDS 8TH: Perez grounded out (third to first); McRae made an out to center; Helms grounded out (shortstop to first); 0 R, 0 H, 0 E, 0 LOB. Phillies 4, Reds 0.

PHILLIES 9TH: CLINE REPLACED CARROLL (PLAYING LF); GRANGER REPLACED MCRAE (PITCHING); Montanez made an out to center; Freed struck out; Vukovich singled to center; Wise forced Vukovich (shortstop to second); 0 R, 1 H, 0 E, 1 LOB. Phillies 4, Reds 0.

REDS 9TH: STEWART BATTED FOR CONCEPCION; Stewart was called out on strikes; Cline grounded out (second to pitcher); Rose lined to third; 0 R, 0 H, 0 E, 0 LOB. Phillies 4, Reds 0.

Final Totals	R	H	E	LOB
Phillies	4	7	0	5
Reds	0	0	0	1

CHAPTER NINETEEN

April 18, 1981/June 23, 1981
Rochester Red Wings at Pawtucket Red Sox

Longest Game of All Time

ON APRIL 18, 1981, AT McCoy Stadium in Pawtucket, Rhode Island, the Pawtucket Red Sox faced the Rochester Red Wings in a AAA minor league game. Not a soul could have predicted that history was about to happen. The Pawtucket Red Sox were the AAA affiliate of the Boston Red Sox, and the Red Wings were the AAA team of the Baltimore Orioles.

Extra inning games happen all the time, but this one went on and on. This game lasted thirty-three innings, and is and probably always will be the longest game ever played in professional baseball.

It would take a lot of crazy elements to match this one. It was actually a mistake that allowed it to happen. The home plate umpire accidentally left his rule book in another city; he had to use a rule book that wasn't up to date. Most leagues have a curfew rule, but there was no indication of one in the rule book that the umpire had. So he kept them playing.

It looked like it would finally end in the twenty-first inning. With Rochester up and Mike Hart the base runner at first with two out, catcher Dave Huppart doubled, scoring Hart. In the bottom of the twenty-first, future Hall of Famer Wade Boggs drove in Dave Koza to once again tie the score. Boggs remembered that long after the game was played.

"A lot of people were saying, 'Yeah, yeah, we tied it, we tied it!' Then they said 'Oh no, what did you do? We could have gone home!' but the game went on.

Finally, after thirty-two innings of play, the league president, Harold Cooper was contacted. He instructed the umpires to call the game and it would be finished at a later date. Shortly after 4AM, the game was halted. There were nineteen fans in the stands. Every one of them was given a season pass to McCoy Stadium.

The first part of the game, the thirty-two inning part played in April began at night and ended in daylight. The players told me that it was shocking to leave the stadium with the sun coming up. Rich Gedman, who caught some of the game for Pawtucket told writer Steve Krasner "When we walked off the field (after the first thirty-two innings) at 4'oclock in the morning, it was like 'you mean we're not done with the game yet'?"

This game was given more attention because by the time it finished on June 23, the major leagues were on strike. There was no major league baseball being played. When it was finished, it was the highlight of baseball. Reporters from all over the world came to Pawtucket to see this game. I was one of them. I was working for a small station in Massachusetts, WEIM. I went down there - I wasn't going to miss this.

I didn't know it at the time, but I was watching two future Hall of Famers. Besides Boggs, who played third base for the Red Sox, the Rochester third baseman was Cal Ripken, Jr. Boggs and Ripken are today in the Baseball Hall of Fame.

Steve Grilli was the losing pitcher for Rochester, but he wasn't even on the team when the game began in April. He was pitching for Syracuse at the time.

There were many records set that night besides most innings. Pawtucket set an all time record with ninety-nine putouts. Both teams combined for 195 putouts. Pawtucket set the record with 114 at-bats. Pawtucket pitchers set the all time record with thirty-four strikeouts in a game. Both teams combined for 219 at-bats and both teams combined for sixty strikeouts. There were a total of 882 pitches thrown in that game, 459 for Pawtucket and 423 for Rochester. Three Pawtucket players, Dave Koza, Lee Graham, and Chico Walker set the record for at-bats with fourteen. Three Rochester players, Tom Eaton, Cal Ripken Jr., and Dallas Williams set the record with fifteen plate appearances.

Dallas Williams of Rochester had no hits in thirteen at-bats. This is a professional record for the most at-bats with no hits. He discussed this game with Steve Krasner. "It sank in the next day. Man, we just played thirty-two innings of baseball. We joked about it. We had smiles on our faces. I was thankful I was a baseball player and on the field that night. As time went by, I appreciated it more."

The best pitcher of the night was Jim Umbarger. He pitched ten scoreless innings for Rochester, striking out nine.

The winning manager was Joe Morgan. Joe would go on to manage the major league Boston Red Sox in the late 80's and early 90's. Joe was the one guy who was hoping the game would go on longer. "I wanted 40 innings so nobody could ever tie our beautiful record," was what Joe told Krasner.

Former major leaguer Bruce Hurst pitched five scoreless relief innings, striking out seven. He told Krasner "I remember striking out Cal Ripken on a 3 and 2 breaking ball at 4 o'clock in the morning, and I don't think he ever forgave me." Ripken, who played the whole game at third base, had a funny exchange with relief pitcher Jim Umbarger at one point in the game. Umbarger shouted over to Ripken to watch for the bunt. "I've been watching for the bunt for twenty-three innings now!" was Ripken's tired response.

When the game resumed in June, the atmosphere was incredible. I was down on the field before the game interviewing many of the players before the game. One guy that I met was the Rochester Manager Doc Edwards. Doc was a former major league catcher and a future big league manager with the Cleveland Indians. I never met a nicer guy in baseball than Doc.

When the 33rd inning began, I was sitting up on the third base side. Then it was over very quickly. It took only eighteen minutes to end it. All that was needed was one inning. Rochester batted in the top of the inning. Cal Ripken, Jr. reached base, but that was all. Then in the last of the 33rd, everything went Pawtucket's way. Marty Barrett was hit by a Steve Grilli pitch. Then Chico Walker singled, sending Marty to third. Russ Laribee was next and he was intentionally walked. Rochester wanted to set up a force play at any base. Then the batter was Dave Koza. Koza singled, scoring Barrett and the historic game was over. The crowd went crazy and the Pawtucket players celebrated on the field. After his winning hit, Koza said, "Nothing I ever do in life will probably compare to this."

After the game ended, I went down to the Rochester dressing room. It was very somber. I went up to Doc Edwards, who had been so nice to me before the game and shook his hand. He just sat at his desk and stared for a few minutes. He really wanted this win. I also remember having a long talk with Tom Eaton, the Rochester second baseman. He never made it to the major leagues. This game for him was the pinnacle of his pro baseball career.

After a brief break, both teams took to the field again to play the regular scheduled game for that evening. It was a thrill for me because Joe Morgan let me stay in the Pawtucket dugout the whole game. I got an up close look at what goes on in the dugout during the game. Some of it is not meant to be seen by the fans. I remember one player, Mike Ongarato, who was the designated hitter. In the sixth inning, he doubled. Then, the Rochester pitcher Pete Torrez lobbed the ball to Dan Logan at first and Ongarato was called out, as he did not touch first base. He was well composed until he got right under the dugout roof and then threw his helmet crashing against the wall. All the other players didn't get thrown by it like I did. They seemed to understand. Rochester won this game by a score of 7-6.

In short, the thirty-three inning game was just what baseball needed at that time. It was poetic justice that the finale of this game occurred during the major league players' strike. All eyes of the baseball world were on this game. It was a reminder of what baseball was supposed to be. These minor leaguers, most of whom never made it in the major leagues showed everybody that baseball is a game and is supposed to be the American Pastime.

There is a display of the game at the Hall of Fame in Cooperstown, New York. One thing in the display is Steve Grilli's hat. The losing pitcher donated the hat to the Hall. Even though he got the "L," it's a source of pride that he was in this game. That's the way it should be.

BOX SCORE

ROCHESTER

PLAYER	POS	AB	R	H	RBI
Tom Eaton	2B	10	0	3	0
Dallas Williams	CF	13	0	0	0
Cal Ripken	3B	13	0	2	0
Mark Corey	DH	5	1	1	0
Tom Chism	PH	1	0	0	0
Floyd Rayford	CF	5	0	0	0
Dan Logan	1B	12	0	4	0
John Valle	1B	1	0	0	0
Chris Bourjos	LF	4	0	2	1
John Hale	LF	7	0	1	0
Keith Smith	LF	0	0	0	0
Drungo Hazewood	RF	4	0	0	0
Mike Hart	RF	6	1	1	0
Bob Bonner	SS	12	0	3	0
Dave Huppart	CF	11	0	1	1
Ed Putman	PH	1	0	0	0
TOTALS		105	2	18	2

PAWTUCKET

PLAYER	POS	AB	R	H	RBI
Lee Graham	CF	14	0	1	0
Marty Barrett	2B	12	1	2	0
Chico Walker	LF	14	1	2	0
Russ Laribee	DH	11	0	0	1
Dave Koza	1B	14	1	5	1
Wade Boggs	3B	12	0	4	1
Sam Bowen	RF	12	0	2	0
Rich Gedman	C	3	0	1	0
Mike Ongarato	PH	1	0	0	0
Roger LaFrancois	C	8	0	2	0
Julio Valdez	SS	13	0	2	0
TOTALS		114	3	21	3

Pitcher	IP	H	ER	R	BB	SO
Larry Jones	8 2/3	7	1	1	2	5
Jeff Schneider	5 1/3	2	0	0	0	8
Steve Luebber	8	6	1	1	2	4
Jim Umbarger	10	4	0	0	0	9
Steve Grilli	0	1	1	1	1	0
Cliff Speck	0	1	0	0	0	0

Pitcher	IP	H	R	ER	BB	SO
Danny Parks	6	3	1	1	4	3
Luis Aponte	4	0	0	0	2	9
Manny Sarmiento	4	3	0	0	2	3
Mike Smithson	3 2/3	2	0	0	3	5
Win Remmerswaal	4 1/3	4	1	1	3	3
Joel Finch	5	3	0	0	1	3
Bruce Hurst	5	2	0	0	3	7
Bob Ojeda	1	1	0	0	0	1

Winning Pitcher: Bob Ojeda (9-5)
Losing Pitcher: Steve Grilli ((0-3)

SCORE BY INNINGS

	1	2	3	4	5	6	7	8	9	10	11	12	13	14	15	16	17	18	19	20	21
ROCHESTER	0	0	0	0	0	0	1	0	0	0	0	0	0	0	0	0	0	0	0	0	1
PAWTUCKET	0	0	0	0	0	0	0	0	1	0	0	0	0	0	0	0	0	0	0	0	1

	23	24	25	26	27	28	29	30	31	32	33	R	H	E
ROCHESTER	0	0	0	0	0	0	0	0	0	0	2	18	3	
PAWTUCKET	0	0	0	0	0	0	0	0	0	1	3	21	1	

PLAY BY PLAY

FIRST INNING. ROCHESTER. Eaton was hit by a pitch. Williams flied out to left. Ripken forced Eaton at second, second baseman to shortstop, Ripken reaching first. . Corey struck out. NO RUNS, NO HITS, NO ERRORS, ONE LEFT.

FIRST INNING. PAWTUCKET. Graham grounded out to second. Barrett grounded out, first baseman to pitcher. Walker lined out to second base. NO RUNS, NO HITS, NO ERRORS, NONE LEFT.

SECOND INNING. ROCHESTER. Logan grounded out to second. Bourjos popped out to the first baseman. Hazewood flied out to center. NO RUNS, NO HITS, NO ERRORS, NONE LEFT.

SECOND INNING. PAWTUCKET. Laribee struck out. Koza grounded out to third. Boggs grounded out to shortstop. NO RUNS, NO HITS, NO ERRORS, NONE LEFT.

THIRD INNING. ROCHESTER. Bonner grounded out to the pitcher. Huppart struck out. Eaton flied out to center. NO RUNS, NO HITS, NO ERRORS, NONE LEFT.

THIRD INNING. PAWTUCKET. Bowen singled. Gedman singled, Bowen taking second. Valdez struck out. Graham struck out. Barrett forced Gedman at second, second baseman to shortstop. NO RUNS, TWO HITS, NO ERRORS, TWO LEFT.

FOURTH INNING. ROCHESTER. Williams flied out to right. Ripken singled. Corey grounded into a double play, third to second to first. NO RUNS, ONE HIT, NO ERRORS, NONE LEFT.

FOURTH INNING. PAWTUCKET. Walker flied out to center. Laribee grounded out to second. Koza doubled. Boggs flied out to left. NO RUNS, ONE HIT, NO ERRORS, ONE LEFT.

FIFTH INNING. ROCHESTER. Logan walked. Bourjos popped out to the first baseman. Hazewood struck out. Bonner walked. Huppart grounded out to third. NO RUNS, NO HITS, NO ERRORS, TWO LEFT.

FIFTH INNING. PAWTUCKET. Bowen singled. Gedman struck out. Valdez forced Bowen at second, second baseman to shortstop, Valdez taking first. Graham forced Valdez at second, shortstop to second baseman. NO RUNS, ONE HIT, NO ERRORS, TWO LEFT.

SIXTH INNING. ROCHESTER. Eaton walked. Eaton was caught stealing, catcher to shortstop. Williams grounded out to shortstop. Ripken grounded out to third. NO RUNS, NO HITS, NO ERRORS, NONE LEFT.

SIXTH INNING. PAWTUCKET. Barrett grounded out to third. Walker flied out to left. Laribee struck out. NO RUNS, NO HITS, NO ERRORS, NONE LEFT.

SEVENTH INNING. ROCHESTER. Corey walked. Logan singled, Corey taking second.

Bourjos singled, Corey scored, Logan stopping at second. Luis Aponte now pitching for Pawtucket. Hazewood struck out. Bonner struck out. Huppart struck out. ONE RUN, TWO HITS, NO ERRORS, TWO LEFT.

SEVENTH INNING. PAWTUCKET. Koza grounded out to third. Boggs flied out to left. Bowewn grounded out to third. NO RUNS, NO H ITS, NO ERRORS, NONE LEFT.

EIGHTH INNING. ROCHESTER. Eaton walked. Williams bunt sacrificed Eaton to second, Williams thrown out, third baseman to first baseman. Ripken struck out. Corey struck out. NO RUNS, NO HITS, NO ERRORS, ONE LEFT.

EIGHTH INNING. PAWTUCKET. Gedman grounded out to the pitcher. Valdez singled. Graham grounded into a double play, shortstop to second baseman to first baseman. NO RUNS, ONE HIT NO ERRORS, NONE LEFT.

NINTH INNING. ROCHESTER. Logan struck out. Bourjos walked. Bourjos was caught stealing, catcher to shortstop. Hazewood struck out. NO RUNS, NO HITS, NO ERRORS, NONE LEFT.

NINTH INNING. PAWTUCKET. Barrett grounded out to shortstop. Walker doubled. Walker took third on a wild pitch. Laribee hit a sacrifice fly to right, Walker scoring. Koza singed. Boggs walked. Bowen walked. Jeff Schneider now pitching for Rochester. Mike Ongarato pinch hit for Gedman and struck out. ONE RUN, TWO HITS, NO ERRORS, THREE LEFT.

TENTH INNING. ROCHESTER. Roger LaFrancois now catching for Pawtucket. Bonner was hit by a pitch. Bonner was caught stealing. Huppart struck out. Eaton struck out. NO RUNS, NO HITS, NO ERRORS, NONE LEFT.

TENTH INNING. PAWTUCKET. Valdez grounded out to shortstop. Graham struck out. Barrett singled. Walker forced Barrett at second, shortstop to second baseman. NO RUNS, ONE HIT, NO ERRORS, ONE LEFT.

ELEVENTH INNING. ROCHESTER. Manny Sarmiento now pitching for Pawtucket. Williams popped out to third. Ripken flied out to right. Corey struck out. NO RUNS, NO HITS, NO ERRORS, NONE LEFT.

ELEVENTH INNING.PAWTUCKET. Laribee struck out. Koza flied out to left. Boggs singled. Bowen struck out. NO RUNS, ONE HIT, NO ERRORS, NONE LEFT.

TWELFTH INNING. ROCHESTER. Logan flied out to center. Bourjos singled. Bourjos singled. Bourjos was caught stealing, catcher to second. Hart struck out. NO RUNS, ONE HIT, NO ERRORS, NONE LEFT.

TWELFTH INNING. PAWTUCKET. LaFrancois struck out. Valdez struck out. Graham grounded out to third. NO RUNS, NO HITS, NO ERRORS, NONE LEFT.

THIRTEENTH INNING. ROCHESTER. Bonner singled. Huppart bunt sacrificed Bonner to second, pitcher to first. Eaton walked. Williams flied out to left. Ripken grounded out to third. NO RUNS, ONE HIT, NO ERRORS, ONE LEFT.

THIRTEENTH INNING. PAWTUCKET. Barrett flied out to right. Walker struck out. Laribee was hit by a pitch. Koza grounded out to second. NO RUNS, NO HITS, NO ERRORS, ONE LEFT.

FOURTEETH INNING. ROCHESTER. Corey singled. Logan sacrificed Corey to second, pitcher to first. John Hale pinch hit for Bourjos and struck out. Hart walked. Bonner flied out to right. NO RUNS, ONE HIT, NO ERRORS, TWO LEFT.

FOURTEENTH INNING. PAWTUCKET. John Hale now playing left field for Rochester. Boggs flied out to left. Bowen struck out. LaFrancois popped out to the shortstop. NO RUNS, NO HITS, NO ERRORS, NONE LEFT.

FIFTEENTH INNING. ROCHESTER. Mike Smithson now pitching for Pawtucket. Huppart struck out. Eaton singled. Williams struck out. Ripken walked. Tom Chism pinch hit for Corey and became the designated hitter. Chism struck out. NO RUNS, ONE HIT, NO ERRORS, TWO LEFT.

FIFTEENTH INNING. PAWTUCKET. Steve Luebber now pitching for Rochester. Valdez singled. Graham forced Valdez at second, second baseman to shortstop. Graham was caught stealing catcher to shortstop. Barrett lined out to second. NO RUNS, ONE HIT, NO ERRORS, NONE LEFT.

SIXTEENTH INNING. ROCHESTER. Dan Logan singled. Hale popped out to third. Hart struck out. Bonner flied out to right. NO RUNS, ONE HIT, NO ERRORS, ONE LEFT.

SIXTEENTH INNING. PAWTUCKET. Walker grounded out to second. Laribee struck out. Koza singled. Boggs flied out to center. NO RUNS, ONE HIT, NO ERRORS, ONE LEFT.

SEVENTEENTH INNING. ROCHESTER. Huppart grounded out to third. Eaton popped out to shortstop. Williams popped out to third. NO RUNS, NO HITS, NO ERRORS, NONE LEFT.

SEVENTEENTH INNING. PAWTUCKET. Bowen struck out. LaFrancois struck out. Valdez reached on an error by the second baseman. Graham singled. Barrett walked, bases loaded. Walker forced Barrett at second, shortstop to second baseman. NO RUNS, ONE HIT, ONE ERROR, THREE LEFT.

EIGHTEENTH INNING. ROCHESTER. Ripken grounded out to second. Chism walked. Logan struck out. Hale walked, Chism going to second. Win Remmerswaal now pitching for Pawtucket. Hart walked, loading bases. Bonner grounded out, shortstop to catcher. NO RUNS, NO HITS, NO ERRORS, THREE LEFT.

EIGHTEENTH INNING. PAWTUCKET. Laribee grounded out to the shortstop. Koza reached on a error by the first baseman. Boggs grounded into a double play, pitcher to shortstop to first baseman. NO RUNS, NO HITS, ONE ERROR, NONE LEFT.

NINETEENTH INNING. ROCHESTER. Huppart grounded out to second. Eaton singled, but was thrown out going to second, right fielder to second baseman. Williams lined out to the shortstop. NO RUNS, ONE HIT, NO ERRORS, NONE LEFT.

NINETEENTH INNING. PAWTUCKET. Bowen grounded out to the shortstop. LaFrancois singled. Valdez grounded into a double play, short to second to first. NO RUNS, ONE HIT, NO ERRORS, NONE LEFT.

TWENTIETH INNING. ROCHESTER. Ripken flied out to right. Floyd Rayford batted for Chism and became the designated hitter. Rayford flied out to left. Logan struck out. NO RUNS, NO HITS, NO ERRORS, NONE LEFT.

TWENTIETH INNING. PAWTUCKET. Graham grounded out to short. Barrett grounded out to short. Walker grounded out to second. NO RUNS, NO HITS, NO ERRORS, NONE LEFT.

TWENTY-FIRST INNING. ROCHESTER. Hale struck out. Hart singled. Bonner grounded out to third, Hart going to second. Huppart doubled, scoring Hart. Eaton grounded out to short. ONE RUN, TWO HITS, NO ERRORS, ONE LEFT.

TWENTY-FIRST INNING. PAWTUCKET. Laribee flied out to left. Koza doubled. Boggs double, scoring Koza. Bowen grounded out to short. LaFrancois walked. Valdez struck out. ONE RUN, TWO HITS, NO ERRORS, TWO LEFT.

TWENTY-SECOND INNING. ROCHESTER. Williams grounded out to first. Ripken popped out to third. Rayford walked. Logan singled. Hale walked, loading bases. Hart struck out. NO RUNS, ONE HIT, NO ERRORS, THREE LEFT.

TWENTY-SECOND INNING. PAWTUCKET. Graham grounded out to the pitcher. Barrett grounded out to the shortstop. Walker grounded out to the pitcher. NO RUNS, NO HITS, NO ERRORS, NONE LEFT.

TWENTY-THIRD INNING. ROCHESTER. Joel Finch now pitching for Pawtucket. Bonner singled. Huppart bunt sacrificed Bonner to second, pitcher to first. Eaton grounded out to third. Williams grounded out to second. NO RUNS, ONE HIT, NO ERRORS, ONE LEFT.

TWENTY-THIRD INNING. PAWTUCKET. Jim Umbarger now pitching for Rochester. Laribee struck out. Koza struck out. Boggs grounded out to second. NO RUNS, NO HITS, NO ERRORS, NONE LEFT.

TWENTY-FOURTH INNING. ROCHESTER. Ripken grounded out to short. Rayford grounded out to third. Logan grounded out to shortstop. NO RUNS, NO HITS, NO ERRORS,

NONE LEFT.

TWENTY-FOURTH INNING. PAWTUCKET. Bowen grounded out to shortstop. LaFrancois singled. Valdez struck out. Graham grounded out to the third baseman. NO RUNS, ONE HIT, NO ERRORS, ONE LEFT.

TWENTY-FIFTH INNING. ROCHESTER. Hale grounded out to second. Hart grounded out to short. Bonner singled. Huppart struck out. NO RUNS, ONE HIT, NO ERRORS, ONE LEFT.

TWENTY-FIFTH INNING. PAWTUCKET. Barrett grounded out to third. Walker struck out. Laribee struck out. NO RUNS, NO HITS, NO ERRORS, NONE LEFT.

TWENTY-SIXTH INNING. ROCHESTER. Eaton grounded out to shortstop. Williams grounded out to second. Ripken popped out to third. NO RUNS, NO HITS, NO ERRORS, NONE LEFT.

TWENTY-SIXTH INNING. PAWTUCKET. Koza flied out to right. Boggs struck out. Bowen flied out to left. NO RUNS, NO HITS, NO ERRORS, NONE LEFT.

TWENTY-SEVENTH INNING. ROCHESTER. Rayford struck out. Logan singled. Hale grounded out to second. Hart walked. Bonner struck out. NO RUNS, ONE HIT, NO ERRORS, TWO LEFT.

TWENTY-SEVENTH INNING. PAWTUCKET. LaFrancois grounded out to the pitcher. Valdez grounded out first baseman to pitcher. Graham struck out. NO RUNS, NO HITS, NO ERRORS, NONE LEFT.

TWENTY-EIGHTH INNING. ROCHESTER. Bruce Hurst now pitching for Pawtucket. Huppart grounded out to second. Eaton walked. Williams bunt sacrificed Eaton to second, pitcher to first. Ripken grounded out to third. NO RUNS, NO HITS, NO ERRORS, ONE LEFT.

TWENTY-EIGHTH INNING. PAWTUCKET. Barrett grounded out to the first baseman. Walker struck out. Laribee struck out. NO RUNS, NO HITS, NO ERRORS, NONE LEFT.

TWENTY-NINTH INNING. ROCHESTER. Rayford walked. Logan struck out. Hale struck out. Hart struck out. NO RUNS, NO HITS, NO ERRORS, ONE LEFT.

TWENTY-NINTH INNING. PAWTUCKET. Koza grounded out to short. Boggs singled. Bowen forced Boggs at second, second baseman to shortstop, Boggs taking first. LaFrancois flied out to left. NO RUNS, ONE HIT, NO ERRORS, ONE LEFT.

THIRTIETH INNING. ROCHESTER. Bonner grounded out to second. Huppart struck out. Eaton struck out. NO RUNS, NO HITS, NO ERRORS, NONE LEFT.

THIRTIETH INNING. PAWTUCKET. Valdez grounded out first baseman to pitcher. Graham grounded out third to first. Barrett singled. Walker flied out to right field. NO RUNS, ONE HIT, NO ERRORS, ONE LEFT.

THIRTY-FIRST INNING. ROCHESTER. Williams grounded out pitcher to first. Ripken walked. Rayford struck out. Logan grounded out to the pitcher. NO RUNS, NO HITS, NO ERRORS, ONE LEFT.

THIRTY-FIRST INNING. PAWTUCKET. Laribee grounded out to the pitcher. Koza grounded out to second. Boggs singled. Bowen popped out to the shortstop. NO RUNS, ONE HIT, NO ERRORS, ONE LEFT.

THIRTY-SECOND INNING. ROCHESTER. Hale singled. Hart sacrificted Hale to second, catcher to first. Bonner reached on a fielders choice. Ed Putnam pinch hit for Huppart and struck out. Eaton singled, but Hale was thrown out at home left fielder to catcher. NO RUNS, TWO HITS, NO ERRORS, TWO LEFT.

THIRTY-SECOND INNING. PAWTUCKET. Floyd Rayford now catching. Jim Umbarger now put in the batting order in the ninth position. LaFrancois grounded out to second. Valdez grounded out to third. Graham flied out to center. NO RUNS, NO HITS, NO ERRORS, NONE LEFT.

THIRTY-THIRD INNING. ROCHESTER. Bob Ojeda now pitching for Pawtucket. Williams popped out to short. Ripken singled. Rayford struck out. John Valle pinch hit for Logan and flied out to left. NO RUNS, ONE HIT, NO ERRORS, ONE LEFT.

THIRTY-THIRD INNING. PAWTUCKET. Valle now playing first for Rochester. Keith Smith now playing left for Rochester. Steve Grilli now pitching. Barrett was hit by a pitch. Walker singled, Barrett going to third. Laribee was intentionally walked, bases loaded. Cliff Speck now pitching for Rochester. Koza singled, scoring Barrett.

CHAPTER TWENTY

June 29, 1905
New York Giants at Brooklyn Superbas

August 19, 1951
Detroit Tigers at St. Louis Browns

Two guys, two games, no at-bats

CUP OF COFFEE PLAYERS. THAT'S what we call guys who come up to the major leagues for just a brief period of time and then are never heard from again. It's like they came to the major leagues for a "cup of coffee" and then went back to the minors.

This chapter will be about two games rather than one. For both of these games, only the box score is available, not the play by play.

In both cases, the game contained one player who played briefly in one and only one game without ever getting an official at-bat.

This chapter is about the two most interesting "cup of coffee" players that ever played the game.

The first one is 'Moonlight' Graham. If you saw the movie "Field of Dreams," you will know who I am talking about. He's the guy that was played by Burt Lancaster.

"Field of Dreams" is a great baseball movie written by W. P. Kinsella. It was great fantasy. The name of the main character played by Kevin Costner is Ray Kinsella. He owns a farm in Iowa and gets an inspiration from the great beyond that he should build a baseball field on his acreage. He kept hearing the message "If you build it, they will come." He realizes that he must build the field so that the banned White Sox players from the 1919 Black Sox scandal can come back and play baseball.

"Shoeless" Joe Jackson (played by Ray Liotta) appears through the cornfields and existed on this field only. They can play ball again, but Ray Kinsella gets some more inspiration. He needs to go to Boston to pick up one of the heroes of his life, fictitious author Terrence Mann (played by James Earl Jones). While they're in Boston, they catch a game at Fenway Park and up on the scoreboard Ray gets a message that he must go pick up Archie 'Moonlight' Graham. Graham was a former baseball player who only got into one game in the major leagues with the New York Giants. He did not get to bat. All they know is that he is from Chisholm, Minnesota. So, off they go to pick up this guy. They not only go to Minnesota, they also go back in time. Graham was indeed deceased. But they travel back through time and greet an aged medical doctor in Chisholm, 'Doc' Graham. When Kinsella and Mann realize who it is, they call to him by his baseball nickname, 'Moonlight'. Just then, Graham spins around and says back to them, "No one's called me 'Moonlight' for fifty years."

The three of them talk it over, and Doc Graham tells them "Well, you know I...I never got to bat in the Major Leagues. I would have liked to have that chance. Just once. To stare down a big-league pitcher. To stare him down and just as he starts his windup, wink. Make him think you know something he doesn't. That's what I wish for. That's my wish Ray Kinsella. That's my wish." Ray tells the Doc that he feels it's a tragedy that he never got his chance. Doc Graham responded, "If I'd only gotten to be a doctor for five minutes, now that would have been a tragedy."

So, Doc Graham stays behind in Chisholm, Minnesota, and Kinsella and Mann go to Ray's farm in Iowa. Along the way, they see a young guy hitch-hiking. They pick up the young guy who introduces himself as 'Archie' Graham. Realizing that 'Moonlight' Graham's real name is Archibald, they realize the young guy they picked up was indeed a young 'Moonlight' Graham.

On to Iowa they go, and 'Moonlight' does get his turn at bat. He hits a sacrifice fly to drive in a run. He came through! Shortly after that, in the small grandstand section that is in the foul area, Ray's little girl starts to choke. 'Doc' Graham, standing there on the field comes over to help, realizing that once he crosses the foul line, he becomes the Doctor, and cannot go back. He crosses the line, helps the little girl spit out a piece of hot dog stuck in her throat and then goes off the save more lives. As he leaves, 'Shoeless' Joe Jackson shouts to him "Hey Rookie! You did good."

That's the way it happened in the movie. But where there was a lot of fiction in the movie, there really was an Archibald 'Moonlight' Graham. He did indeed play baseball and did reach the major leagues and get into one and only one game. He did not get to bat, and did go on to become the town doctor in Chisholm, Minnesota. It wasn't just a fictitious character at all.

The real 'Moonlight' Graham played minor league baseball near where I live. I live in northern Massachusetts, not far from southern New Hampshire. The baseball field that I go to watch baseball most at is in Nashua, New Hampshire. It has been through the years a minor league park. The Brooklyn Dodgers had a team there, so did the California Angels and the Pittsburgh Pirates. It is presently the home of an independent team, The Nashua Pride.

But in the year 1903, Doc Graham played in Nashua. He was most known for his blazing speed. That's how he got the nickname 'Moonlight'. His teammates gave him that name because he was a "Fast as a flash." There was a publication back then called *Sporting Life*. In the July 18, 1903 edition, it states "Graham of Nashua is the fastest man in the league on a long sprint. He easily makes two bases on many hits other men would count on but a single."

Speed he had, but perhaps he needed other tools. In the Lowell (Massachusetts) Courier of May 14, 1904 (Lowell is a large city near Nashua), it states "Graham has fallen off badly in hitting. He stands up to the plate with less confidence and swings weakly. All the teams are on the lookout for bunts when Graham goes to bat. No faster runner in league but a fast runner must have more than one trick up his sleeve."

Graham had a good year in the minors in 1901, batting .323 for Manchester in the New England League.

While he was playing in the minors, Doc Graham was studying to become a doctor at the Baltimore Medical College in Maryland, He missed spring training in 1905 because of his studies, but the New York Giants did plan on him playing in the majors that year. In *The Sporting Life* issue of March 25, 1905, there was an article about the New York Giants spring training. In that article it is mentioned, "All hands are now in except Graham, the New England League outfielder who is finishing his studies in Baltimore." The same article later refers to him as "Dr. Archie Graham."

Well, he did finish his studies, and made it to the major league roster on May 23, 1905. For some reason that no one seems to know, he didn't get into a game until June 29. This game was the one and only game he played in with the Giants. And in the game, he got to play the last two innings in right field. No fly balls were hit to him, but he may have handled the ball. There was a base hit while he was in right field by Charlie Malay. Malay was a switch hitter, and the pitcher at the time was a righty, Claude Elliott. So, I assume Malay was batting left at the time and he may have pulled a single to right, but we don't know for sure.

Graham did not get an at-bat, but he nearly did. He was on deck when the last out was made by the Giants in the top of the ninth.

On July 15, 1905, Graham was sent to Scranton, back in the minors. He played a bit in 1906 for Memphis and went back to Scranton in 1907. He was the first player in the league to get 100 hits that year.

It appears that it was in 1909, that Graham, now a full fledged medical doctor, got the chance to be the town doctor in Chisholm, Minnesota. He took it and lived there for the rest of his life. He passed away in 1965.

His baseball career was seldom referred to after it ended. His career in medicine is what he was all about. In the 1966 edition of *The Sporting News Baseball Guide,* Archie Graham's death in 1965 is not even mentioned in their annual necrology.

Today, there is a scholarship fund in Doc Graham's name and on June 29, 2005, 100 years to the day after Graham's one and only game, there was a ceremony at the Minnesota Twins game. Is there any way anyone could have predicted all this way back in 1905.I think not.

The play by play is not available for this game, but the box score is:

NEW YORK GIANTS AT BROOKLYN SUPERBAS
JUNE 29, 1905

NEW YORK

PLAYER	POS	AB	R	H
George Brown	RF	3	2	1
Moonlight" Graham	RF	0	0	0
Mike Donlin	CF	4	2	2
Dan McGann	1B	3	1	2
Sammy Strang	1B	2	0	0
Sam Mertes	LF	3	1	0
Bill Dahlen	SS	4	2	3
Art Devlin	3B	3	0	0
Billy Gilbert	2B	4	1	2
Frank Bowerman	CF	3	1	1
Boileryard Clarke	CF	2	1	1
Christy Mathewson	P	3	0	1
Claude Elliott	P	2	0	0
TOTALS		36	11	13

BROOKLYN

PLAYER	POS	AB	R	H
John Dobbs	CF	4	0	1
Bob Hall	LF	4	0	0
Harry Lumley	RF	4	1	1
Emil Batch	3B	4	0	0
Charlie Malay	2B	4	0	1
Charlie Babb	SS	0	0	0
Fred Mitchell	1B	4	0	1
Lew Ritter	CF	3	0	0
Mal Eason	P	1	0	0
Joe Doscher	PP	2	0	0
Bill Bergen	PH	1	0	0
		31	1	4

PITCHER	IP	H	R	BB	SO
Christy Mathewson	5	2	0	2	7
Claude Elliott	4	2	1	3	6

PITCHER	IP	H	R	BB	SO
Mal Eason	3	8	7	4	1
Joe Doscher	6	5	4	5	3

Left on Base: Brooklyn, 8; New York, 7
Home Runs: McGann, Clarke
Triples: McGann, Bowerman
Doubles: Donlin
Stolen Bases: Lumley, Mertes (2), Dahlen (2), Devlin
Umpire: Mr. Emslie
Time of Game: 1:55
Attendance: 2000

TEAM	1	2	3	4	5	6	7	8	9	R
New York	0	1	6	0	0	3	0	0	1	11
Brooklyn	0	0	0	0	0	0	0	0	1	1

Now the story of another guy who played in one and only one game and did not get an official at-bat. This guy, however did get a plate appearance. He walked in his only time at bat. This is the story of Eddie Gaedel, the shortest and lightest man ever to play major league baseball.

This was the greatest all time stunt. It was pulled off by Bill Veeck, the owner of the St. Louis Browns in 1951.

Frank Saucier was a fabulous minor league outfielder in the late 40's. He batted .446 for Wichita Falls of the Big State League in 1949. He got his chance to play in the majors in 1951 for Veeck and the St. Louis Browns. However, he came down with acute bursitis and had bad bloody blisters on his hands. This shortened his total major league career to only 18 games. But he had a part to play in this goofiest of all major league games.

Saucer was the starting right fielder for the Browns against the Tigers in their game on August 19, 1951. It was played in St. Louis, so Detroit batted in the top of the first and Saucier played that half inning in right field. He was also set to lead off the last of the first, but was lifted for a pinch hitter.

This is where is gets crazy. The pinch hitter was somebody that no one ever heard of. He had never played before in the majors or the minors. This would be his professional debut and it would be in the major leagues. Everyone was expecting to see a legitimate player come out of the St. Louis dugout, but what they saw was a seven-foot tall papier-mâché cake. Then, Eddie Gaedel popped out of the cake with a bat in his hand and he was ready to face pitcher Bob Cain of the Detroit Tigers.

What makes this whole thing crazy is that Gaedel was only 3'7" tall and weighed only 65 pounds. He was a midget, he had a tiny bat, and the number on his uniform was 1/8. The crowd went nuts. So did the Tigers' pitcher and catcher, Bob Cain and Bob Swift. They were cracking up.

The game was halted and home plate umpire Frank Hurley had to try to figure out what was going on. The Browns presented a legitimate contract signed by them and Gaedel and convinced Hurley that the league was properly notified. More about that later. But with Hurley being satisfied, Gaedel took his place in the batters box. He hunched over with the tiny bat and stood there like a statue. Cain was cracking up on the pitchers mound, and he actually tried to hit the half-inch strike zone that existed. But after ball two, he just lobbed two more high balls to his catcher and Gaedel trotted off to first. The crowd was roaring. After he hit the bag, Jim Delsing, the regular Browns center fielder came out of the dugout to pinch run for Gaedel. Gaedel patted Delsing on the behind and returned to the Browns dugout, waving to the crowd as he went. He got a pat on his own behind by the first base coach. That was Max Patkin, the famous "Crown Prince of Baseball." He was coaching first - that was another stunt by Veeck.

Gaedel didn't swing at any pitch. Veeck told him beforehand "Eddie, I'm going to be up on the roof with a high powered rifle watching every move you make. If you so much as look as if you're going to swing, I'm going to shoot you dead."

Gaedel was paid $100 for his day's work.

If you're wondering how Veeck got away with the paperwork, knowing that he had to slip it through, he wired the signed contract to the American League office just after the office had closed. Veeck's wife Mary Francis said "We knew that when (American League president) Will Harridge went to lunch on Friday that meant that he finished work for the week. So we wired it along and it wasn't like they weren't going to approve it - his size wasn't printed anywhere on that contract."

The next day, Harridge went crazy, voided Gaedel's contract, and accused Veeck of "making a mockery of the game."

Playing left field that day for the Browns was Ken Wood. Ken was a veteran major leaguer and I had the pleasure of talking to him about this game.

"Well he went up to bat when his turn came. And they walked him of course, four pitches, and he didn't go to the base to run, one of the players (Jim Delsing) ran for him."

"They brought him on the field in a truck and I don't remember what it was, he climbed out of a cake or a pumpkin or something...It was simply to draw fans...Bill Veeck, what a promoter he was...and that's simply what it was."

I asked Ken if he knew about it beforehand.

"Yes, oh yes. They had to get approval from the league, the president."

Ken didn't get to know Eddie Gaedel very well.

"I just shook his hand and that was about it."

Ken went on to tell me that they really weren't surprised by the stunt because Veeck was always trying something to get the fans to the park. "I was telling someone not long ago, we put a wooden basketball court on the infield and played the Globetrotters in an exhibition game just to draw a crowd. Also, from the grandstand behind home plate they ran a wire to the right field wall, a guy slid down holding something in his teeth, and of course they stopped him with a rope between his legs when he got too close. And such things as that. They had a big crowd that day and the fans loved it."

I also had the opportunity to talk to Dick Kryhoski. Dick was the first baseman that day for the Detroit Tigers. When I brought up the game to Dick, he chuckled.

"Funny thing is, Bob Swift our catcher with Detroit that day came out to the mound to talk to Cain. Of course, with Gaedel in the batters box, I had to hear what he had to say. He said to Cain 'You brag about your pinpoint control, lets see how you do with a one inch strike zone!"

Interestingly, Dick Kryhoski and Bob Cain were traded from Detroit to the Browns after this season. Dick got to know Bill Veeck, his new boss. They talked about the Gaedel game.

"He mentioned he paid him a hundred bucks. He told him 'If you swing, I won't give you your hundred bucks!'" He said that Veeck told him how he schemed to get this prank past the American League president.

"If you were activating a player, you had to call the American League office before midnight. So what Bill did, he called them about 11:30. Of course, there was no one there. And he told his own office 'If someone calls for me today, tell them I'm not in.'"

He told me that Bill Veeck was always trying to think of a scheme to draw the fans in.

"He did a lot of things. He had the fans manage the team one day. He had his traveling secretary holding placards that would say BUNT, STEAL, HIT AND RUN, with a question mark."

Eddie Gaedel was 26-years-old on this day. After his major league appearance, be continued to work for Bill Veeck. Veeck would sell the Browns and later buy the Chicago White Sox. Gaedel made frequent appearances in Chicago on the field in non-playing stunts.

Eddie didn't do too well in the years that followed, though. He became a serious drinker and in 1961, ten years after his big game, Eddie was mugged in a bar and died from a heart attack a short time later. This occurred on June 19, 1961. When they found him in his Chicago apartment, there were bruises around his knees and on his face. A sad ending.

Nevertheless, here we will celebrate the joint effort of Bill Veeck and Eddie Gaedel, two guys who pulled off the greatest stunt in the history of baseball. Here's the box score.

AUGUST 19, 1951

DETROIT TIGERS (AWAY)

PLAYER	POS	AB	R	H	RBI
Jerry Priddy	2B	5	1	1	1
Dick Kryhoski	1B	4	1	1	0
George Kell	3B	4	1	3	0
Vic Wertz	RF	2	0	0	0
Charlie Keller	RF	2	0	1	2
Pat Mullin	CF	5	1	3	2
Bud Souchock	LF	4	0	1	1
Bob Swift	C	4	0	1	0
Johnny Lipon	PH	0	1	0	0
Joe Ginsberg	C	0	0	0	0
Neil Berry	SS	4	0	0	0
Bob Cain	P	2	1	0	0
Dizzy Trout	P	0	0	0	0
TOTALS		36	3	11	6

ST. LOUIS BROWNS (HOME)

PLAYER	POS	AB	R	H	RBI
Frank Saucier	RF	0	0	0	0
Eddie Gaedel	PH	0	0	0	0
Jim Delsing	CF	3	0	1	0
Bobby Young	2B	4	0	1	0
Cliff Mapes	CF-RF	5	0	2	0
Sherm Lollar	CF-RF	5	1	0	0
Ken Wood	LF	3	0	2	1
Hank Arft	1B	4	0	0	0
Fred Marsh	3B	4	1	1	0
Bill Jennings	SS	4	0	0	0
Duane Pillette	P	2	0	0	0
Jim Suchecki	P	0	0	0	0
Jack Maguire	PH	1	0	0	0
TOTALS		35	2	7	1

PITCHER	IP	H	R	BB	SO
Bob Cain	8 1/3	7	6	5	1
Dizzy Trout	02/03	0	0	0	1

PITCHER	IP	H	R	BB	SO
Duane Pillette	6 2/3	9	2	4	3
Jim Suchecki	2 1/3	2	0	0	0

Winner: Cain (10-9)
Losing Pitcher: Pillette (5-13)

Johnny Lipon ran for Bob Swift in the eighth
Eddie Gaedel batted for Frank Saucier in first
Jack Maguire batted for Suchecki in ninth

Errors - Kell (2), Berry, Young
Doubles-Mullin (2), Delsing, Wood, Marsh
Home Runs-Priddy
Sacrifice-Cain, Keller
Double Play-Kell and Kryhoski
Left on Base-St. Louis 11, Detroit 9
Passed Ball-Lollar
Umpires: Eddie Hurley, Art Passarella, Joe Paparella
Time: 2:34, Attendance: 18,369

DETROIT	0	0	0	1	0	1	3	1	0	6
ST. LOUIS	0	0	0	0	0	2	0	0	0	2

CHAPTER TWENTY-ONE

July 7, 1963
Chicago White Sox at Boston Red Sox

The Unsung Hero

IN EARLY 1963, I WAS nine years old when I was hit with the baseball 'bug'. I became a slave to the game. I bought the cards, read all the stats on them and listened to every game that was on the radio.

My Dad was not a big fan. He read the sports pages and knew who the stars were, but didn't closely follow the game. He had other interests and hobbies. I never saw him sit down to watch a baseball game.

Knowing how much baseball meant to me, he looked at the Red Sox schedule early in the season and got an idea. He asked my Mom to send away for four tickets to the July 7, 1963 Sunday game. I think the tickets were about $3.00 at that time. When the tickets arrived, it was Dad, me, my older brother Jim and my Uncle Teeks off to the game.

When we arrived at the game, we parked the car and made our way to the field. I remember walking up the ramp and stretched out before me, in all its glory, Fenway Park. That beautiful, green Cathedral grabbed me and the memory still grabs me today,

The game went into extra innings and we stayed to the end. Knowing how much it meant to me, there would be no way Dad would want to leave before the final out was made.

I remember when I spoke to Chuck Schilling about this game. Chuck was the second baseman for the Red Sox that day. I rattled off the starting lineup to him. I didn't have to memorize it; I just knew it then and still do. Each time I go to Fenway Park, the memory of that day comes back to me. Part of me is still surprised that Bressoud, Mantilla, Geiger, Mejias and the others are not there. The Red Sox ended up losing more than they won and finished seventh out of ten teams that year, but none of that matters. The 1963 Red Sox are the number one team I will always remember.

Overall, it was just another game. No records were set. Nothing notable occurred. My Dad took me to many more games after that, including a doubleheader the following year. The second game of the doubleheader went into extra innings. We stayed until the end. After that, Dad said he'd be glad to take me to more games, but no more doubleheaders.

On July 7, 1963, the first game I ever went to, there were no heroes on the field; however there was, in fact, one hero attending the game; the big guy sitting next to me, the guy who got me there, Ralph J. Pallotta.

The 'big guy' passed away in 1989, I was 34 and as a veteran local sports reporter had made a few contacts. Before he passed, my dad received get-well wishes from Rico Petrocelli and Frank Malzone. They made him smile; thanks Rico and Frank.

Dad would have enjoyed seeing this book published. From where I am now to where he is now, I just know my Dad can hear me say what I should have said that Sunday back in 1963...' Thanks Dad... Love Ya. Rip."

Chicago White Sox 4, Boston Red Sox 1

Game Played on Sunday, July 7, 1963 (D) at Fenway Park

```
CHI A    0  0  0    0  0  0    1  0  0    0  0  3  --   4  15  3
BOS A    0  0  0    0  0  0    0  0  1    0  0  0  -    1   4  1
```

BATTING

Chicago White Sox	AB	R	H	RBI	BB	SO	PO	A
Landis cf	6	1	3	0	0	1	2	0
Weis ss	5	1	2	1	1	0	2	6
Ward 3b	5	1	2	0	1	1	2	3
Robinson lf	6	0	2	0	0	0	3	0
Hershberger rf	6	1	3	1	0	2	0	0
Fox 2b	5	0	3	2	1	0	2	3
McCraw 1b	6	0	0	0	0	1	13	0
Martin c	4	0	0	0	1	1	12	2
Wilhelm p	4	0	0	0	0	3	0	1
Brosnan p	0	0	0	0	0	0	0	2
Lemon ph	1	0	0	0	0	1	0	0
Pizarro p	0	0	0	0	0	0	0	0
Totals	48	4	15	4	4	10	36	17

FIELDING -
DP: 1. Martin-Fox.
E: Weis (7), Ward (21), McCraw (3).

BATTING -
2B: Robinson (15,off Lamabe); Hershberger (12,off Lamabe); Fox (11,off Monbouqu
3B: Landis (4,off Radatz).
IBB: Fox (1,by Lamabe); Martin (4,by Monbouquette).
Team LOB: 12.

BASERUNNING -
SB: Weis (10,2nd base off Radatz/Tillman).

Boston Red Sox	AB	R	H	RBI	BB	SO	PO	A
Schilling 2b	5	0	0	0	0	0	1	3
Geiger cf	3	0	0	0	0	0	1	0
Mejias cf	2	1	0	0	0	1	1	0
Yastrzemski lf	5	0	2	1	0	0	2	1
Malzone 3b	5	0	1	0	0	1	3	0
Stuart 1b	4	0	0	0	1	0	7	2
Clinton rf	5	0	0	0	0	2	4	0
Bressoud ss	5	0	0	0	0	2	3	3
Tillman c	4	0	1	0	0	1	12	0
Lamabe p	1	0	0	0	0	0	0	3
Mantilla ph	1	0	0	0	0	1	0	0
Radatz p	0	0	0	0	0	0	0	0

Williams ph	1	0	0	0	0	1	0	0
Monbouquette p	1	0	0	0	0	0	2	0
Totals	42	1	4	1	1	9	36	12

FIELDING -
DP: 1. Schilling-Bressoud-Stuart.
E: Tillman (4).

BATTING -
2B: Yastrzemski (22,off Wilhelm).
Team LOB: 6.

PITCHING

Chicago White Sox	IP	H	R	ER	BB	SO	HR
Wilhelm	9	3	1	0	1	6	0
Brosnan	1	0	0	0	0	0	0
Pizarro W(11-4)	2	1	0	0	0	3	0
Totals	12	4	1	0	1	9	0

Boston Red Sox	IP	H	R	ER	BB	SO	HR
Lamabe	6	8	0	0	2	5	0
Radatz	2	2	1	1	1	3	0
Monbouquette L(11-6)	4	5	3	3	1	2	0
Totals	12	15	4	4	4	10	0

IBB: Lamabe (5,Fox); Monbouquette (3,Martin).

Umpires: Red Flaherty, Eddie Hurley, Lou DiMuro, Sam Carrigan

Time of Game: 2:50   **Attendance:** 17611

Starting Lineups:

Chicago White Sox		Boston Red Sox	
1. Landis	cf	Schilling	2b
2. Weis	ss	Geiger	cf
3. Ward	3b	Yastrzemski	lf
4. Robinson	lf	Malzone	3b
5. Hershberger	rf	Stuart	1b
6. Fox	2b	Clinton	rf
7. McCraw	1b	Bressoud	ss
8. Martin	c	Tillman	c
9. Wilhelm	p	Lamabe	p

WHITE SOX 1ST: Landis struck out; Weis walked; Ward struck out; Robinson doubled to left [Weis out at home (left to catcher)]; 0 R, 1 H, 0 E, 1 LOB. White Sox 0, Red Sox 0.

RED SOX 1ST: Schilling popped to catcher in foul territory; Geiger grounded out (second to first); Yastrzemski made an out to left; 0 R, 0 H, 0 E, 0 LOB. White Sox 0, Red Sox 0.

WHITE SOX 2ND: Hershberger struck out; Fox singled; McCraw grounded into a double play (second to shortstop to first) [Fox out at second]; 0 R, 1 H, 0 E, 0 LOB. White Sox 0, Red Sox 0.

RED SOX 2ND: Malzone made an out to third; Stuart grounded out (shortstop to first); Clinton made an out to left; 0 R, 0 H, 0 E, 0 LOB. White Sox 0, Red Sox 0.

WHITE SOX 3RD: Martin grounded out (pitcher to first); Wilhelm was called out on strikes; Landis singled; Weis grounded out (second to first); 0 R, 1 H, 0 E, 1 LOB. White Sox 0, Red Sox 0.

RED SOX 3RD: Bressoud grounded out (shortstop to first); Tillman singled; Lamabe forced Tillman (catcher to shortstop); Schilling grounded out (second to first); 0 R, 1 H, 0 E, 1 LOB. White Sox 0, Red Sox 0.

WHITE SOX 4TH: Ward made an out to shortstop; Robinson made an out to right; Hershberger doubled; Fox singled [Hershberger to third]; McCraw forced Fox (shortstop to second); 0 R, 2 H, 0 E, 2 LOB. White Sox 0, Red Sox 0.

RED SOX 4TH: Geiger grounded out (second to first); Yastrzemski made an out to left; Malzone singled; Stuart forced Malzone (shortstop to second); 0 R, 1 H, 0 E, 1 LOB. White Sox 0, Red Sox 0.

WHITE SOX 5TH: Martin made an out to left; Wilhelm grounded out (pitcher to first); Landis singled; Landis was picked off first (pitcher to first); 0 R, 1 H, 0 E, 0 LOB. White Sox 0, Red Sox 0.

RED SOX 5TH: Clinton struck out; Bressoud grounded out (shortstop to first); Tillman struck out; 0 R, 0 H, 0 E, 0 LOB. White Sox 0, Red Sox 0.

WHITE SOX 6TH: Weis made an out to third; Ward singled; Robinson singled [Ward to second]; Hershberger made an out to center [Ward to third, Robinson to second]; Fox was walked intentionally; McCraw struck out; 0 R, 2 H, 0 E, 3 LOB. White Sox 0, Red Sox 0.

RED SOX 6TH: MANTILLA BATTED FOR LAMABE; Mantilla struck out; Schilling grounded out (shortstop to first); Geiger popped to catcher in foul territory; 0 R, 0 H, 0 E, 0 LOB. White Sox 0, Red Sox 0.

WHITE SOX 7TH: MEJIAS REPLACED GEIGER (PLAYING CF); RADATZ REPLACED MANTILLA (PITCHING); Martin struck out; Wilhelm struck out; Landis tripled; Weis singled [Landis scored]; Weis stole second [Weis to third (error by Tillman)]; Ward walked; Robinson made an out to right; 1 R, 2 H, 1 E, 2 LOB. White Sox 1, Red Sox 0.

RED SOX 7TH: Yastrzemski grounded out (shortstop to first); Malzone grounded out (third to first); Stuart walked; Clinton struck out; 0 R, 0 H, 0 E, 1 LOB. White Sox 1, Red Sox 0.

WHITE SOX 8TH: Hershberger was called out on strikes; Fox made an out to center; McCraw popped to third in foul territory; 0 R, 0 H, 0 E, 0 LOB. White Sox 1, Red Sox 0.

RED SOX 8TH: Bressoud made an out to shortstop; Tillman reached on an error by Weis; WILLIAMS BATTED FOR RADATZ; Williams struck out; Schilling grounded out (third to first); 0 R, 0 H, 1 E, 1

LOB. White Sox 1, Red Sox 0.

WHITE SOX 9TH: MONBOUQUETTE REPLACED WILLIAMS (PITCHING); Martin made an out to shortstop; Wilhelm struck out; Landis grounded out (shortstop to first); 0 R, 0 H, 0 E, 0 LOB. White Sox 1, Red Sox 0.

RED SOX 9TH: Mejias reached on an error by Ward [Mejias to second]; Yastrzemski doubled [Mejias scored (unearned)]; Malzone reached on an error by McCraw; Stuart forced Yastrzemski (pitcher to third) [Malzone to second]; Clinton popped to catcher in foul territory; Bressoud struck out; 1 R, 1 H, 2 E, 2 LOB. White Sox 1, Red Sox 1.

WHITE SOX 10TH: Weis made an out to left; Ward popped to third in foul territory; Robinson grounded out (first to pitcher); 0 R, 0 H, 0 E, 0 LOB. White Sox 1, Red Sox 1.

RED SOX 10TH: BROSNAN REPLACED WILHELM (PITCHING); Tillman grounded out (pitcher to first); On a bunt Monbouquette grounded out (pitcher to first); Schilling made an out to center; 0 R, 0 H, 0 E, 0 LOB. White Sox 1, Red Sox 1.

WHITE SOX 11TH: Hershberger singled; Fox grounded out (second to first) [Hershberger to second]; McCraw made an out to right; Martin was walked intentionally; LEMON BATTED FOR BROSNAN; Lemon struck out; 0 R, 1 H, 0 E, 2 LOB. White Sox 1, Red Sox 1.

RED SOX 11TH: PIZARRO REPLACED LEMON (PITCHING); Mejias struck out; Yastrzemski singled; Malzone struck out while Yastrzemski was out trying to advance to second; 0 R, 1 H, 0 E, 0 LOB. White Sox 1, Red Sox 1.

WHITE SOX 12TH: Landis popped to catcher in foul territory; Weis singled; Ward singled [Weis to second]; Robinson made an out to right [Weis to third]; Hershberger singled [Weis scored, Ward to second]; Fox doubled [Ward scored, Hershberger scored]; McCraw grounded out (first to pitcher); 3 R, 4 H, 0 E, 1 LOB. White Sox 4, Red Sox 1.

RED SOX 12TH: Stuart made an out to center; Clinton grounded out (third to first); Bressoud was called out on strikes; 0 R, 0 H, 0 E, 0 LOB. White Sox 4, Red Sox 1.

Final Totals	R	H	E	LOB
White Sox	4	15	3	12
Red Sox	1	4	1	6

BIBLIOGRAPHY

1918 American Medical Directory

1940 American Medical Directory

Baseball America, August-September 2006

Boston Herald, March 21, 1906; May 19, 1906; August 31, 1907

Bouton, Jim. *Ball Four, the Final Pitch*. Champaign, IL: Sports Publishing Inc., 2000

Brooklyn Eagle, March 22, 1905

Cataneo, David. *Tony C.* Nashville, Tenn.: Rutledge Hill Press, 1997

Coleman, Ken and Valenti, Dan. *The Impossible Dream Remembered*. Lexington, Mass: 1987

Crehan, Herbert and Ryan, James W. *Lightning in a Bottle*. Boston. Branden Publishing Co 1992

Krasner, Steve, *The Longest Game.* WWW.PAWSOX.COM

Lowell (Mass.) *Courier.* May 14, 1904

Marazzi, Rich and Fiorito, Len. *Aaron to Zuverink.* New York: Avon 1982

Marazzi, Rich and Fiorito, Len. *Aaron to Zipfel.* New York: Avon 1985

Miller, Doug. "'Moonlight' Still a Star 100 Years Later." www.majorleaguebaseball.com

New York Times, June 30, 1905; August 20, 1951

Nowlin, Bill. *Mr. Red Sox.* Cambridge, Ma. Rounder Books, 2004

Olberman, Keith. "Moonlight Graham Remembered." www.msnbc.com

Pappas, Milt, Mausser, Wayne, and Names, Larry. *Out at Home.* Oskhosh, Wi. LKP Group 2000

Piersall, Jimmy and Whittingham, Richard. *The Truth Hurts* Chicago: Contemporary Books 1984

Reynolds, Bill. *Lost Summer.* New York: Warner Books 1992

Rovell, Darren. "Short on Size, Long on History." espn.go.com

Society of American Baseball Research. "The Real 'Moonlight' Graham." WWW.SABR.COM

Seattle Times. January 26, 2005

Sporting Life. July 13, 1903, March 25, 1905, July 15, 1905, September 16, 1905.

Sporting News. October 16, 1965; April 29, 1967; July 10, 1971.

Tellis, Richar. "Once Around the Bases". WWW>SABR.COM

Thompson, Dick and Simon, Tom. "Moonlight in the News." WWW.SABR.COM

Walker, Ben. "Between the Seams: Moonlight's Day in the Sun." www.sabr.com

www.baseballalmanac.com "Eddie Gaedel obituary"

www.baseball-fever.com "Emmet Ashford"

www.baseballlibrary.com. "Emmet Ashford"

www.baseballlibrary.com. "Jim Piersall"

www.cmgww.com. "Satchel Paige"

www.historicbaseball.com "Eddie Gaedel"

www.retrosheet.org. All box scores and play by play except in Chapters 19 and 20 came from this excellent organization.

Www.sbeen.com "Forgotten in time-Rocky Colavito"

www.seth.com "Satchel Paige"

www.winipedia.org "Eddie Gaedel"

www.winipedia.org "Satchel Paige

Printed in the United States
79612LV00006B/116

9 781425 978990